The Use/Nonuse/Misuse of Applied Social Research in the Courts

Contributing Authors

Clark C. Abt, *Abt Associates Inc.*
David C. Baldus, *University of Iowa*
Charles H. Baron, *Boston College Law School*
Stephen Breyer, *Harvard University*
Ken Carlson, *Abt Associates Inc.*
Paul Chernoff, *Massachusetts District Court*
James Coleman, *University of Chicago*
Shari Seidman Diamond, *University of Illinois*
Bernard Grofman, *University of California*
Robert J. Hallisey, *Superior Court of Massachusetts*
Donald L. Horowitz, *Duke University School of Law*
Sue Johnson, *Administrative Office of the New York State Courts*
Arthur Kantrowitz, *Dartmouth College*
Orm W. Ketcham, *National Center for State Courts*
Michael P. Kirby, *Southwestern College*
Arthur F. Konopka, *National Science Foundation*
Richard Light, *Harvard University*
Allan Lind, *Federal Judicial Center*
Teb Marvell, *National Center for State Courts*
George Michaels, *private practice lawyer*
Stephan Michelson, *Econometric Research Inc.*
Joseph Mitchell, *Superior Court of Massachusetts*
Stuart S. Nagel, *University of Illinois*
Geoffrey W. Peters, *National Center for State Courts*
Robert Post, *Williams & Connolly*
Paul L. Rosen, *Carleton University*
H. Laurence Ross, *State University of New York at Buffalo*
Peter Rossi, *University of Massachusetts*
Michael J. Saks, *National Center for State Courts*
Austin Sarat, *Amherst College*
Leonard Saxe, *Boston University*
Howard Scarrow, *State University of New York at Stony Brook*
Stephen L. Wasby, *State University of New York at Albany*
Adam Yarmolinsky, *Kominers, Fort, Schlefer, & Boyer*

The Use/Nonuse/Misuse of Applied Social Research in the Courts

edited by

Michael J. Saks
Charles H. Baron

Published for
The Council for Applied Social Research
by
Abt Books
Cambridge, Massachusetts

Library of Congress Cataloging in Publication Data

Conference on the Use/Nonuse/Misuse of Applied Social
    Research in the Courts, Washington, D.C., 1978.
    The use/nonuse/misuse of applied social research
in the courts.

    Bibliography: p.
    Includes index.
    1. Social science research—Law and legislation—
United States. 2. Courts—United States—Congresses.
3. Sociological jurisprudence—Congresses. 4. Social
psychology—Congresses. 5. Psychology, Forensic—
Congresses. I. Saks, Michael J. II. Baron,
Charles H., 1936-   III. Title.
KF4280.S6C66 1978   347.73'1'0724   79-55776
ISBN 0-89011-544-3

Printed in the United States of America

CONTENTS

PREFACE

The Conference on the Use/Nonuse/Misuse of Applied Social Research in the Courts was conceived in a telephone conversation between Clark Abt and Michael Saks in the spring of 1978. Several meetings and a well-attended preconference gave shape to the final meeting, which was sponsored by the Council for Applied Social Research and held in October 1978 in Washington, D.C. The proceedings were masterfully transcribed by the Withers Reporting Service and were subsequently edited by Michael Saks and Charles Baron, as well as by the individual participants, who revised, updated, and in some cases rewrote their papers.

The papers and dialogues contained in this volume reflect the current state of interchange between the applied social research community and the legal/judicial community. That relationship is marked by mutual ignorance and misunderstanding, but also by the promise of more and better utilization of social research findings in the courts. Use of such findings in a legal context has increased considerably in recent years and will almost certainly continue to do so. We hope that this volume will serve to narrow the gap in understanding between the two communities and enhance the critical and intelligent use of applied social research in and by the courts.

Michael J. Saks
Washington, D.C.

Charles H. Baron
Wellfleet, Massachusetts

OPENING REMARKS

CLARK C. ABT*

Judicial intervention in social policy has been increasing in the last decade; judge-made law is expanding to encompass social problem solving, whether it is health cost containment, welfare reform, school and housing desegregation, or environmental and consumer issues. The courts are shaping, controlling, or attempting to control the behaviors of many social groups, including some not often brought before the courts, such as program administrators and employers. The decisions of the courts affect what they can do in the future concerning social issues. Moreover, the courts are involved not only in the formulation and interpretation of U.S. social policies and programs, but also in their implementation.

The legitimacy of this expanded role of the courts, as well as their ability to adjudicate social policy, is being questioned, and of course we recognize the interdependence between legitimacy and capability.

Resolution of social policy issues, I think we are probably all agreed, benefits from social policy knowledge, including information on program needs, costs, processes, benefits, and impacts. Social policy knowledge is currently obtained by federal, state, and local governments in the form of program evaluations and social experiments. From these we derive estimates of the social costs and benefits and the comparative equity and efficiency of alternative social programs and policies.

The courts' capacity to generate knowledge of social programs and policies has been extremely limited. Often, the findings of courts are based only on the input of expert witnesses and perhaps briefs or memoranda. Seen from the perspective of a social scientist conducting program evaluations and experiments, major social programs in the United States are evaluated and their effects estimated by individual experts who explain their views to the courts for a few hours, rather than by thousands of experts conducting research on social problems over the course of many years in diverse locations.

It is this limited ability of the courts to mobilize social program and policy knowledge that has led to a questioning of their ability to resolve social issues and ultimately their legitimacy in doing so. One of my hopes for this discussion is that through the discourse between officers of the courts and leading social researchers we will move toward a more effective application of social research findings to the court process, in the interests of greater equity and efficiency in the administration of justice in the United States.

---

*President of Abt Associates Inc., a social science research firm in Cambridge, Mass., and past president of the Council for Applied Social Research.

1

History and State of the Art
of Applied Social Research
in the Courts

STEPHAN MICHELSON
PAUL L. ROSEN
STEPHEN L. WASBY

STEPHAN MICHELSON*

A 1969 report from the National Academy of Sciences chastized lawyers for their failure to pay attention to social science and even encouraged employment in law schools of such misfits who chose to practice it (National Academy of Sciences 1969). That same year Friedman and Macauley produced an interesting collection titled *Law and the Behavioral Sciences* (1969). It contains a number of analyses critical of the legal system. In one, the defense attorney is portrayed as part of the court bureaucracy, practicing a confidence game on his client (Blumberg 1967). This bore out Arnold Rose's observation in an earlier essay (1967) that because sociologists study law as a subject, because they have funny notions about the law and lawyers, they pose something of a threat that, say, doctors or biologists do not. It's easy to see how the relationship could be as tense as was summarized recently by Sharon Collins:

> Above all, the profound differences in perspective between social scientists and lawyers have laid an unstable foundation for the alliance between social science and law. . . . There still remains a skepticism verging on hostility that pervades the legal attitude toward social science—a condition that in turn frustrates social science research. . . . (Collins 1978, p. 18)

According to these statements, then, lawyers are hostile and social scientists are frustrated. But not all lawyers are hostile; some, apparently, are just slow. Ovid Lewis, in reviewing the Friedman-Macauley book, said:

> The primary criticism that emerges from a reading of *Law and the Behavioral Sciences* is not of the text but of the law schools. They are not ready for this text. The faculties are generally neither prepared nor interested in deviating radically from the traditional approach that has made legal education what it is today. (Lewis 1970, p. 149)

Since judges come from law schools, one might expect the same intransigence in the courts. In 1968 Arthur S. Miller argued that the Court would "diminish in power and importance unless certain improvements are made in its method of operation." He went on:

> No one should be sanguine about the likelihood of the high bench making necessary and desirable changes to improve its methodology; if a prediction had to be made, it would be that the Court will continue in its time-honored manner, making some incremental alterations, and that it will dwindle into an essentially impotent organ of government. (Miller 1968, p. 208)

One could almost say that these writers are explaining why Oliver Wendell Holmes's prediction in 1897 about the future of the law has been so slow in coming. Holmes was on the supreme court of Massachusetts at the time. In an address delivered at Boston University he talked about the excessive use of history, as opposed to analysis, in deciding cases:

---

*President of Econometric Research Inc., Washington, D.C.

> For the rational study of law the black-letter man may be the man of the present, but the man of the future is the man of statistics and the master of economics. (Holmes 1897, p. 469)

Roscoe Pound, Felix Frankfurter, Benjamin Cardozo, and others made similar predictions in the 1920s. And yet after forty or fifty more years, if you believe the people I have been quoting, neither the courts nor the law schools have changed much.

Another criticism of the courts has been made by Nathan Glazer, Eleanor Wolf, and Donald Horowitz, who assert that the courts have gone *too far* in adopting social science. Wolf, for example, in the 1977 version of the *Supreme Court Review*, argued "The reasoning of the Courts on the entire issue of the relationship between school and residential segregation is illogical and confused" (Wolf 1978, p. 83). She laid a good deal of blame on sociologists who knew better but did not enter the fray to argue that the courts were misusing social science. Horowitz seems to argue that the courts have adopted a faulty theory of society: they cannot effect the changes they want (Horowitz 1977). Glazer argues that the courts have no business being involved with certain issues in the first place (Glazer 1978). I think these are interesting and legitimate, though incorrect, points of view.

There would be an easy way to reconcile the view that the law is too slow to utilize social science with the view that it is too hasty. That would be to conclude that it has accepted faulty social science because it has neglected to institute procedures to incorporate good social science. I think this reconciliation is true but trivial. I will dwell on it only briefly.

In an interesting note in the *Harvard Law Review* in 1948, an argument was made about the procedures by which legislative facts are determined by the court. Discussing the use of judicial notice in determining adjudicative facts, the author remarks:

> Unfortunately, there is no comparable device for supplementing judicial notice when the court is seeking to learn broad social and economic facts pertinent to the rule of law to be applied, rather than to the issue of what took place between the particular litigants. This inadequacy of judicial machinery restricts investigation to notorious and indisputable facts, shutting off the judge from much pertinent information. (*Harvard Law Review* Note 1948, p. 693)

The author refers to Pound, Cardozo, Isaacs, and Winfield—the writers who in the 1920s advocated (and predicted) an enlarged role for social science in the courts. The problem that prompted this note is that judicial notice and independent investigation by the court do not subject these legislative facts to the adversary process. The solution, of course, is to allow expert testimony on such issues.

As we know, the National Association for the Advancement of Colored People (NAACP) was doing exactly this. In the 1954 *Brown* decision we have the famous footnote 11, referring to studies by Kenneth Clark—but not studies of the particular children involved in the lawsuit. Clearly this is a case of social science evidence—whatever people consider its force to have been—presented in support of judicial notice. Jack Greenberg of the NAACP Legal Defense Fund soon thereafter wrote on the general question of social scientists appearing as expert witnesses (Greenberg 1956). He did not suppose, as Holmes had, that lawyers would be of social science stock but rather that lawyers would utilize social scientists and that their testimony would be influential in deciding more cases in the future.

Eleanor Wolf contends that this has happened but that the adversary system has failed to bring forth the necessary debate. She notes, for example, that in the Detroit desegregation case the city took the position that "evidence" of residential segregation was irrelevant. The judge then adopted the plaintiffs' social science evidence as fact (Wolf 1976). Cases may be lost because lawyers make incorrect strategic decisions, but this seems to be a flimsy basis on which to attack the system. If neither independent research nor the adversary system is adequate, what would be the best institutional system for presenting that evidence which the court needs for an understanding of the nonadjudicative aspects of a case? Unfortunately, Wolf offers no answer.

What I have been talking about so far is the introduction of evidence of legislative fact, following the notion that courts do something broader than compare the facts of a particular case with a traditional rule of law. I accept that—though others may not—without accepting Brooks Adams's conclusion in 1913 that "our courts have ceased to be true courts, and are converted to legislative chambers, thereby promising shortly to become, if they are not already, a menace to order" (Adams 1913, p. 112). Just as the *Brown* case is in some sense the culmination of social science as legislative fact, *Muller v. Oregon* (1908) is recognized as the opening of that era. There were cases before *Muller* in which social science argument was presented, and there have been cases since *Brown* (1954). But it is convenient to look at that period—1911 through 1954.

Since Paul Rosen will discuss this era, I will move to four other areas in which social science is used in the courts. The first is antitrust. In all the reviews of statistics and social science in the law I have seen, antitrust is hardly mentioned at all. Yet the determination of what a market is, what a monopoly is, what predatory behavior is, and other such issues is inherently based on social science theory and analysis. In graduate school in economics, if I can remember that far back, we thought the Morton Salt Case, Standard Oil, A&P, and Alcoa represented what social scientists did in the courts. I suspect the reason antitrust is treated separately is that social science research in general is a *skill* (or set of skills), whereas antitrust is a particular well-developed *field* in which these skills and special knowledge are used together.

The second area is the procedural aspect of the judicial system. After all, social science is supposed to be an analysis of the manner in which institutions serve or don't serve the people. The judicial system is such an institution.

A third use of social science has been the calculation of the value of harm done, when the harm is proved in some other way. There is an industry out there that sells services to attorneys, calculating the expected future earnings of persons killed by accident or, I suppose, on purpose; calculating the lost profit from predatory behavior by a monopoly; even calculating the losses to a firm caused by a strike. The economic loss suffered from proved discrimination is another example of calculation of the value of harm, apart from proof of harm itself.

That leads me to the fourth area, from which I will make my concluding points. The fourth area of social science activity in courts is determination of adjudicative fact. This occurs by means of statistical analysis of pertinent data, where the issue is inherently statistical. A major point is that if the issue is inherently statistical, it is the legislature which made it so. If laws require statistical proof, can the court deny them? The activist court is applying modern method—maybe not enough, maybe not as well as one would like—but it is accepting statistical proof of fact or, more precisely, proof of the improbability of the fact having a random (noninvidious) explanation. I think, whether we have recognized it or not, this major step from the legislative, background, what-the-world-looks-like use of social science to the adjudicative, foreground, what's-happening-in-this-case use has generated increased interest in the role of social science in the courts.

Remember, Holmes linked statistics and economics—and so do I. Social science conclusions *are* statistical conclusions. Most statistical analyses rely on social science conceptions. Apart from the history of social science in legislative fact, there is an interesting history behind the attempt to prove or at least support the facts of a case by statistical analysis. Here is a brief list of well-known cases:

1. *Howland Will* (1870)—were the changes in the will authentic?
2. *People v. Risley* (New York, 1915)—were court document changes made on an attorney's typewriter "borrowing" the documents from the court?
3. *Maxwell v. Bishop* (1966–67)—an attempt at showing that blacks who raped whites were sentenced to death more than any other race combination in rape cases (that is, the particular jury was a sample from a biased universe).
4. *State v. Snead* (Minnesota, 1966)— use of telephone book to estimate frequency of name.
5. *People v. Collins* (California, 1968)—interracial couple in yellow car.
6. *Griggs v. Duke Power* (1970)—invalid employment requirement.
7. *Hobson v. Hansen II* (1971)—allocation of school resources, reportedly the first use of regression analysis in a federal court.
8. *Serrano v. Priest* and successor cases—public school finance system correlates wealth and per-pupil expenditure.
9. *Hawkins v. Town of Shaw*—unequal allocation of municipal facilities.
10. *Castaneda v. Partida* (1977)—unrepresentative jury list.

Note that in *Norris v. Alabama* (1934) and other jury exclusion cases the disparities between the percentage of a minority in the community and the percentage on juries were so gross that statistical analysis was not required. In other cases the system was so rigged the unfairness was apparent. But *Castaneda* (1977) has a footnote of comparable notoriety to footnote 11 of *Brown*—footnote 17, the two or three standard deviation rule.

Note the shift from statistics as an adjunct to a conceptually nonstatistical case, to statistics as the only way to picture what is wrong. Conceptually, one could have seen a forger changing a will or a court document; and one could have seen and identified persons who committed a crime. One cannot see discrimination in jury lists in the same way—unless it is contended that an original draw was fair and someone changed the names. No particular draw, no particular name that appears or does not appear, is suspect. Although a law saying "Don't drive through a red light and strike a pedestrian" looks grammatically like "Don't discriminate in hiring or pay on the basis of race, sex, or national origin," the way in which one would observe these actions is entirely different. For example, we do not need to observe a car which does not hit a pedestrian to know when a pedestrian has been hit.

Statistical propositions are not new to courts. Fingerprint classifications, for example, have no biological basis that I know of. It is merely highly improbable for two people to have the same combination of print characteristics, assuming the characteristics are independent. I don't even know of a biological model that says why the characteristics used to define a print should be independent, but apparently they act as if they are.

In addition to the history of cases, we have the explosion of literature. Finkelstein, Kaplan, and Sigal wrote major law review articles in the mid-1960s, discussing statistical proofs (Finkelstein 1966; Kaplan 1968; Sigal 1969-70).[1] In the early 1970s there was a stimulating debate between Finkelstein and Fairley, on the one hand, and Lawrence Tribe, on the other, about the use of Bayesian analysis as proof in criminal cases (Finkelstein and Fairley 1970; Tribe 1971; Finkelstein and Fairley 1971). Recently an entire issue of the *Villanova Law Review* discussed statistical proofs (*Villanova Law Review* 1977-78). Articles too numerous to mention and certainly too numerous to read appear regularly. Frank Morris, a Washington attorney, has published an interesting book bearing virtually the same name as this conference—substituting "statistics" for "applied social research" (Morris 1978). David Copus published his famous paper, "The Numbers Game is the Only Game in Town" (Copus 1977). For good or ill, the art today is statistical proof.

I don't contend that this new area is a tidal wave sweeping the law. Suits filed as class actions represent less than 3 percent of all federal filings, although that percentage has been growing over time (U.S. Courts 1977).[2] Thus, statistical proof of adjudicative fact is hardly the major thrust of litigation today. My claim is only that this area of litigation places the social scientist in the role of partner with the attorney in proving or disproving the alleged facts of the case at hand. Statistical proof challenges the court to assess a social

7

science/statistical analysis in order to understand the basic factual assertions or denials. One consequence of this challenge is that class actions are a larger percentage of cases pending than of cases filed in U.S. district courts.

Despite the differences I have pointed out, class actions and statistical proof do not reflect a change in the focus of court action on the individual; they reflect a change in the nature of the action of the individual that the government intends to regulate. We cannot say *which* Mexican-Americans in Hidalgo County were excluded from the grand jury list, but we can say that too many of them were and that the sheriff did it. The proof is not in a parade of people saying, "I was excluded," "So was I," and "Me too." There simply aren't such individual people who were excluded, though there is a class which contains excluded people.

This is very different from, say, a cashier who steals a dollar a day and is apprehended a year and $200 later. Stealing the first dollar was a crime. Not hiring a particular black, Hispanic, female, or maybe an Anglo isn't even conceptually a crime (if you'll pardon the civil/criminal confusion) in the typical class action. In the "numbers game" there is a different conception of what the problem is and therefore of how to demonstrate it. The government has chosen to regulate behavior inherently observable only in relative terms and only when there are multiple observations.

This is a long way from the remarks of Judge Henley of Arkansas:

> As a matter of fact, the Court doubts that such discrimination, which is a highly subjective matter, can be detected accurately by a statistical analysis such as was undertaken here. Statistics are elusive things at best, and it is a truism that almost anything can be proved by them. (*Maxwell v. Bishop* 1966, p. 720)

I have nothing against good intelligent skepticism. But the language of the Supreme Court in *Teamsters* seems more appropriate:

> . . . statistics are not irrefutable; they come in infinite variety and, like any other kind of evidence, they may be rebutted. In short, their usefulness depends on all of the surrounding facts and circumstances. (*International Brotherhood of Teamsters v. United States* 1977, p. 340)

So what is the state of the art? Miserable, of course. It is easy to go to a museum and admire French Impressionist paintings, but how many paintings of that period and type were any good? For every great rock band of the 1960s there were twenty lousy ones; and for every great song from a band that same band produced twenty lousy ones—except, of course, the Beatles. If you ask about the state of *any* art from the *average* practice of it, no era, no art looks very good. Working in this field every day, I find that the average quality of statistical analysis, social science, case theory, data, concept, and preparation is really bad.

Let's not talk about the average. But in one corner—3 percent of the cases—the prediction of Holmes, the hope of Frankfurter, and the fear of many is coming true: the courts are receiving and applying analytic method as direct factual proof. Law journals are bursting with the news. Many of these articles are foolish, some are wrong, most are merely vacuous; but they are there. And I trust all the foregoing explains why we are here.

PAUL L. ROSEN*

More than seven decades have passed since the Boston attorney Louis Brandeis formally introduced the fledgling social science, or what was then perceived to be social science, to the venerable institution of law. Justice David Brewer of the U.S. Supreme Court accorded legitimacy to the innovative union of social science and law when he stated, "It may not be amiss, in the present case, before examining the constitutional question, to notice the course of legislation as well as expressions of opinion *from other than judicial sources*" (emphasis added). This extralegal or social science data, Brewer went on to note, "may not be, technically speaking, [legal] authorities, and in them is little or no discussion of the constitutional question presented to us for determination, yet they are significant of a widespread belief that woman's physical structure, and the functions she performs in consequence thereof, justify special legislation restricting or qualifying the conditions under which she should be permitted to toil" *(Muller v. Oregon* 1908, pp. 419-420). Brewer was in effect opening the Court, which with its insular mechanical jurisprudence had long blocked progressive social welfare legislation, to fresh insights, assumptions, and perspectives, which in time would revolutionize American constitutional politics. Brewer had issued what later came to be construed as a judicial invitation to social science to play a more active role in the courtroom. For as he made clear on behalf of the Court in this regard, "when a question of fact is debated and debatable, and the extent to which a special constitutional limitation goes is affected by the truth in respect to that fact, a widespread and long continued belief concerning it is worthy of consideration. We take judicial cognizance of all matters of general knowledge" *(Muller v. Oregon* 1908, pp. 420-421). Brandeis's successful linkage of social science and law, however, did not generate widespread attention. Nor did it stimulate pronounced interest among social scientists until more than forty years later. In the celebrated 1954 school desegregation case the Supreme Court cited social science as "modern authority" in what is probably the most controversial footnote in American constitutional law *(Brown v. Board of Education* 1954).[3]

Thus, while social science had an unheralded and modest impact on constitutional adjudication between 1908 and 1954, the Brown case marked the beginning of a trend toward greater judicial utilization of social science knowledge. Today this trend has developed into a substantial, sometimes critical, and frequently controversial component of the legal process. However, problems remain to be resolved. Some are implicit in the inherent differences between social science and law. Other, perhaps more fundamental, problems relate to the administration and application of social science research.

In the first instance, to be sure, Brandeis's original match of social science and law was not without its legal and epistemological eccentricities. Because the prototypical sociological or Brandeis brief was submitted in support of

*Associate professor of political science, Carleton University, Ottawa, Canada.

contested legislation, Brandeis argued that the Court need only note the existence of a reputable body of knowledge from which it could surmise the reasonableness of the legislation in question. He disavowed any need for the Court to ponder the far more nettlesome scientific issue of the reliability and validity of the research it was being asked to consider. In effect, Brandeis claimed that social science could be of invaluable assistance to the Court regardless of whether or not such research met conventional standards of scientific credibility. For the purpose of law, then, legal presumption and not scientific credibility became established as the extrascientific canon which would primarily determine the utility and efficacy of the judicial use of social science.

Today, of course, the courts are much more inclined to scrutinize the quality of the social science research they are requested to note. Nevertheless, it must be realized that courts will use social science as they and not necessarily social scientists see fit. Therefore, legal presumptions require study when social science is considered as a legal resource, because anomalous adjudicatory consequences may sometime follow from them. As Donald Horowitz has shrewdly observed, "a court, using behavioral studies, can find as a 'fact' what the studies cannot and do not show with anything approaching the degree of consistency required to generate confidence in the findings, and no one can impeach the results" (Horowitz 1977, p. 145). With regard to the judicial use of less disputable social science (or in terms of Brewer's dictum, research which confirms "widespread and long continued belief"), though presumably safe and nonproblematic, what application aside from a mere legitimating function can such data have? If social science is to play a meaningful role in adjudication, it will invariably offer findings or hypotheses which contravene common knowledge or challenge the taken-for-granted world. However, radical social science which flies in the face of common definitions of social reality and which is applicable only to concrete and narrowly drawn legal controversies is likely to be in short supply. Also, more often than not such information will be considered tentative.

In other words, the social science which can have the greatest impact on law, that which buttresses the case for progressive change, will pose a pressing ideological question which, curiously enough, will be debated in alternative methodological terms. By and large the most consistent critics of the judicial use of social science are not only conservative judges but equally conservative social scientists who fundamentally object to courtrooms being used as vehicles of social change. Conservative social scientists tend to view all of social science as a liberal conspiracy, almost as if they themselves and their establishment journals did not exist. As Daniel Patrick Moynihan writes, for example, social science "attracts persons whose interests are in shaping the future rather than preserving the past. In any event, the pronounced 'liberal' orientation of sociology, psychology, political science, and similar fields is well established" (Moynihan 1979, pp. 19-20). Accordingly, the argument runs, social science must be a most tentative enterprise. However, the judgment of what is tentative is not made with reference to the standards of social science as a whole. Nor is it made in the context of understanding the way human affairs are conducted. Instead, it is made by spuriously comparing social science to physical science as if it were commonplace to make legal, political, and economic decisions only when these decisions are verifiably in accord with the laws of physical science. Making this comparison, Moynihan remarks, "The explanatory power of the various [social science] disciplines is limited. Few serious permanencies are ever established. In a period of civilization in which the physical sciences are immensely advanced, when the methodology of proof is well established, and when discoveries rush one upon the other, there are not many things social science has to say" (Moynihan 1979, p. 20).

Perhaps it would be more accurate to say that it is not the volume of judicially available social science insights which is problematic, but rather the political consequences of these explanations, which for some is the critical disquieting factor inherent in the judicial application of social science knowledge. It is not the fact that social science is always likely to chart a liberal course which make critics politically wary of it. This would be to prejudge the results of social science research before it is even undertaken. Social science engenders conservative suspicion simply because liberal courts and counsel are likely to be the proponents of social science findings as justification of substantive legal change, whereas conservatives with precedent ready at hand have less need for additional ammunition to fight change. Precedent or the lack thereof can always be cited in the place of social science to question the wisdom and constitutionality of fundamental social change. This is not to suggest, however, that the adequacy of social science findings is ipso facto a moot question. Needless to say, courts must apprise themselves of the adequacy of the data and findings they are urged to apply to particular cases. Jurists certainly need to give more thought to the question of whether the courts should enter the legal wilderness with incomplete social science maps. That is, should the courts fashion new legal rules on the basis of less-than-compelling evidentiary data? Conversely, should the courts ignore wrongs and proposed remedies simply because illustrative social science hypotheses have not been certified as methodologically pure in all quarters?

Surely, this is a judgmental quandary, one which no doubt contributed to the judiciary's reluctance in the first instance to rush fully into the embrace of social science. The Brandeis brief may well provide a deluge of facts, but facts which a court may perhaps not wish to recognize. Speaking in the Adkins case in 1923, Justice Sutherland observed, "A mass of reports, opinions of special observers and students of the subject, and the like, has been brought before us in support of this statement [the relationship between female earnings and female morality], all of which we have found interesting but only mildly persuasive" (*Adkins v. Children's Hospital* 1923, p. 560). In the same case Chief Justice Edward D. White is reported to have lifted the Brandeis brief and remarked, "Why, I could compile a brief twice as thick to prove that the legal profession ought to be abolished" (Mason 1964, p. 31). But this was a court with a restrictive view of judicial powers. In retrospect it is clear that the courts have undergone a veritable revolution; they now make not only law but social policy, and there is hardly an area of the public bureaucracy that remains immune from what is in effect administrative supervision by the courts. This judicial activity is characteristically predicated on the basis of legislative or social facts. Accordingly, during the past twenty years the relationship between social science and law has become not only familiar but routinized. As Judge John Minor Wisdom observed:

> What seemed at first to be antagonism between social science and law has now developed into a love match. What began in the field of education spread to many other fields. In case after case the Fifth Circuit, among other courts, has relied on studies developed by social scientists and other scientists to show pollution, unlawful exclusion of blacks from the jury system, employment discrimination, arbitrary or discriminatory use of the death penalty, discrimination against women, the need for reapportionment, and the cure for malapportionment of various public bodies. (Wisdom 1975, pp. 142-143)

This may indicate the nature and scope of the relationship, as well as the need for communication, between two disparate and autonomous disciplines. But it should not be inferred that the judicial process is now fully open to ministrations from social science. To the extent that social science formally relates to law, it must for the most part be filtered through the adversary system, and this system, it has been widely noted, does not work well to clarify competing social science hypotheses. Opposing counsel produce highly partisan versions of the facts, and courts must choose between two one-sided and necessarily conflicting statements. Counsel's objective is to win a favorable verdict rather than to establish a record of scholarly detachment and commitment to truth. Thus, there is present within the adversary system a positive incentive for lawyers to manipulate social science data or to use them with less than a scrupulous concern for scientific method.

Social scientists may also be tempted to stray from the principle of objectivity when they put their learning at the service of a worthwhile but nonetheless partisan cause. One sociologist familiar with this problem has written, "The social science researcher has a fear of his being captured subtly, and, perhaps even unconsciously, by the desire to prove his case, to show the kinds of evidence he believes and wants to believe exist" (Wolfgang 1974, p. 241).

It is difficult to deny that the clash of ideas and concepts and the delivery of partisan social science testimony can obfuscate rather than explain critical factual problems. This is particularly true when courts are subjected to opposing methods of statistical analysis. In *Hobson v. Hansen*, for example, Judge J. Skelly Wright addressed this specific imbroglio and extricated the court by remarking, "the court has been forced back to its own common sense approach to a problem which, though admittedly complex, has certainly been made more obscure than was necessary. The conclusion I reach is based upon burden of proof, and upon straightforward moral and constitutional arithmetic" (*Hobson v. Hansen* 1971, p. 859). Justice Brennan, in the case of *Craig v. Boren*, observed in the same vein, "It is unrealistic to expect either members of the judiciary or state officials to be well-versed in the rigors of experimental or statistical technique. But this merely illustrates that proving broad sociological propositions by statistics is a dubious business, and one that inevitably is in tension with the normative philosophy that underlies the Equal Protection Clause" (*Craig v. Boren* 1976, p. 204). Nevertheless, this did not deter the high bench from finding unconstitutional a gender-based traffic safety law on the grounds that the statistical reasoning underlying the statute was methodologically inadequate.

While the adversary system and rules of evidence are intended to insulate the courtroom from unfounded factual assumptions, this does not mean that facts cannot be introduced in circuitous ways. Judges have been known to conduct what Justice Brennan called "independent research." "It is better to have witnesses," Frankfurter has remarked, "but I did not know that we could not read the works of competent writers" (Friedman 1969, p. 63). Judicial research may be undertaken in an even more unorthodox fashion. Some Supreme Court justices have been known to consult *in camera* with the executive branch on the course of a case under deliberation. For that matter, there are many ways that different kinds of less reliable extralegal data are brought into the courtroom and translated into law. The somewhat ironical point is that social science findings regarded as apposite to law are always open to criticism because they are subjected to the inadequate testing procedure of the adversary system, while other extralegal data—and perhaps the very assumptions on which a case may actually turn—escape adversarial scrutiny and are accepted at face value.[4]

A related though technical problem is that the judiciary has severely limited resources for the job of fact-finding. Despite the impressive volume of social policymaking by the courts, this situation has hardly improved over the years. As long ago as 1921 Benjamin Cardozo called attention to this judicial deficiency. He suggested that a ministry of justice be established to gather facts from all sources, particularly from social science, which would be relevant to the judicial decision-making process (Cardozo 1921). Courts do appoint experts in some instances to present findings on technical matters, and there are various proposals for creating and putting at the disposal of courts better fact-finding machinery. But how this might be done without threatening the highly prized autonomy of the courts to find facts for themselves has not been made clear. And while it is a necessary activity, fact-finding, after all, is not the end of the judicial decision-making process. As Justice Frankfurter remarked somewhat trenchantly, "I do not care what any associate or full professor in sociology tells me. If it is in the Constitution, I do not care about what they say. But the question is, is it in the Constitution?" (Friedman 1969, p. 65).

In the final analysis the Brandeis brief, with all its limitations, remains for the courts their best link to social science. This suggests that the ultimate responsibility for insuring that the courts are informed of apposite social science findings rests with counsel. "There are many things that courts would notice if brought before them that beforehand they do not know," Justice Holmes once remarked, adding that "It rests with counsel to take the proper steps, and if they deliberately omit them, we do not feel called upon to institute inquiries on our own account" (*Quong Wing v. Kirkendall* 1912, p. 64).

Attorneys, however, anxious to buttress their cases, are not likely to know how to gain access to the findings they require. Those without social science training or ties to research organizations must rely on their own limited resources in locating relevant findings. Source books prepared for lawyers are of some assistance, but much remains to be done to improve the access of the legal community to the archives of social science.

If all the problems of access and delivery were solved, there would still be concern over the political impact or lack of impact of social science on the law. Recall Edmund Cahn's reaction to the Supreme Court's use of social science in *Brown*: Should fundamental rights, he asked, be tied to the tenuous and changing findings of social science (Rosen 1972)? Most recently, it has been argued that the absence of clear and conclusive social science findings in several important areas of litigation has served for the judiciary as a justification for cautious and status-quo-oriented decisions (Daniels 1978). For example, despite extensive social science research on the deterrent effect (that is, the lack of effect) of capital punishment, no court has yet found the death penalty to be in contravention to the restriction on cruel and unusual punishment contained in the Eighth Amendment.

It is questionable, though, whether there are valid grounds for complaint just because social science does not always fit easily into every man's legal brief. Some of this disappointment is based on a misconception of what social science is and what it can do. Advocates would like to think of social science as empirical hardtack, a no-nonsense nutrient which would permit every man to conquer his own personally chosen legal frontier. Because statistical evidence ostensibly lends itself best to specific controversies, statistical argumentation has often been relied on by courts, reinforcing the mistaken notion that social science is more or less a statistical science. The fact is that the common identity of social science is a loose one; social science is a variegated science extending from statistically informed, narrow-gauge studies to grand Weberian or Marxian projections which are often statistically barren. The latter variation has usually been the more creative and insightful form of social science, but it tends to be articulated at such a high level of abstraction that it is not applicable to concrete legal disputes. The former may be more amenable to judicial use, but it is also more vulnerable to methodological criticism and is in the long run less useful in extending the sweep of the judicial mind.

The courts may use the absence of convincing social science findings or a professed inability to understand social science explanation as an excuse not to endorse a particular social policy. An example is the Supreme Court's cautious and conservative approach to affirmative action in the *Bakke* case. Fearful of problematic cases that might be spawned by too strong an endorsement of affirmative action, Justice Powell pointed out the difficulties that the courts would encounter if they had to classify various deprived minority groups: "The kind of variable sociological and political analysis necessary to produce such rankings simply does not lie within the judicial competence—even if they otherwise were politically feasible and socially desirable" (*Regents v. Bakke* 1978, p. 775). Nevertheless, we know that the courts will undertake intricate remedial social planning (for example, busing programs) without the assistance of social science (*Northcross v. Board of Education* 1973, pp. 16-17). Therefore, we should not be too quick to fault social science for the varying rate of judicial activism or restraint.

Social science may at times mesh well with the needs of the law. But it is not prudent to expect too much from social science inasmuch as in its full creative bloom it bears little likeness to a problem-solving discipline. In a concrete dispute contract research may contribute immeasurably to an adversarial objective; whether such research makes any contribution to social science is another matter. If social science is to maintain its creative energy it must not become too ensconced in the legal marketplace. Law and social science ought to be encouraged to cohabit but in so doing should not sacrifice their own identities.[5] Law and social science need to get on with their business, and inevitably these lines of business will intersect. The higher business of both, however, is civilization, and thus we are faced with a question far larger than that of the best technique. Social science and law need to remain conscious of their service to civilization, and the primary lesson for both may perhaps be found in the words of Learned Hand: "Of those qualities on which civilization depends, next after courage, it seems to me, comes an open mind, and, indeed, the highest courage is, as Holmes used to say, to stake your all upon a conclusion which you are aware tomorrow may prove false" (cited in Dillard 1959, p. 148).

STEPHEN L. WASBY*

We may be asking the wrong question when we inquire about the quality of social science data used in the courts. Even when they are of the highest quality, the issue may be more centrally that of judicial attitudes toward the data, that is, the willingness of judges to use them. A closely related issue is jurisprudential: When is the use of such data appropriate?

Courts continue to be ambivalent about the use of social science evidence. I think that this is in part a reflection of the general public's misunderstanding—or lack of understanding—of social science, coupled with the failure to train lawyers in the social sciences. Even if most lawyers have majored in the social sciences as undergraduates, training in social science methods and techniques tends to be the province of graduate schools.

Criticisms of the courts, such as those appearing in law reviews, could benefit substantially if law students or their professors knew more social science. Part of the problem is that they don't know when they have a social science problem, just as lawyers say that citizens don't know when they have a legal problem. And then they aren't sure how to deal with the methods, even if they know they have a social science problem.

*Professor of political science, State University of New York at Albany.

The attitude that Justice Frankfurter expressed in the *Brown* case—if a proposition is true, I don't need sociologists to tell me that it is true (D'Amato, Metrailer, and Wasby 1977, pp. 73-74)—is still quite prevalent. Judge Henley's remarks, cited by Stephan Michelson in his presentation, are of the same general tone. We still find this attitude on the Supreme Court. Justice Rehnquist complained in *Craig v. Boren* that Justice Brennan had subjected the state to a doctoral dissertation examination in statistics (*Craig v. Boren* 1976). And Justice Powell commented on the use of numerology in the five-person jury case (*Ballew v. Georgia* 1978).

Judges will use social science findings when they reaffirm the judges' positions. In this regard, we ought to be well aware of Don Horowitz's point that competing social science findings provide judges with the flexibility to do what they want to do (Horowitz 1977, Wasby 1978). They are like legislators who, faced with competing constituent demands, are better able to go their own way than if the constituent demands pointed in a single direction. An example of this use of social science evidence to fit a particular position is Chief Justice Burger's dissent in *Bivens v. Six Unknown Federal Narcotics Agents* (1971, p. 416). Burger used Dallin Oakes's study of the exclusionary rule in his first call that the rule be repealed (Oakes 1970).

To be sure, one can find more appealing uses of social science evidence. *Castaneda v. Partida* (1977) has already been mentioned. One ought to look as well at Thurgood Marshall's discussion of sociological theory concerning repression by minority group members who have made it into positions of authority. Countering Justice Powell's passing remark that this would not be likely to happen, Marshall cites Allport, Yinger, and footnote 11, which of course he had something to do with in the first place.

We should also look at the jury cases, comparing, for example, Justice Powell's use of the Kalven jury studies in the nonunanimous-vote cases. We have tended to pay too much attention in the last couple of years to the jury size cases. But let's not overlook *Johnson v. Louisiana* (1972) and *Apodaca* (1972). And note, in the same case, Justice Douglas's more effective use of those data. It happens to fit with my predispositions, but I also think it is more effective.

Some justices appear to have a good knowledge of social science. Perhaps the material was well presented in the brief and/or the law clerks knew how to handle it. Examples are Justice Blackmun on statistical decision theory in *Castaneda* (1977) and Justice Brennan's critique of the Oklahoma surveys on drunk driving accidents by young males in *Craig v. Boren* (1976). But again keep in mind Justice Brennan's warning that it is unrealistic to expect members of the judiciary or state officials to be well versed in the rigors of experimental or statistical technique.

I would add that perhaps the high point in the courts' use of social science data was reached in the jury size cases. I think the movement from *Williams v. Florida* (1970) to *Ballew v. Georgia* (1978) is fascinating in that social scientists responded to a concern stated by the court. Studies were used to do more than just provide a footnote stating that the evidence is inconclusive, which is often the way in which such data are used, for example, in the exclusionary rule cases.

We also need to recognize the use of social science around the courts, not merely as evidence in cases. This includes what many people would call court reform, but it is not limited to that. Social scientists can assist courts in obtaining perspectives on themselves. My own experience, largely based on a study of the U.S. Court of Appeals for the Ninth Circuit, suggests that under proper conditions judges may be open to the presence of social scientists and may learn that they have something to contribute to the law. As I noted earlier, judges don't know much about social science; part of the reason is that they don't know many social scientists and have not seen them at work.

What I am suggesting is difficult to carry off; it requires an entree and the right sort of circumstances. Probably the most critical requirement is a receptive chief judge. I rank judges along a continuum from "open" to "closed" in terms of their attitude toward having extra people, "furriners," around the courts. Social scientists who don't have law degrees—and I fall into that category—clearly are foreigners.

What can a person do in that situation? Judges are simply too busy to develop perspectives on themselves. Indeed, a court may learn about itself by reading what social scientists say or write on the basis of interviews with the judges. That may seem a rather roundabout way of doing it, but the judges simply don't have the time. They talk business over lunch; they don't ask, "How do we look to each other?"

An independent social scientist, by interviewing lawyers, can provide the court with the lawyers' views on sensitive matters, for example, the question of whether the court is perceived as discouraging oral argument. Most lawyers wouldn't dare say that directly to a judge, but they might funnel it through a social scientist.

It is also possible that in this circumstance a social scientist could provide some input with respect to the court's problems, but again only if the judges are open in their attitudes. A question, however, that bothers me is whether a social scientist who is successful in getting proposals adopted has been co-opted.

The courts may be unwilling to accept findings which run counter to their conventional wisdom, particularly where they have publicly advocated a specific reform. An example is the Civil Appeals Management Project in the Second Circuit. Jerry Goldman's findings simply do not bear out Judge Kaufman's often touted position that settlement conferences are going to help (Goldman 1977). And there will be further embarrassment when Goldman's findings appear in the *Columbia Law Review* right under the judges' noses. They are not happy about that.

Another example is the study of judges' evaluations of lawyer competence in their courts. While the findings of the Federal Judicial Center (FJC) study, *The Quality of Advocacy in the Federal Courts* (Partridge and Bermant 1978), suggest that some judges, and indeed some lawyers, think that some lawyers are inadequate, the findings are not nearly as strong as the Chief Justice suggested in his earlier remarks. And that is going to cause a problem.

Since I have mentioned the FJC, let me make a comment about the sort of studies that it is able to carry out so well. The FJC can obtain access to information because it is official; it can collect data very quickly. But one should be aware in reading FJC materials that there are rumblings out there. The judges have been known to say, "Oh, another one of those FJC surveys."

I don't know whether there are actually distortions in the data, but it is possible. There is also the question of whether the FJC, where the Chief Justice is the chairman of the board, might have to pull its punches or be tempted to keep some of its findings beneath the surface because of his position.

Now let me say something about what we do or do not know about the use of social science evidence in the courts. That we are having this conference suggests that we need to know more. I would point out that the program of which I am in charge this year has funded several studies concerned with the use of social science material in the courts. But they have barely begun to take us down the necessary path.

Levin and Askin have made some useful observations about social science data in privacy cases. Let me just quote a paragraph from a draft manuscript:

> For all the social scientists now researching and writing about personal privacy, it is clear that their impact on the law has been minimal. Privacy as a phenomenological concept rests at a relatively high level of abstraction and research is still embryonic. Courts and lawyers are understandably hesitant to venture into such a milieu for hard answers. (Levin and Askin 1977)

Victor Rosenblum's more general study presents some basic information about the use of social science data in various types of Supreme Court cases. Rosenblum offers a fairly good picture in terms of frequency of use by judge, by issue, by majority and minority types of opinions. Although this is essentially a citation count, it is a necessary first step. The Barron and Miller study examines the flow of information to the court, but its thrust is somewhat different (Barron and Miller 1975). We need many more such studies, although that should not be read as an official call for proposals.

DISCUSSION

Alan Paller *(Applied Urbanetics)*: It seems to me that each of you is talking about a few cases that you think are social science applications. Stephan drew the economists in with the statisticians from Holmes's statement and thereby sort of jumped into everything that economists do in antitrust cases. But where do you think the limits are? At what point are we talking about social science and at what point are we talking about the law, not social science?

Stephen Wasby: I'm not sure we ought to impose limits when only beginning to examine a topic. I think the temptation is to focus, for example, on the jury size cases, and they certainly deserve attention, to focus on Title VII cases, which, as Stephan pointed out, are one of the cutting edges. But then we tend to forget about antitrust, as you have just recognized, and the exclusionary rule cases. We have been trying to suggest the wide variety of areas in which social science is applicable.

Ron Anson *(National Institute of Education)*: Do you think there is any problem in limiting this discussion to the courts? There is growing interaction between courts and legislatures, and the courts really have to take off from what legislatures give them. There is also more interaction between the courts and the regulatory or administrative agencies which must implement what the courts say. The interaction between applied social research and these other arenas probably has a lot to do with what has happened and will happen in the courts.

Wasby: If you think the state of the art is bad in this area, don't even begin to think of the state of the art with respect to legislatures, most of which are poorly staffed, if staffed at all. They simply do not have the requisite time, personnel, or expertise.

I agree with you that many of the problems faced by the courts stem from legislative problems and compromises. But the state of the art in terms of the use of applied social research by legislatures is much worse.

Stephan Michelson: I think that is a good point for two reasons. First, a very large percentage of cases filed are not decided by the court; they are otherwise disposed of.

Second, in the Title VII area many more cases are handled in negotiation between the Equal Employment Opportunity Commission (EEOC) and companies or defendants, and compliance with the Executive Order for federal contractors, which is similar to Title VII, almost never gets into court. So there is a lot of activity going on outside the courts which resembles what you think of as the forefront cases. Of course, ideally the people running EEOC, the Office of Federal Contract Compliance Programs (OFCCP), the Federal Trade Commission, and other such agencies should have training in both social science and the law. It is a sad state of affairs.

Another point: lawyers have a peculiar notion that you have a set of rules and you have facts which are applied against the rules. They think that the district courts look only at facts; the rules are set somewhere else. But it never happens this way. You never know when you are talking about a fact and when you are talking about a rule, which means that you can't draw that boundary.

Clark Abt *(Abt Associates Inc.)*: Steve Wasby mentioned the primitive state of social research application to the legislature. Consider the implication of this for the degree of specialization among lawyers, judges, and particularly the courts versus the degree of specialization among social scientists, at least with respect to the federal legislature.

Donald Horowitz's excellent book, *The Courts and Social Policy* (1977), speaks to this point. Discussing problems in adjudication of social issues and the contrast between rights and alternatives, Horowitz claims that the adjudicative process inhibits the presentation of an array of alternatives in the court and an explicit matching of benefits and costs that is available to legislatures:

> Legislators and administrators . . . have a wider range of tools in their kit. They may resort to the same kinds of sanctions judges invoke or they may use taxation, incentives and subsidies of various kinds, interventions in the market place, the establishment of new organizations or the takeover of old ones, or a number of other ways of seeking to attain their goals. The judiciary, on the other hand, having no budget save for administrative expenses, no power to tax or to create new institutions, has much less ability to experiment or to adjust its techniques to the problems it confronts. The courts can forbid, require, or permit activity, but in general they cannot permit activity conditionally, for example by taxing something so as to discourage it. Many of the tools that are favored by economists in particular are missing from the judicial black bag.

What that says to me is basically that, with the increasing reliance on litigation in the resolution of social issues, we have one of the primary wellsprings of the increasing use of government regulation, as opposed to the system of incentives that Charles Schultz talked about in his Godkin Lectures as a highly preferable form of persuasive social action, because the courts generally have to make decisions that result in regulation of social behavior rather than creation of incentives for productive social behavior.

I think in that sense the legislative bodies have a superior armamentarium of more diverse tools which are more consistent with American pluralistic democratic practice, that is, the preference for incentives rather than coercive measures to implement public policy.

Wasby: Clark, I think we are talking about two different things. Potentially, legislatures can do a lot more. That line of analysis I don't have trouble with. But what I am talking about is whether or not they use applied social research. There are an increasing number of social scientists on Capitol Hill because of the academic unemployment rate. Political scientists are finding that that is a place to go. Job insecurity comes with the territory and you don't sit there for five years and not get tenure. I think that there are more people there.

But those of us in Washington, D.C., have a seriously distorted view of legislative staffing, which is reinforced if we happen to come from New York or Florida or California. State legislatures are in an exceptionally sorry state in terms of staffing. I have worked with them and I know a lot of staff people. Even if they have the range of weapons to apply and do apply them, that doesn't mean they do it on the basis of applied social research.

Abt: I would agree with Steve Wasby's opinion of most state legislatures. I think we differ mainly with respect to the Congress and some of the more advanced states, like California and Michigan and New York. I'm afraid I can't say anything very good about my native state of Massachusetts in that regard.

Carol Werner *(University of Utah)*: Any social service agency receiving federal funding is required to provide some statistical evidence that it is using the money properly and adequately and that its program is productive. That requirement seems to be of value in terms of evaluation research. Perhaps we could devise a mechanism for getting more evaluation research into the courts. Is that a possibility?

Michelson: You certainly don't want to get me off on the sorry state of evaluation research. God help us, it's bad enough now. If it went into the courts, there would be no end.

Werner: Those of us who are in the forefront wouldn't agree.

David Baldus *(University of Iowa)*: Is there anything special about the problems of the courts dealing with applied social research, or could we generalize our question to the problems of courts dealing with any sort of scientific research?

Michelson: Don't you think social science is a contradiction in terms and that the courts are bothered by this? There is a lot of argument on the other side.

It is difficult to answer the question of what constitutes different kinds of knowledge. But surely most lay people think that physics knowledge is different from social science knowledge and medical knowledge. One of the points I made was that some things that we think are scientific, like fingerprinting, are in fact statistical.

But I can't get over the belief from my childhood that there are different kinds of knowledge, and what we think we know about society tends to be wrong, even though we know that many physicists have been wrong over time.

Wasby: I like David's suggestion. Look at the suggestions about the science court. Judges are not trained in the physical sciences either. Although this is not done systematically, sometimes judges pick as their law clerks people who have majored in chemistry or physics as undergraduates, and cases are assigned to those judges for writing, interestingly enough, because nobody else can handle them. In that sense the question of whether judges can deal with scientific input can be posed for both hard science and social science.

Abt: What we are talking about is the use of applied social research in the courts, and that is a little bit different from social science. It includes social science, but it also includes the physical sciences. In other words, you can define applied social research in terms of the intellectual disciplines it uses or the kinds of problems it addresses. Applied social research uses the physical sciences, mathematics, statistics, and sometimes engineering, although most of the people who practice applied social research are trained in the social sciences.

I would also like to reaffirm the unity of the sciences in general and point out that the quantitative methods used in the social sciences are not fundamentally different from the quantitative methods used in the physical sciences. I speak with a little bit of authority on this, having been trained in both.

It is also not widely understood by either social scientists or laymen that much of the basis of our knowledge in the physical sciences is statistical. Specifically, a great deal of the knowledge in theoretical physics is based on statistical analyses, very much as knowledge in the social sciences is based on statistical knowledge.

We could get into a long, complicated discussion of the similarities and differences between the social and physical sciences, which is probably an excellent topic for another conference. Suffice it to say here that we should not exclude the use of information from the physical sciences or engineering in court decisions, but our concern here is mainly with the social sciences because of the topics of concern, rather than the methods alone.

Garth Taylor *(University of Chicago)*: I have a question for Stephan: whose responsibility is it to produce information for the court? What are the current trends in judicial notice, and what do you think would be the right way to do it?

Michelson: One of the interesting trends is the addition of appendage organizations to the federal judicial system. The first was the conference; I forget what it was originally called, but it was an official gathering of justices. I think that started in the 1920s. It is now an annual judicial conference. Then the Administrative Center of the Courts was established to gather data and help administrate the courts. In 1968 the Federal Judicial Center was founded to meet the need for another institution.

That should raise the question of whether there will be yet another institution to do research on a confidential basis, for example, to provide justices with a good social science analysis of diminution of jury size. Considering our recent history of adding institutions, this is conceivable. But I don't think it will happen. I think that, had the Court asked for a social science analysis of the diminution of jury size, it would have been given the same analysis. You will be surprised to know that when my book is published by the Urban Institute, it will support the Court and not the critics. I will claim that the social science analysis was wrong.

That will be a continuing problem: an institution will do social science analysis for the court, and somebody will say it's wrong. I don't have an answer. The obvious answer, which would be a new institution added to the two that the federal judicial system has already, won't work. The adversary process is going to have to be improved.

Richard Goldstein *(Center for Community Economic Development)*: I have two questions. The first one concerns Stephan's discussion of inherently statistical cases. Are there cases that never get to court or that fail in court because they are inherently statistical from the defense point of view; that is, the aggrieved party would actually have to be suing a class of people, something that doesn't appear to have happened?

Second, is there a distinction to be made in the context in which social science is used? In the context of a particular case an analysis may be good, whereas in some other context, it may not.

Michelson: To answer your first question, I'm sure there are situations where you have nobody to sue, but I don't know of any. People are always in organizations. When employees go on strike, their employers sue the union.

Robert Hallisey *(Superior Court of Massachusetts)*: In the case of deaths caused by air pollution, everybody contributed.

Paul Rosen: I think the problem is that, generically speaking, social science doesn't deal with particular cases.

Michelson: Regarding the second question, this is the forefront. Social science traditionally deals with groups; we come into the courts and talk about particular cases. Certainly some of the proofs used in court wouldn't be used for large-scale research projects.

Sue Johnson *(New York State Court System)*: I think we use different criteria when we move from research viewed as research to research used in the courts; the criterion for judging whether it was successful in a court case is whether the side for which it was presented won or lost. In the courts research plays an advocacy role.

NOTES

1. See also Broun and Kelly (1970).
2. In some of these cases class certification is dropped or denied, but in others amended complaints make class claims that are not picked up in the data.
3. For a discussion of the Court's epoch-making use of social science in *Brown* and the events leading to it, see Rosen (1972).
4. See Barron and Miller (1975).
5. See Rosen (1977).

REFERENCES

Adams, Brooks. 1913. *The Theory of Social Revolutions*. New York: MacMillan.

Adkins v. Children's Hospital, 261 *U.S.* 525, 560 (1923).

Apodaca, 404 *U.S.* 404 (1972).

Ballew v. Georgia, 46 *U.S.L.W.* 4217 (1978).

Barron, Jerome A. and Miller, Arthur S. 1975. The Supreme Court, the Adversary System, and the Flow of Information to the Justices: A Preliminary Inquiry. 61 *Virginia Law Review* 1187-1245.

Bivens v. Six Unknown Federal Narcotics Agents, 403 *U.S.* 388 (1971).

Blumberg, Abraham S. 1967. The Practice of Law as Confidence Game: Organizational Cooptation of a Profession. l *Law and Society Review* 15-39.

Broun, Kenneth and Kelly, Douglas G. 1970. Playing the Percentages and the Law of Evidence. 1970 *University of Illinois Law Forum* 23-48.

Brown v. Board of Education, 347 *U.S.* 483 (1954).

Cardozo, Benjamin N. 1921. A Ministry of Justice. 35 *Harvard Law Review* 113-26.

Castaneda v. Partida, 97 *S. Ct.* 1272 (1977).

Collins, Sharon. 1978. The Use of Social Research in the Courts. In *Knowledge and Policy*, Laurence E. Lynn, ed. Washington, D.C.: National Academy of Sciences.

Copus, David. 1977. The Numbers Game is the Only Game in Town. 20 *Howard Law Journal* 374.

Craig v. Boren, 429 *U.S.* 190 (1976).

D'Amato, Anthony, Metrailer, Rosemary, and Wasby, Stephen L. 1977. *Desegregation from Brown to Alexander: An Exploration of Supreme Court Strategies*. Carbondale, Ill.: Southern Illinois Univ. Press.

Daniels, Stephen. 1978. Civil Liberties and Civil Rights on the Shifting Sands of Social Science. Paper delivered at annual meeting of the American Political Science Association, New York, N.Y., September 3.

Dillard, Irving, ed. 1959. *The Spirit of Liberty*. New York: Vintage Books.

Finkelstein, Michael O. 1966. The Application of Statistical Decision Theory to the Jury Discrimination Cases. 80 *Harvard Law Review* 338-76.

Finkelstein, Michael O. and Fairley, William B. 1970. A Bayesian Approach to Identification Evidence. 83 *Harvard Law Review* 489-517.

———. 1971. A Further Critique of Mathematical Proof. 84 *Harvard Law Review* 1810-20.

Friedman, Lawrence and Macauley, Stewart, eds. 1969. *Law and the Behavioral Sciences*. Indianapolis: Bobbs-Merrill.

Friedman, Leon, ed. 1969. *Argument*. New York: Chelsea House.

Glazer, Nathan. 1978. Should Judges Administer Social Services? 50 *The Public Interest* (Winter) 64-80.

Goldman, Jerry. 1977. *An Evaluation of the Civil Appeals Management Plan: An Experiment in Judicial Administration*. Washington, D.C.: Federal Judicial Center.

Greenberg, Jack. 1956. Social Scientists Take the Stand: A Review and Appraisal of Their Testimony in Litigation. 54 *Michigan Law Review* 953-70.

Hallock, M. M. 1977-78. The Numbers Game—The Use and Misuse of Statistics in Civil Rights Litigation. 23 *Villanova Law Review* 5-34.

Hobson v. Hansen, 327 F. Supp. 844, 859 (USDC D.C. 1971).

Holmes, Oliver Wendell. 1897. The Path of Law. 10 *Harvard Law Review* 457-78.

Horowitz, Donald. 1977. *The Courts and Social Policy*. Washington, D.C.: The Brookings Institution.

International Brotherhood of Teamsters v. United States, 431 *U.S.* 324, 340 (1977) (Mr. Justice Stewart for the Court).

Johnson v. Louisiana, 404 *U.S.* 356 (1972).

Kaplan, John. 1968. Decision Theory and the Factfinding Process. 20 *Stanford Law Review* 1065.

Levin, H. A. and Askin, F. 1977. Privacy in the Courts: Law and Social Reality. 33 *Journal of Social Issues* 138.

Lewis, Ovid C. 1970. Book review of *Law and the Behavioral Sciences*. 22 *Case Western Law Review* 144-49.

Mason, Alpheus Thomas. 1964. *The Supreme Court from Taft to Warren*. New York: W. W. Norton.

Maxwell v. Bishop, 257 F. Supp. 710, 720 (E. D. Ark. 1966).

Miller, Arthur S. 1968. *The Supreme Court and American Capitalism*. New York: The Free Press.

Morris, Frank C., Jr. 1977. *Current Trends in the Use (and Misuse) of Statistics in Employment Discrimination Litigation*. Washington, D.C.: Equal Employment Advisory Council.

Moynihan, Daniel Patrick. 1979. Social Science and the Courts. 54 *The Public Interest* 19-20.

Muller v. Oregon, 208 *U.S.* 412 (1908).

National Academy of Sciences and Social Science Research Council. 1969. *Report on the Behavioral and Social Sciences: Outlook and Needs*. Washington, D.C.

Northcross v. Board of Education, 489 F. 2d 15, 16-17 (1973).

Oakes, Dallin. 1970. Studying the Exclusionary Rule in Search and Seizure. 37 *University of Chicago Law Review* 655-757.

Partridge, Anthony and Bermant, Gordon. 1978. *The Quality of Advocacy in the Federal Courts*. Washington, D.C.: Federal Judicial Center.

Quong Wing v. Kirkendall, 223 *U.S.* 59, 64 (1912).

Regents v. Bakke, 57 *L.Ed. 2d* 750, 775 (1978).

Rose, Arnold. 1967. The Social Scientist as an Expert Witness in Court Cases. In *The Uses of Sociology*, Paul F. Lazarsfeld, William H. Seweel, and Harold L. Wilensky, eds. New York: Basic Books.

Rosen, P. L. 1972. *The Supreme Court and Social Science*. Urbana, Ill.: Univ. of Illinois Press.

_____ . 1977. Social Science and Judicial Policy Making. In *Using Social Research in Public Policy Making*, C. Weiss, ed. Lexington, Mass: D.C. Heath and Co.

Sigal, Paul. 1969-70. Comment: Judicial Use, Misuse, and Abuse of Statistical Evidence. 47 *Journal of Urban Law* 165-90.

Note, Social and Economic Facts—Appraisal of Suggested Techniques for Presenting Them to the Courts. 1948. 61 *Harvard Law Review* 692-702.

Tribe, Lawrence H. 1971. Trial by Mathematics: Precision and Ritual in the Legal Process. 84 *Harvard Law Review* 1329-93.

U.S. Courts, Administrative Office. 1977. *Report of the Administrative Office, U.S. Courts*. Washington, D.C.

23 *Villanova Law Review* (1977-78).

Wasby, Stephen L. 1978. Book review of *The Courts and Social Policy*. 31 *Vanderbilt Law Review* 727-61.

Williams v. Florida, 399 *U.S.* 78 (1970).

Wisdom, John M. 1975. Some Remarks on the Role of Social Science in the Judicial Decision Making Process in School Desegregation Cases. 39 *Law and Contemporary Problems* 134, 142-43.

Wolf, Eleanor P. 1976. Social Science and the Courts: The Detroit Schools Case. 42 *The Public Interest* (Winter) 102-20.

_____. 1978. Northern School Desegregation and Residential Choice. In *Supreme Court Review*, P. B. Kurland and G. Casper, eds. Chicago: Univ. of Chicago Press.

Wolfgang, Marvin E. 1974. The Social Scientist in Court. 65 *Journal of Criminal Law and Criminology* 239, 241.

2

Misuses of Applied
Social Research

TEB MARVELL

ALLAN LIND

AUSTIN SARAT

SUE JOHNSON

ADAM YARMOLINSKY

TEB MARVELL[*]

Let me begin with two examples. The first is *Larry P. v. Riles*, a 1972 federal district court decision in California. Judge Peckham issued a preliminary injunction prohibiting the use of IQ tests when placing students in special classes for the educable mentally retarded, on the grounds that blacks were overrepresented in the special classes largely because the IQ tests were biased against blacks. To reach this result, Judge Peckham had to answer a key question: whether the IQ tests were actually a major factor in placement decisions. The schools were supposed to use many types of information and tests before placing students in special classes. The judge decided that even though the IQ tests were only one element they were very important. His reasoning was based, among other things, on *Pygmalion in the Classroom*, a 1968 study which claimed to show that informing a teacher of the IQ of a student often influences the way the teacher acts toward the student and eventually affects the student's performance (Rosenthal and Jacobson 1968). But attempts to replicate this study reached different results, and the conclusions in the Pygmalion study may well be inaccurate.[1] Even in 1972, at the time of the *Riles* decision, the failure to replicate was well known.

The second example is Judge Jerome Frank's dissent in *Triangle Publications v. Rohrlich*, a 1948 Second Circuit case. The publisher of *Seventeen Magazine* brought an unfair-competition suit against Miss Seventeen Foundations in order to get the name "Seventeen" removed from the latter's girdles. The publisher won; Judges Clark and Augustus Hand said the names were too similar.

Judge Frank dissented, claiming that it was uncertain whether the buyers—mothers and teenagers—really confuse these brand names. He complained that the parties hadn't done a survey to find out whether there was confusion. So Frank did a survey himself. He "questioned some adolescent girls and their mothers and sisters, persons I have chosen at random," and was told by all of them that no one would confuse the girdles with the magazine. He concluded that the court should rule for the girdle makers.

On the surface, these examples look like pretty bad misuses of social science. And they are misuses, not just for one reason, but for several, as I will explain later. But arguments can also be made that they are not misuses; this will also be discussed later. The point is that misuse of social science in the courts is a very complex topic. One must study each instance in depth to decide whether a misuse has occurred; often there is no clear-cut answer.

Misuse of social science in courts usually brings to mind the misinterpretation of social science information by the courts, the use of inaccurate studies, or the use of studies that do not actually address the issues decided. These are the typical attacks, often by social scientists, on footnote 11 in *Brown v. Board of Education*, the jury size cases, *Miranda, Rodriquez*, and so on.

---

[*]Staff attorney, National Center for State Courts, Williamsburg, Virginia.

However, the accuracy and relevancy of the research used are often not the key questions. Many other issues are involved. Use of a bad social science study may not be a misuse; use of a good and relevant study may be quite a bad misuse.

Much depends on the type of use. Courts allow for using inaccurate and incomplete information by presuming that a certain outcome should result based on what is currently known. Social science information in support of such a presumption, therefore, need not be particularly accurate. The original Brandeis briefs are an example; although much of their material was questionable, these briefs were not a misuse of social science information, because they were used to bolster a presumption of the validity of the statutes attacked. In a similar vein, the social science material in the *Riles* case was used only as a means to shift the burden of proof to the defendants with respect to issuing a preliminary injunction. This still left open the possibility that it would be refuted at the preliminary injunction hearing (which the defendant did not do) or in a later hearing for a permanent order.

Another factor in determining whether there is a misuse is the obvious one of determining whether there is a use. Often, when a court receives or cites questionable research findings, one cannot tell whether the materials were actually used in the decision. For example, there have been many debates about whether the Supreme Court in *Brown v. Board of Education* placed any reliance on the studies in footnote 11. Much of the social science in opinions is in footnotes, which are typically considered ancillary to the court's reasoning. Also, the social science evidence may be just one of many reasons given for a holding, and as such it may be only makeweight. In *Larry P. v. Riles* the court actually gave several arguments, in addition to that based on *Pygmalion in the Classroom*, to substantiate the contention that IQ tests are the predominant factor in decisions to place children in classes for the educable mentally retarded. That study may have had no effect on the ruling. Thus, the complexity of judicial decision making often turns the question of misuse into one of use/nonuse.

Much that can be classified as misuse of social science occurs in minority opinions. This is not a use by the court, by the actual decision makers in the case. One can even say that when a minority opinion misuses social science information, the majority is pretty shrewd, because it had the information and did not use it. This could be said about the Second Circuit in *Triangle Publications*, for Judges Hand and Clark didn't buy Judge Frank's little survey.

In determining whether there is, or may be, a misuse, it is often important to distinguish the type of fact involved. Facts used by the courts can be categorized as case facts, which are the facts of the immediate dispute, social facts, which are the facts used by courts when making law, and supporting case facts, which are used to establish case facts but are themselves not facts about the immediate dispute.[2] Each type of fact has a particular key problem concerning misuse. For case facts, the problem is that the research is almost always done specifically for the case in question (for example, a study of citizen attitudes in venue questions and economic analysis of company activities in antitrust cases). Because the research is done with the case in mind, there is bound to be uncertainty about whether the research is objective,[3] especially when much of the underlying data (for example, responses to survey questionnaires) are under the control of the litigant or his hired researcher. It may thus be a misuse to permit social science research into the court under these circumstances. The research may in fact be accurate and objective, but whether it is typically cannot be determined. Debates in this area have generally been in terms of whether the policy reasons behind the hearsay rules apply to social research.

In the case of social facts, the major issue concerning misuse is similar: Are questions about accuracy so substantial that judges should refrain from using social science material? Here the problem results from the uncertainty of the social sciences in general, as opposed to the lack of objectivity that may be caused by the adversary situation, compounded by the fact that appellate judges may not be familiar with the social sciences and may not scrutinize studies presented to them. Hence, some have suggested that social science findings should not be used to establish social facts, except in very restricted circumstances.[4]

As for supporting case facts, social science data are typically introduced in the form of expert testimony about how case fact testimony should be interpreted. This appears to be the area where social science information is most used in courts, and it is certainly the fastest growing area, largely because evidentiary restrictions are loosening. The most publicized example is psychologists' testimony about the reliability of eyewitness identifications—often lengthy testimony that includes descriptions of prior research about eyewitness mistakes. What concerns me most about social science information as supporting case facts is the floodgate problem: such information could be used in innumerable circumstances, overloading the courts and vastly increasing litigant expense. Moreover, to the extent that this testimony is successful, it gives the advantage to the litigant with the most resources. A solution in many instances is to turn the supporting case fact issues into social fact issues, such that the social science information can be used to make new law that obviates its use in numerous cases as supporting case facts. In the case of eyewitness identification, the psychologists' findings should be presented to appellate courts to support contentions that tight cautionary instructions be given juries about the general inaccuracy of eyewitness testimony (for example, when the witness did not formerly know the defendant) and that defense attorneys be allowed to emphasize this problem in their closing statements. The trial courts would then not be burdened by the psychologists' testimony, and defendants who cannot afford psychologists would also receive protection against overreliance on eyewitness testimony.

Another important question concerning misuse of social science research is how the research should be presented to or obtained by the courts, especially whether the information should come in through the adversary system. The distinction between the three types of facts is crucial here. Unless stipulated, case facts must come in through the adversary system, and the opposing party must have a chance to answer them. Case facts must be introduced by testimony, thus permitting cross-examination. "Judicial notice" of social science research used as case facts is virtually always a misuse of the research by the court, because the technical requirements for judicial notice—that the fact be commonly known or readily verified from an authoritative source—cannot be met. This is the most important reason why Judge Frank's survey in *Triangle Publications* was a misuse of social science research; it was obtained outside the record. It makes no difference that the social science research happens to be accurate; the misuse occurs because it is unfair not to give the opposing party a chance to contest the information.

Whether courts can (or should) obtain supporting case facts outside the record is uncertain. The law seems to say a judge can go outside the record if he wants to,[5] but again it may be unfair to the opposing party. In *United Shoe*, a famous antitrust case, Judge Wyzanski hired an economist as his law clerk to analyze the competitive situation in the shoe industry.[6] This provoked a lot of criticism, because it was done outside the adversary system and the lawyers had no input. Also, at one time there was talk about having technical experts as clerks in the U.S. circuit courts (Commission on Revision of the Federal Court Appellate System 1975) but the suggestion was squelched because it was felt that lawyers should have a chance to answer any information presented. The issue, I think, still remains unclear. Does a judge misuse social science research if, when hearing a criminal case without a jury, he goes home and reads about the research on eyewitness testimony? I don't know the answer.

Most of the debate about how social science information should come to the courts is in the area of social facts. Some say a court misuses social science material not included in the record. That's absurd, I think. The record is an awful place to get social science information when making law; the testimony is unorganized, presented in question-and-answer format, and often out of date by the time it gets to the final appellate court. It's hard to get the best experts to testify. And there are often large imbalances in the amount of material brought in by the opposing sides. Others claim that the court can go outside the record but not outside the briefs; but you get some of the same problems here, especially lack of competent expert information from both sides.

In my opinion, a judge misuses social science information as social facts if he fails to do a lot of work on his own to investigate it; the chances of being misled are great, and because new law is made, the consequences of using misleading information can be substantial. This is one of the key problems in *Larry P. v. Riles*. Only the plaintiff presented social science information, and the judge apparently did not check out the plaintiff's material. He should have, even though the result was only a temporary injunction (which, by the way, remained in effect for seven years).

I have been talking about misuse by judges. Attorneys and social scientists appearing in the courts can also misuse social research. These are ethical questions, by and large, having to do with whether, and if so when, there is an obligation to present information adverse to the party's position. These obligations are set forth in ethical rules that are taken more or less seriously and that may or may not define whether there is a misuse. Lawyers, except prosecutors and government lawyers, are not obliged to bring forth adverse case facts, and there appear to be no ethical rules concerning supporting case facts and social facts (Weinstein 1966). But they are obliged to bring forth important adverse legal authority, although this obligation is not taken seriously by many lawyers (Marvell 1978). Social scientists' obligation to present adverse information also does not always seem to be taken seriously. In all, I don't think that the ethical rules should define when there is a misuse. The adversary system is totally implanted when the information presented—case fact and supporting case fact information—determines the winner of a dispute. Presentation of social science testimony is directed by the attorney, who would certainly not facilitate testimony that aids his opponent. Thus, the social scientist is too caught up in the adversary system to present balanced testimony, which in any case would not be expected by the court.

When social facts are involved, however, the stakes are much higher because creation of law, not just who wins a case, is at issue. This is the reason why attorneys are obliged to bring forth adverse legal authority. Therefore, I think—and this may be wishful thinking—that it should be considered a misuse of social science when lawyers or social scientists do not attempt to give a balanced presentation of social facts. (Social scientists can—but never have, as far as I know—present their own amicus briefs whenever lawyers insist on maintaining an adversary stance.) A major reason for this position is that there is often a large imbalance in the amount of social fact information presented by opposing sides, such as in *Larry P. v. Riles*. Again, judges must do their own research, but they would be much better off if helped by the lawyers and social scientists.

ALLAN LIND[*]

I would like to speak from the perspective of some research that I have done with John Thibaut and Laurens Walker on perceptions of justice and the psychology of dispute resolution.[7]

Stephan Michelson noted that lawyers often seem to think of legal cases as simply a matter of finding the facts and matching them to some sort of template of law. I think that social scientists often adopt a similar point of view in thinking that what a specific legal case is about primarily is finding the truth.

I would like to present as an alternative point of view the notion that people in legal cases, particularly in civil disputes, are interested not just in truth, but also in the feeling that they have been treated fairly, that the procedures for resolution of their dispute are fair and match their notions of what should be done.

I think that this idea is relevant to the distinction that we have made between adjudicative, case-specific social research and more general social research about legislative or supporting facts.

---

[*]Research social psychologist, Federal Judicial Center, Washington, D.C.

Case-specific social research is not conducted just to find some general truth; it is also intended to advance the arguments that are being made on one side or the other. The tone of the remarks so far has suggested that such adversariness is not necessarily a pleasant thing for a social scientist, or not always a desirable thing for the use of social research. I would like to suggest that in terms of case-specific research facts using an adversary procedure may well enhance, if not the finding of truth, at least the perception that justice is being done, that people are being treated fairly in the particular case at hand. There is some research evidence that an adversary procedure enhances the feeling that one is being treated fairly in a court and that this is not entirely a bad thing, even in situations where the social research being presented is somewhat distorted by the adversary process.

My argument is that people want not only to have the truth found in the case, they also want to be able to present their arguments and to have a judgment made on the basis of those arguments, to have some sort of essential weighing of claims in the context of the specific case.

With regard to supporting or more general legislative facts, I don't think that an adversary approach is necessarily best. Our research on psychological perceptions of justice suggests that adversariness does not necessarily carry the importance in terms of general decisions that it does in terms of specific decisions.[8]

I have just one comment about the particular procedures that one might use to get supporting or legislative facts before a trial judge or before an appeals court. The general social research that is cited often comes from law journals. I wonder if as social scientists we haven't been somewhat neglectful of these media. They offer an opportunity to present research findings in a nonadversary context and to make them available to legal decision makers. I think we might get around some of the problems we have noted by making our research available to the legal profession in this way.

AUSTIN SARAT*

I would like to begin by advancing a proposition, namely, that the use of applied social research in the courts is not just a problem for courts, it is also a problem for social researchers. It seems to me that one can advance the following rather simple and not very enlightened argument: as courts reach out for applied social research, as they adopt a paradigm of legal decision making which purports to include us, we have an increased responsibility.

Others have spoken and written about some of the ethical concerns that might impinge upon the role of a social scientist in the court. I would like to address the role of a social scientist outside the court doing research that might be of interest to judges rather than the role of expert witness in court proceedings.

*Associate professor of political science, Amherst College, Amherst, Massachusetts.

Let me begin with an anecdote about my own involvement. After *Furman v. Georgia* was decided, I undertook to do Justice Marshall a favor. His opinion contained a very interesting hypothesis about the nature of public opinion in America on the death penalty (*Furman v. Georgia* 1972). The hypothesis was quite simple: the American public appeared to be overwhelmingly supportive of the death penalty. Marshall, being only theoretically a democrat, said that such opinion was uninformed. If it were informed by what he knew about the death penalty, the American public would support his position. I regarded that as an invitation to social research.

I was at that time a Russell Sage Fellow at Yale Law School, where I was learning how to speak to lawyers and was concerned that I should write articles good enough to get into law reviews. That concern is an important part of my story.

A colleague, who will remain nameless so as not to implicate him, and I designed the following study. We decided that we would cull through Marshall's writings and his opinions to determine what he considered to be correct information about the death penalty. We would then present this information in a before-and-after design to a randomly selected group of residents of a representative community in America, namely, Amherst, Massachusetts. Amherst was convenient because I lived there and the funding came from Amherst College.

We planned what I will call, for want of knowledge in the area, a quasi-experimental design. We thought there were two types of information that Marshall had considered relevant. One type, which we called utilitarian, referred to the death penalty and the deterrence argument. Marshall wrote at the time of *Furman v. Georgia* that all of the reputable social science evidence suggested that the death penalty was not a deterrent. The other type of information, which we called humanitarian, suggested that the death penalty was a cruel and inhumane way of dealing even with convicted murderers.

We constructed our design, went into the field, and asked people about their attitude toward the death penalty. We then presented them with short summaries of what Marshall considered to be relevant. Then we asked about their attitudes again.

What we found, perhaps not surprisingly, was that people's attitudes changed, but in a very interesting way. Social psychologists can have all kinds of fun with this particular finding. We found that people became more uncertain; unlike what Marshall believed, that people would reject their previous position, they became more uncertain when presented with this information.

We subsequently went out and reinterviewed the same people approximately nine months later. To our great surprise, there was little movement backwards; the people who had become more uncertain remained so.

In the course of writing about our results, we introduced another part of the evidence, which had to do with feelings about retribution or the retributive motive. What we found was that feelings about retribution were more important in determining what people felt about the death penalty than either utilitarian or humanitarian information. The determining factor was whether they felt that the death penalty was morally warranted.

35

We rushed into print in the *Wisconsin Law Review* (Sarat and Vidmar 1976), anticipating the decision which was to come in *Gregg v. Georgia*. And, lo and behold, Justice Marshall's dissenting opinion in footnote 1 of *Gregg v. Georgia* cited the study which confirmed his prior proposition, namely, that an informed public would reject the death penalty on the grounds that it is inhumane (*Gregg v. Georgia* 1976).

The study we did was probably not very good; that is to say, I don't think it was a very good research design, and I don't think it was executed with great sophistication. Did I have a responsibility to do a better study for the purposes of pure science? Surely. Did I have a responsibility to do a better study for the purposes of my desired audience? Imagine, Justice Marshall was citing a study of 200-and-some-odd residents of Amherst, Massachusetts. That is front-page news in Amherst, Massachusetts.

My first inclination is to say that I ignored my responsibility as a social researcher. Perhaps ignored is the wrong word; I was not as conscious of it as I should have been. But one thing that intrigues me is the way that Justice Marshall read our article and used our argument. He got the finding that he wanted, ignored Sarat's argument about retribution, and cited this article as supporting his position.

Is this an example of the misuse of social science research by a judge? I don't know. I have talked to judges in the past about this issue. One judge in Colorado told me that he thought social science research was "inbetween." Coming from a judge, I thought this might be quite good. I asked, "Inbetween what, Judge?" He said, "Inbetween the pits and mediocre." And he hadn't even read my study on the death penalty.

In *Furman v. Georgia*, Marshall talks about the Sellin studies in rather glowing and general sentences. There is no critique of the research design nor is there any consideration of whether this method of assessing the deterrent capability of the death penalty is good or bad. He just cites the research with approval.

If you read Marshall's critique of Ehrlich in *Gregg v. Georgia*, you get the sense that Justice Marshall took a course at the University of Wisconsin in social research methods. The judge states that Ehrlich's regression techniques are inadequate and that his time series biases his results. That is to say, reading Sellin, there is no question in Marshall's mind of research design and the execution of research. Having read Ehrlich and the discussions of Ehrlich, Marshall feels an obligation to present a detailed social science critique, the likes of which we all read in the *American Sociological Review*. He thinks that as a judge it is his responsibility to critique.

Is this an example of misuse? I don't know. There are, however, three explanations for the misuse or the potential misuse of social science evidence. The first is the one that I've illustrated, namely, the qualifications of the audience. We are trying to influence judges and juries. Why should they pay any more attention to our work than we pay to theirs? Why is it that we expect that judges will be able to decipher the points, the arguments, of our work?

Indeed, the paradigm of social science research is itself a dialectic. I write my study, somebody else writes his study; we build incrementally and often through a conflict. But judges have to make decisions. Social science researchers usually don't make decisions. The judge has to invoke the rule of finality and come down on one side or the other.

In *Commonwealth v. O'Neal* (1975) in Massachusetts, decided between *Furman* and *Gregg*, Justice Reardon, writing in dissent, dismissed the deterrence argument. He didn't care what the social scientists say; common sense dictates that people are afraid to die, and therefore if you execute people or threaten to execute them and carry those threats out, they will be deterred.

Is that a misuse? I don't know, but it doesn't reflect a close reading of the social science evidence.

The second variable in determining when or why there is misuse is embedded in the adversary system. The best book I know of on the adversary system is written by the most extreme proponent of ethics in the profession of law, and that is Monroe Freedman. As Freedman understands the adversary system, the good lawyer is dedicated to the concept of human dignity embodied in winning for your side.

Is the adversary system an appropriate way for social science research to be communicated to judges and juries? That question leads to consideration of evaluation research for policymakers, which is typically no good to them and really not what they want to hear (Lindbloom and Cohen 1979). They typically say, "I've got to make a decision. If you do good evaluation research, it is going to come to me too late." How many of us get to do pure experiments and how many use true experimental design? Even when we do, Judge Kaufman doesn't like the results.

The kind of presentation of information in the adversary system is inappropriate to evaluation research—testing hypotheses and presenting data—that most of us typically do, even when we do it well. When I was a graduate student at Wisconsin Karl Deutsch said that if social science research explains 10 percent of the variance, we're doing well. Even when we explain 10 percent of the variance, most of us ignore that. Are judges supposed to ignore the fact that 90 percent is unexplained? Lawyers do. In terms of these considerations, social scientists are like "hired guns."

After I wrote my Amherst article, I was invited by a group called Team Defense in Atlanta, Georgia, to come and testify as an expert witness. They considered me an expert on public attitudes toward the death penalty on the basis of a flawed research design. I was put on the stand as the third of three expert witnesses. The case was really simple, but ingenious from the point of view of law. A defendant named Jesse Lewis Pulliam had been sentenced to death by a Georgia jury between *Furman* and *Gregg*. The people at Team Defense said that the jury, when they sentenced him, could not have taken the sentence seriously. They were asking for a resentencing. The jury would know that the sentence would be carried out or that it was constitutional. When the original jury sentenced him, there was doubt in their minds. I was called in because these people had read my article and they read something about uncertainty or doubt.

The Team Defense lawyer told me what he wanted me to say. He had done a Justice Marshall to my article; he had a précis of it that didn't have anything to do with its essential argument. I explained that there were qualifications and hedges. And he said, "First of all, the judge is not going to be listening to you. And second of all, if you start with qualifications and hedges, you will be of no use to me at all."

I was in a precarious ethical position. I didn't want to see Jesse Lewis Pulliam executed and I had a contribution to make. So I testified.

Unfortunately, from the point of view of Pulliam and our case, the judge slept but the district attorney was awake. He asked me one question. In a Georgia accent he said to me, "Professor Sarat, where was this study carried out?" And I said, "Well, before I answer that, let me tell you that I believe—" He said, "Where was the study carried out?" At this point the judge woke up and said to me, "Answer the question." I said, "It was carried out in Amherst, Massachusetts." The judge said, "Witness excused."

Was I a hired gun or was I an expert witness? I don't know.

There are one or two other problems worth noting. The first thing is that using social science research in court decision making is dangerous because social science findings change. Suppose that in 1952 *Brown v. Board of Education* had been based on the proposition that blacks learn better in classes with whites. We now read the educational literature and learn that nobody learns anything anywhere in the public schools and that integrating blacks and whites makes no difference. Let's say that that is true. Are we now prepared as social scientists to rewrite the meaning of the equal protection clause?

I think the idea that there are boundaries between law and fact doesn't work in identifying the province of social science. Again taking the death penalty as an example, to determine whether it is unconstitutional, you have to determine whether it is cruel and unusual. To determine whether it is cruel, you have to determine whether it is excessive, whether it is unnecessary in relation to its purposes. That leads to the deterrence question.

My fear is that the use of social research in deciding law-making questions, whether something is constitutional or not, will lead us to the point where we will ask the judges to revise their opinions quickly or not so quickly, depending upon the area of law in question.

For a year I was not a free-floating social scientist. I worked for the Office for Improvement in the Administration of Justice (OIAJ). This office is committed to using social science in the service of improving justice. I tried to use applied social research not as evidence in litigation, but as a tool for improving the courts. But, even here one might ask whether information about their operation per se is good for the courts?

Geoff Peters gave a talk to the Office for Improvement staff on the activities of the National Center for State Courts. He mentioned that the center is interested in getting state court systems to adopt minimal personnel systems. As Geoff said, in some states if you ask who is working for the courts you're told, "Well, there is Joe over there and somebody else down the hall and somebody else." But I wonder if the National Center for State Courts is doing a service to the courts? Is there some effect that we can anticipate in the courts that we would want to produce by allowing them to generate information about themselves or by generating information for them?

We adopt the model, at least they did in OIAJ, that the best courts are the most efficient courts. Then the function of applied social research is to increase the efficiency of courts. There are, however, obvious costs to efficiency in courts. For example, maybe Joe is eighty years old and he is the only one who knows the filing system for that courthouse. We adopt a modern personnel system; we decide sixty-five is the retirement age; and we fire Joe. In the interim we cause undue heartache to litigants and lawyers and social researchers who don't have Joe to steer them around the courthouse. Have we done a service by increasing the informational capabilities of courts but perhaps contributing to Joe's loss of employment?

In conclusion I go back to where I started from; if we take ourselves seriously, and it is apparent that there is a movement out there among judges and court administrators to take us applied social researchers seriously, then we have new responsibilities. I hope that we will address the question of how as social researchers we can improve our capabilities, whether or not our capabilities are to be used by the courts, but in the expectation or the fear that they might be.

SUE JOHNSON*

I guess it is appropriate for me to respond since I represent a state court in a sense.

I would just like to assure you that, considering the way state courts function as political animals, it is unlikely that Joe, who is eighty and knows the filing system, would be fired when we instituted the modern personnel system. We would create a unique title for Joe and he could stay till he died.

We have discussed two areas where social research is applied—or misapplied—in the courts. One area is litigation, with the discussion focused on the federal appellate courts. The second area is court reform, which we have barely discussed at all. There are substantial differences between the two areas which will affect the use, misuse, and nonuse of social research.

As one who is neither a lawyer nor a social scientist, but a court administrator, I am not sure that I have anything to contribute except perhaps to comment briefly on the uses or nonuses of research applied to issues of court improvement.

Examples of applied social research in litigation suggest that the problems addressed are those which have matured and where there is some agreement as to what is confirmed knowledge. Here the problems are apparently ones of misuse created by bringing research findings into the adversary process, where findings are shaped into arguments to support an advocate's position and where all the hedges around the conclusions may be buried along with any contradictory findings.

---

*Assistant state administrator of the courts, New York State, and a former research engineer.

Reasons for Nonuse of Research Findings Aimed at Court Reform

By contrast, the application of social research to court reform is relatively new. Consequently, the conclusions are still tentative in many important areas, such as sentencing, and have reached the mature stage in relatively few areas, such as jury research. However, the application of scientific research methods to policy issues dates back to World War II. The experience in applying research to illuminate policy issues in other social areas, such as defense, health, education, and welfare, among others, suggests that the principal problem here, even when research is more fully developed, will be one of nonuse of research findings. There are at least four reasons for this which may provide some lessons for practitioners.

Failure to Address Key Policy Issues. First of all, we must all recognize that it is seldom possible to address the key policy issues in any policy-oriented research. Thus, as applied to court improvements, it has been noted that research focuses on secondary issues of efficiency rather than primary issues of effectiveness. The aim of the courts is to provide justice, but so far only the research mentioned by Allan Lind has been explicitly concerned with this goal. Because the quality of justice is difficult to measure, researchers tend to use approximate measures, such as speed. Although all courts wish to provide fair and speedy justice, we are also very concerned with the relation between fairness and delay and the point at which speed detracts from fairness. This would be a useful topic for research to address and would assist policymakers in evaluating judicial productivity (which is court productivity) on a more realistic basis.

In addition to seldom addressing the key policy issues, research often applies one-dimensional measures to evaluating justice when multidimensional measures are required. Research on jury selection, for example, has been aimed at improving fairness, but the outcome of such procedures may be to increase delay because the legal correctness of the jury selection procedures has to be adjudicated prior to commencing trial. Furthermore, jury selection and size are second-order concerns with respect to court reform since the jury trial is the exception rather than the norm.

All of this is not to suggest that the research is not useful because it is limited, but rather to suggest that researchers cannot be satisfied by dealing with what is measurable but must try to illuminate the dimensions that are not so easily measurable.

The Problem of Timeliness. A second reason for nonuse of policy-oriented research is that it tends to lag behind the real decisions that must be made in a timely fashion. Our court of appeals in New York State acted on jury size and selection procedures in the 1960s, before the research was confirmed knowledge.

Irrelevance of Research to User Concerns. A third reason for nonuse of much policy-oriented research derives from the way research is initiated. It has been fashionable in the last two decades to believe that the best way to solve public sector problems is to finance research; indeed this is the explicit mission of many public agencies. Implementation is then left to the surprised user. Surprised users make poor consumers for several reasons. One is that the research is irrelevant to their concerns: it addresses a problem which the funding agency thinks is of concern to policymakers when the policymakers have a different interest. For example, one of the more warmly debated topics at the most recent meeting of the Council of State Court Administrators concerned research on civil case processing by the National Center for State Courts (1978), which measured delay from the filing of the case. The view of most courts, however, was that there is no public interest in expediting the resolution of civil disputes among private parties until one of the parties demands a trial. As a consequence of this view, many courts as a matter of policy will not use research aimed at reducing pretrial delays in civil actions.

Prevalence of Bad Research. A fourth reason for nonuse is that there is a Gresham's Law in policy research. Bad research so turns off decision makers that good research is ignored. We have already concluded that, on the average, research is inappropriate or incomplete, and research aimed at court improvement is no exception. A recent article in *Judicature* is illustrative. In "Building a Theory of Case-Processing Time," Mary Lee Luskin (1978) documents some serious but common defects in research on court delay:

> Analysis is insufficient to rule out plausible alternatives, and many examples can be cited where the practical or political realities of the court setting precluded adequate experimental controls, thereby making causation unclear.
> Critical elements of problems are excluded, for example, the common failure to examine the motives of participants in the court process.
> The framework is static and descriptive (because this assumption provides a mathematically tractable framework) as in most process models of courts, which are based on steady state assumptions, whereas the problem is dynamic and complex.
> Relevant and important variables are omitted because they are not analytically tractable, as in some sentencing research.
> Changes in structure and parameter, as well as unique elements, are not accounted for or are assumed away in time series studies. Researchers often ignore the changes in the penal law or in court procedures that occur at least annually in most jurisdictions.

As long as the research findings keep the shortcomings of techniques in view, the results can still be useful in providing insights to decision making. But when the inadequacies are not highlighted, the research can be dangerous. The danger here is a familiar one.

Analytic Tools from Other Fields

We are starting to see in court reform research the phenomenon of researchers with solutions from other fields looking for problems in the court area. This leads to proposals for using fashionable but inappropriate tools of analysis or modeling of the kind that has been largely discredited as inapplicable to policy research in other fields. The examples are legion but a few will be indicative.

*Queuing Theory.*This theory provides mathematical models of waiting line conditions, which have been used principally in the design of telephone systems. These models are conceptually useful in understanding the influence of such factors as arrival distributions (of cases), service distributions (of dispositions by courts), and the effects of the number of servers (court parts) on waiting line conditions (court delay). They are also used to measure gross effects of changes in filing and disposition rates on pending caseloads (Jennings 1971). Queuing models are so well known to court practitioners that it would be misleading to characterize them as research.

Although some researchers may suggest otherwise (Nagel, Neef, and Munshaw 1978), queuing theory cannot be used in court applications beyond this simple level of approximation, unless one can engage in large-scale and expensive simulations. Real world conditions in courts violate many assumptions required to derive analytically tractable queues:

> Multiple server, nonexponential service time distributions are typical, real court situations.
>
> Court conditions are not steady state; the number of servers and the service time vary over time, as do other parameters, because of adjustments in busy or slack periods.
>
> Arrivals are batch and some service of court cases may be in batch, or batch arrivals may be served singly because defendants may be joined or severed (for example, this happens in as many as 10 percent of all criminal cases in New York).
>
> Service times vary widely from one server to another, as does the type of service provided.
>
> Queue disciplines may be unstructured at some processing points (as they are in New York City criminal courts) because of the ways in which prosecutors and public defenders screen cases.

Optimum Sequencing Models. It is an axiom of operations research in industrial settings that operations which have existed for a long time tend to approach an optimum way of performing. This is also true in the courts: judges and lawyers representing opposing sides naturally prefer to address those cases which can be disposed of most easily and quickly. This is the algorithm of optimum sequencing which researchers propose (Nagel, Neef, and Munshaw 1978; Ryan 1978). But if optimum sequencing is used, the older cases, which take longer to dispose of, will get older and older. Hence, court managers, and indeed sometimes legislators, place limits on the maximum age of cases.

Markov Processes. Markov chain models have been suggested as a means for "predicting subsequent events by knowing the probabilities of one event leading to another." No mention is made of the likelihood that in court settings data will not be available to verify the underlying assumptions about ergodicity and stationarity of the one-step transition matrix.

Analysis of Variance. Standard analysis of variance based on well-designed and well-controlled orthogonal experiments is almost unassailable—even in the courts. Unfortunately, the factors that influence the outcome of experiments in a court setting are not always subject to control or even identifiable.

Regression and Correlation. Mathematicians understand the linear statistical models and structure of the data required to provide decent parameter estimates. One hopes that researchers will be more conscientious in addressing missing data and collinearities of the data, which can produce parameter estimates and apparent correlations that may be spurious and yet may pass conventional statistical tests with flying colors. With respect to the use of correlation coefficients, one might also hope to see a comment concerning assumptions about error randomness and normality and the sample statistic r.

All of this is simply by way of reminder that if the assumptions are not valid, the apparent rigor of the approach is only a facade. Because administrators, unlike judges, do have staffs trained in many disciplines, such research will probably be consigned to the circular files. The research community and the decision-making community will then lose touch, which I think would be regrettable.

Conclusion

How then can the nonuse of social research on court improvements be avoided? A few rather obvious guidelines are suggested by the failures:

Keep in touch with the consumers of the research, not just the sponsors.
Recognize that the consumers will invariably expect too much; avoid disappointment by promising very little in the way of results.
Decision makers typically make decisions with whatever information is at hand, so emphasize the exploratory nature of research and the tentativeness of the findings.
Keep the shortcomings of the research techniques fully in view of the consumer by being your own best critic.
Avoid a mathematical facade which requires assuming reality out of existence.

A few topics of interest to court administrators may suggest how social research techniques can be usefully applied:

the implications for taxation and for efficient public service of unified court budgets and state assumption of financing;
use of cost of living and income statistics in setting salaries for court employees;
use of equal employment opportunity data in establishing hiring practices for court employees;

use of weighted case load statistics as a basis for assigning judges and nonjudicial staff;

forecasting court work loads using community demographic data;

assessing the impact of new laws before and after enactment.

All of these subjects have been addressed recently by the Management and Planning Office, which serves the unified court system in New York State. Although they are not likely to be published in academic journals, the findings have been used in formulating public policy.

ADAM YARMOLINSKY*

I want to say a few words about what I regard as a principal source of difficulty in the use of applied social research by and in the courts, and the principal reason for the misuse of this valuable resource. (I was tempted to say invaluable, but I realized that adjective was not in the proper spirit of applied social science research.) The crux of the difficulty, it seems to me, lies in the essential difference in intellectual background and orientation between lawyers and social researchers—and thus their ability to understand and adopt each other's skills and perspectives. Lawyers may be literate, but they are barely numerate. Despite their reputation—whether deserved or undeserved—of being the only people in the business community who know how to read and write, their legal education does not ordinarily include training in quantitative skills. Social researchers, on the other hand, are generally valued by lawyers for their ability to use numbers. But while social researchers may also have good qualifications in the other two "R's," the great gap in their education is in the use of history, and history is the essence of the judicial process.

One way to describe the judicial process is to say that courts and judges are engaged in the continuous writing and rewriting of history. A judicial opinion is an exercise in reconciling present decisions with the stream of past decisions so as to make the present result appear as close to inevitable as the ingenuity of the legal mind can make it.

The nature of judicial behavior should not be surprising in a branch of government which has neither the authority of the sword nor the power of the purse, but must depend on logic and persuasion to maintain its position vis-à-vis the other two branches. The rare occasions when courts step out of their role as historians are more likely to attract public attention. These are the so-called landmark cases like Brown and Gideon and Miranda. But these cases are the exceptions, and even in these opinions courts have gone far to try to place new ideas in the stream of history.

---

*Lawyer and former counselor of the U.S. Arms Control and Disarmament Agency.

The ordinary course of judicial business and the exercise of legal and judicial skill are intended to reshape the law gradually and almost imperceptibly to keep up with changing times, while simultaneously reaffirming established principles. Applied social research, by contrast, is concerned with making new discoveries about social and economic behavior. It might not be going too far to say that the prestige of the researcher is often a function of the novelty of his or her discoveries—assuming of course that they're solidly based on observed results and are methodologically sound. The authority of the researcher is based on the ability to control or to observe all the variables. The researcher's concern is with present and future events. If the requirements of proof can be satisfied in the present, past behavior is less relevant and less important.

Another way to account for the differences in point of view between lawyers and applied social researchers is to make the classical distinction between truth and proof. The test of proof is whether it satisfies the rules of a closed system. The test of truth is whether it works in the real world. Contrary to what one might suppose, lawyers and judges seem more concerned with proof, that is, producing results that can be justified within the closed system of legal rules, while social researchers are more concerned with truth—testing propositions in the real world. Lawyers' solutions have to work in the real world too, or the legal system will fall apart. And researchers' solutions have to be replicable and testable according to commonly accepted rules. But each researcher tends to pay more attention to his or her particular part of the problem and less attention to what most concerns the other person, with consequent failures of understanding. Lawyers probably tend to overestimate how much social research is able to accomplish, and social researchers probably tend to overestimate how much courts are permitted by the political system to accomplish. The limits in both cases are quite complex, as each group is well aware. For example, courts feel freer to act on constitutional questions than on questions of statutory interpretation, but by the same token they are more hesitant to ask constitutional questions.

I do not have any ready solutions to bridge these gaps. Perhaps it is sufficient in this brief commentary for me simply to call attention to them. I do believe they can be bridged, and I believe that the best way to bridge them is through more extensive and intensive exposure of each species to the other.

I know the results of such exposure can't help but be positive, like the chance meeting many years ago between the late J. P. Morgan and a circus midget. *The New Yorker* cited a newspaper report that the meeting had been an extraordinarily amicable one; in fact, Mr. Morgan had taken the midget on his knee for a conversation. The magazine speculated that Morgan had probably gone home to the bosom of his family and remarked at the dinner table, "I met a midget today. Really quite a decent fellow." Probably the midget had also gone home to his family and said, "You know, I met J. P. Morgan today. Quite a decent fellow." I trust this conference will generate at least equally encouraging reports.

DISCUSSION

Garth Taylor *(University of Chicago)*: I have a question for Dr. Marvell. What steps would be involved in turning adjudicative facts into questions of law so that other people could benefit from them without having to supply all the witnesses and so on?

Teb Marvell: There has been a long-term trend toward changing adjudicative facts—those that are supporting case facts—into social facts, thus expanding the detail of the law. In the eyewitness identification case, I think the lawyer should ask that instruction be given to the jury that they be wary of an eyewitness identification, especially if there is only one eyewitness. Trial courts should be required to give this instruction. In support of this suit, the psychologists who testify at individual trials should pool their efforts and help the lawyer prepare an amicus brief. If the studies offer persuasive evidence that eyewitness identifications are often poor and that jurors may not know this, then the appellate court should make a rule requiring the instructions. This rule would aid defendants throughout the jurisdiction, not just those who get psychologists to testify for them.

Susan Burke *(Syracuse University)*: I have a question for Sue Johnson. Would you expand on your notion of the questions of justice that are beyond the realms of social science? It seems to me that one of the examples you cited, the jury composition and size study, touches directly on questions of justice. And you have relegated them to trivia.

Sue Johnson: I was probably exaggerating when I said that composition is unrelated to fairness. But I think the tendency in examining court reforms from the viewpoint of fairness is to equate fairness to other things. We use a lot of proxy variables which may not be appropriate. For example, court delay is something we can measure, so we tend to think that if we speed things up, we will have fairer courts; fair and speedy justice go together. Well, at some point they don't go together any more. If we speed up the process too much, we lose justice.

Little has been done to illuminate that subject. We tend to say we'll leave fairness to the appellate courts. If something was done that was not fair, they will adjudicate it. But they are going to adjudicate it on a case-by-case basis. What can we do to clarify what we mean by justice and fairness on a much broader scale? I don't know the answer; I am simply posing the question.

Austin Sarat: I think the point just made is a very important one for people who are doing applied social research on courts, and it is one that we beg out of.

We are positivists. We cannot answer the question, "Is the decision just?" That is for someone else to worry about. We tend not to accept the standard for judging the use of applied social research in the courts as whether or not it contributes to decisions which are fairer. As people doing scientific research, we feel we are not equipped to answer the question of whether a decision is just.

What concerns me, and I guess it concerns a court administrator, is that the easier standard is efficiency: Does the judge understand what we have asked him to understand? Can he reproduce it in his opinion accurately?

It is too easy to say we should be worried about whether or not either our court reform research or our involvement in a specific case contributes to more justice in the court system. It is too easy because it is unanswerable. But at least we can be a little more cautious about what it is that we do.

Joseph Mitchell *(Superior Court of Massachusetts)*: I have two comments to make. First, most of the comments that have been made imply that judges can't understand social problems. All of the judges I have met are extremely sensitive to these problems; they know how to use social research findings and they are using them, both in the adversary procedure and in court reform.

Second, social research in court reform is essential. It has a tremendous impact on our whole judicial system.

In Massachusetts we are now trying to establish uniform sentencing because there has been a tremendous disparity in sentencing for the same crime.

Social scientists are making an analysis of all of the sentences that have been given out—let's say over a period of ten years—to whom, and what factors were involved, so that some uniformity can be brought in. We need this kind of research to improve the judicial system. The social scientists cannot back off; they must get involved in such court reforms.

We have also revolutionized the jury system in one county in Massachusetts by randomizing it, doing away with all exemptions, and introducing a one-day-one-trial system that has been tried in other places. Again, social scientists were involved in this. And I think it is essential that they stay involved in reforming our system.

Johnson: On the issue of sentencing, I think it is essential that social scientists stay involved, but carefully involved, because they have come down on all sides of the issue, and people are making decisions based on fragmentary information. I suspect that by the time the studies are done and the information is in, legislatures will have made their laws. The interest will have subsided. The research findings will be available too late to address the problem.

On the jury selection issue, I think the questions are very complicated. Suppose you randomize juries and people start to test that model. I received a telephone call from a defense lawyer representing a Chinese defendant. There were no Chinese on the jury and he wanted to know if there were any on the jury list. The search took three days. It contributed significantly to delay. You are trading off very complicated things that you can't equate on a single scale.

Marvell: I want to second what Judge Mitchell said about judges' knowledge of social science. I am amazed at how much judges know about it, how much experience they have had with social science, and also how skeptical they are of it, for good reason usually.

Clark Abt *(Abt Associates Inc.)*: I am particularly gratified by the remarks of Teb Marvell which demonstrate the need for this conference, because one of the things we are most concerned about is that students of law and the court process, as well as judges and lawyers, might not understand the functioning of social science; some do and some don't. But I think it is an interesting demonstration of ignorance of the social sciences when Teb Marvell says that there are no ethical standards applied.

If the adversary process is believed to achieve truth when practiced by legally trained advocates, why aren't social scientists also accepted as advocates ferreting out the truth in the judicial process, particularly when they are compelled as part of their ethical responsibilities to behave as advocates?

Incidentally, I don't think they always become involved as advocates. Whether they should or they shouldn't is a very complex moral question. One has to differentiate between cases where they should act as advocates and those where they shouldn't. When they are speaking purely as social scientists, not as presenters of data in an advocacy role, I don't believe they should act as advocates.

Regardless of that question, why do you believe that social scientists have no professional ethical standards? Also, why do you find their advocacy less productive than that of legally trained individuals?

Marvell: I think that, as a practical matter, there are no professional ethical standards here. From my experience, the notion that one should present research findings accurately with all the caveats and with all the reasons the researcher thinks the conclusions may not be accurate often—even typically—isn't followed, and there is no enforcement mechanism to ensure that it is followed.

Second, I was stating that social scientists should take both sides of an issue when they get involved in social facts. The reason for this is that a couple of studies of empirical data before appellate courts show major imbalances; usually one side presents a lot and the other side presents nothing. If the court gets information from only one side, unless that side is reasonably objective, the court is in trouble.

Charles Baron *(Boston College Law School)*: To respond to Clark Abt's point very briefly, I think a distinction has to be made between an advocate and a witness. The lawyer is an advocate in the courtroom; he is not there to testify as to facts, he is there to orchestrate one side in terms of presenting evidence and making arguments based on that evidence.

An expert witness, I think, plays a strange role—somewhere between a lawyer, who is an advocate, and a fact witness, who is just somebody who observed the automobile hit the plaintiff on a particular occasion.

The expert witness, whether he is a social scientist or a doctor, is not an advocate. He is in the courtroom to give what he thinks is a justifiable opinion; he is there to infer something from certain facts. If he conducted a study, he is there to talk about what he thinks that study reveals.

He may look a little like an advocate because it is hard to know what objective truth is in social science research. It is also hard to know what objective truth is in medicine. You can find doctors who are willing to testify both ways with respect to almost any medical question. And they are willing to do so in good faith, because although there may be something called objective truth, nobody seems to have an "in" on it.

In the courtroom objective truth is approached asymptotically through the adversary system by permitting expert witnesses to be put on the stand and then allowing opposing expert witnesses to impeach the credibility of these expert witnesses, as was done in the case of Professor Sarat. His is a wonderful story illustrating the adversary system at its best. Counsel puts Professor Sarat on the stand to testify to something he wants to prove. Quite properly, I think, and ethically, he does not ask Professor Sarat to tell about all the problems with his study. Strategically he might have done that, because he would prefer to get this information out on direct examination than have opposing counsel bring it out on cross-examination. But ethically he has no responsibility to bring that out. But then the district attorney, who was not sleeping, impeaches the credibility of the witness by bringing out a major problem with the study.

I think that is exactly what should be done with applied social science research. It should come to the courtroom, and superb advocates ought to have an opportunity to hammer out what is good and bad in the testimony. Over the years, I think, this kind of adjudicative fact evidence will become legislative fact; it will precipitate inclusion of certain accepted facts in the law.

Sarat: What you said characterizes perfectly my dilemma when I was caught in this role. I was appearing as an expert witness, not someone giving an opinion. If I had offered my opinion, they would have said they weren't interested in my opinion, they wanted me to describe my study and tell them what I had observed.

Another point is that you have a lot more faith in the adequacy of the adversary system, as you called it, and the competence of lawyers than I do. I don't like the idea that my work is simply a tool in a game in which most of the players, according to the Chief Justice, are not competent to deal. A more dramatic way of saying it is that putting social science in the hands of lawyers is like putting guns in the hands of children. Sometimes they will hit the mark and sometimes they won't.

Baron: Especially when the barrel is crooked.

Michael Saks *(National Center for State Courts)*: On the subject of ethics and misuses, one issue that was not raised—and I am somewhat surprised that it wasn't, since this has become such a lawyerly discussion—is whether applied social researchers are willing to face certain consequences of doing poor research. If we conduct a study using poor methodology or if we get on the witness stand and report results inaccurately, how willing are we to face professional malpractice suits because we may be causing harm to a great many people? Don't we have some very serious responsibilities, and aren't we subject to liability for the things that we do in the name of delivering truth to the courts?

NOTES

1. For example, see Claiborn (1969).
2. This categorization is from Marvell (1978). Social facts are similar to "legislative facts," and case facts are similar to "adjudicative facts."
3. This problem is discussed by Stephen Breyer and Judge Robert J. Hallisey in chapters five and seven, respectively.
4. For example, see Dworkin (1977). Hearsay rules are not applicable to social facts.
5. See Advisory Committee's Notes on the Proposed Rules of Evidence for the United States Courts, 56 *Federal Rules Decisions* 183, 203 (1973).
6. See Kaysen (1958).
7. For a summary of much of this research, see Thibaut and Walker (1975). The position being advanced here is based on a recent theoretical analysis by Thibaut and Walker (1978).
8. See Thibaut and Walker (1978) for an analysis of the necessity of using different procedures to resolve conflicts about specific cases and general fact conflicts. The function of general research is to address what Thibaut and Walker call "truth conflicts," for which they recommend nonadversary procedures.

REFERENCES

Brown v. Board of Education, 347 *U.S.* 483 (1954).

Claiborn, William L. 1969. Expectation in the Classroom: A Failure to Replicate. 60 *Journal of Educational Psychology* 377-83.

Commission on Revision of the Federal Court Appellate System. 1975. Structure and Internal Procedures: Recommendations for Change (preliminary draft). Washington, D.C.: Government Printing Office.

Commonwealth v. O'Neal, 339 *N.E. 2d* 676 (1975).

Dworkin, Ronald. 1977. Social Sciences and Constitutional Rights—The Consequence of Uncertainty. 6 *Journal of Law and Education* 3-12.

Furman v. Georgia, 408 *U.S.* 238, 364 (1972).

Gregg v. Georgia, 428 *U.S.* 232 (1976).

Jennings, John B. 1971. Quantitative Models of Criminal Courts. Paper presented at 29th national meeting of the Operations Research Society of America, Dallas, Texas.

Kaysen, Carl. 1958. An Economist as the Judge's Law Clerk in Sherman Act Cases. 12 *ABA Antitrust Section Report* 43.

Larry P. v. Riles, 343 *F. Supp.* 1306 (N.D. Calif. 1972).

Lindbloom, Charles and Cohen, David. 1979. *Usable Knowledge*. New Haven: Yale Univ. Press.

Luskin, Mary Lee. 1978. Building a Theory of Case-Processing Time. 62 *Judicature* 114-27.

Marvell, Thomas. 1978. *Appellate Courts and Lawyers*. Westport, Conn.: Greenwood.

Nagel, Stuart, Neef, Marian, and Munshaw, Nancy. 1978. Bringing Management Science to the Courts to Reduce Delay. 62 *Judicature* 128-43.

National Center for State Courts. 1978. Reducing Trial Court Delay Project. 1 *National Center for State Courts Report* (August).

Rosenthal, Robert and Jacobson, Lenore. 1968. *Pygmalion in the Classroom*. New York: Holt, Rinehart, & Winston.

Ryan, John Paul. 1978. Management Science in the Real World of Courts. 62 *Judicature* 144-46.

Sarat, Austin and Vidmar, Neil. 1976. Public Opinion, the Death Penalty, and the Eighth Amendment. *1976 Wisconsin Law Review* 171-206.

Thibaut, John and Walker, Laurens. 1975. *Procedural Justice: A Psychological Analysis*. New York: Halsted Press.

_____ . 1978. A Theory of Procedure. 66 *California Law Review* 541-66.

Triangle Publications v. Rohrlich, 167 *F. 2d* 969 (2d Cir. 1948).

Weinstein, Jack B. 1966. Judicial Notice and the Duty to Disclose Adverse Information. 51 *Iowa Law Review* 541-66.

3

The Science Court

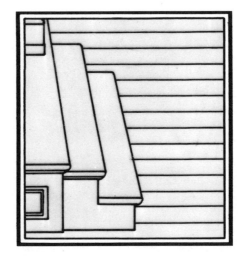

ARTHUR KANTROWITZ

ARTHUR KANTROWITZ*

Since my background is in physical and medical sciences, what I have to say I will relate to those sciences and not specifically to social sciences, about which I understand nothing.

I think a suitable starting point is a decision made in the U.S. Court of Appeals for the District of Columbia in the International Harvester Company case that had to do with exhaust emissions of automobiles. The court was asked to review an Environmental Protection Agency (EPA) ruling. I am not concerned with the decision but only with some of the things that were said in that decision. In particular, I would like to read from the dissent of Chief Judge David Bazelon, who concurred in the result but dissented in the opinions. He said:

> Socrates said that wisdom is the recognition of how much one does not know. I may be wise, if that is wisdom, because I recognize that I do not know enough about dynamometer extrapolations, deterioration factor adjustments and the like to decide whether or not the government's approach to these matters was statistically valid. Therein lies my disagreement with the majority.

I think that it is proper for the courts to recognize this point, and recognize it with utmost clarity, when issues of great social importance are brought before them. This one is an issue of moderate social importance—not negligible, but not the greatest issue that we face involving scientific disputes. But when these issues come to the courts, when they come to the legislature, I think the most important thing in the beginning of wisdom is to recognize that there may be people who understand these issues and have devoted their lives to them and to ask them how information can best be extracted from the scientific community when there is obvious dispute within that community. That is the problem I will deal with today.

Note that what I am proposing has nothing to do with the operation of science when there is no public policy issue involved, and has nothing to do with the operation of the law when there isn't a scientific dispute involved. I am concerned with what I'll call the mixed case—where there is a dispute in the scientific community and there are ethical issues and public policy issues involved.

Let me tell you what our society does today outside of the legal area, which you know all about. We have the institution of the scientific committee. It exists in all parts of the free world under different names. In the United States the highest-level scientific committees that deal with specific issues are

---

*Professor of engineering, Dartmouth College.

epitomized by the National Academy committees, which are formed, frequently at the direct request of the Congress, to provide a scientific, factual basis for legislation.

These committees operate by rules that I will describe very briefly. They operate entirely on noblesse oblige. They are governments of men and not of laws. The committees are appointed by a process that is not public in its details. There are, to be sure, questionnaires that you fill out saying what your interests and conflicts of interests might be and so on. The committees then proceed to deliberate in secret. The National Academy took the step of going to the courts to defend its right to operate in secret, and its defense was successful. They then issue reports, which usually are made public, not only stating what the facts are, but usually also suggesting what to do about the problem under investigation.

Thus the committee recommends action consistent with its own systems of values, which may be very different from the values of other segments of society. When the making of such recommendations is in prospect it is very difficult for the committee to avoid biasing the factual sections of its report so as to provide support for its recommendations.

It is a procedure which I think is comparable to the state of the law at the time of the star chamber. The members of the star chamber were appointed by the king, and occasionally he managed to have some influence on the outcome. The law graduated from this kind of situation in the year 1643.

The scientific decisions that must be made by our society are quite as important as any we face. They have to do with disarmament, with nuclear power, with the advance of chemistry versus carcinogens, and with all kinds of things with which I know you are all familiar. We resolve such issues in the following way. Because the people who make decisions are unable to distinguish the scientist from the magician, we have various kinds of magicians. Some wear white hats and others wear black hats. You may remember that in the Middle Ages it was very important to distinguish between practitioners of white magic, which was beneficial, and black magic; those who practiced the latter were sometimes burned at the stake.

Today, having advanced over the last millennium, we still operate by finding out whether the magicians we are listening to wear white or black hats. So I'm very careful never to wear a hat.

I submit that in order to be able to see through the confusion that exists when there are disputes among scientific experts, we must begin, and begin with all urgency, the development of some sort of credible process for finding out what the state of fact is when there is a dispute. Such a process will not create new knowledge; it will just draw a line between what is known and what is not known. Such a process will make it possible for citizens to express their value systems in making decisions instead of being misled by claimants of the state of scientific fact speaking for partisan purposes, which is nearly all that we hear today.

For the purpose of starting discussion about such a development of due process, I would set forth three principles, none of which are followed by the National Academy today in rendering decisions about issues of enormous importance.

First, I would urge that in these matters we make a clear and sharp separation, to the best of human ability, between facts and values, and that we deal with these two areas in separate ways. In dealing with questions of values, we should use and abide by democratic processes which allow citizens to express their value preferences.

Questions as to scientific fact should be dealt with by a separate organization or a separate procedure which does not proceed by a democratic process but is restricted from introducing its own value systems insofar as that is humanly possible. That's rule number one.

Rule number two is that, in dealing with scientific controversies, we graduate to adopting what was learned in Anglo-Saxon law in the year 1643, that we separate the function of the judge and the function of the advocate. That is not done in scientific committees. If all committee members were unprejudiced people, adequate to be judges, then they wouldn't know enough about the subject. And if they know about the subject in scientific depth and not just superficially, it means only one thing: they have devoted their lives to it. To devote your life to something and to imagine that you can at the same time be unprejudiced is a kind of simplicity that only scientists can aspire to.

That's rule number two. One is to separate facts and values and two is to separate judges and advocates.

Rule number three, also not obeyed by the Academy, is to do the whole damned thing in public. I think that if you respect rules number one and two, you'll have less resistance to number three, which is doing it in public. But if you don't respect one and two, if you want to conceal the impact of your value systems on the factual judgments you make, you do it in secret. If you want to conceal the difference between judges and advocates, you do it in secret. So rule number three is pretty obvious from the first two.

This is an idea that's been around for at least eleven years now. The first time I came to this was in preparation for a Senate hearing held by Senator Fred Harris. He wanted to know about new institutions needed for scientific research and this was my proposal. In the *Congressional Record* for March 16, 1967, you can still find the response he made to this proposal.

He said, "You know, we make decisions all the time without knowing the facts. What, for instance, do we know about China? And we make decisions about China all the time." I submit to you that the costs of proceeding with the kind of ignorance that's operative today are immense. Our present management of technology is much like driving a high-speed automobile in which the windshield is all splattered with mud and you can't see the road ahead. The only reasonable thing to do is to stop, to stop all change, and maybe as soon as you do that, then stop all things that have been changed recently. That's about what we're doing, and the costs for our society have been enormous and are still increasing.

Let me tell you about the reactions in the last eleven years to this proposal. You've got to remember that there are vested interests to be displaced by any new procedure that's introduced. The reaction from the National Academy is very simple. It amounts to just this: if this is right, then what we've been doing all these years is wrong.

During the last months of the Ford Administration a committee (formed by the President) asked Philip Handler, the president of the National Academy, what he proposed to do about the science court proposal, and Handler's answer was, "Yes, we'll try and do something about it, if we get funded." So then Ramo, who was in the chair, turned to Guy Stever, who was then Arthur Konopka's boss, and asked him if he would fund it, and Stever leaned over to whisper to me, "How much is it going to cost?" I said, "Well, probably less than a half million dollars to try it once." So Stever said, "Yes, we'll fund it." I thought I'd gotten someplace, but I really hadn't. The vested interests who would be displaced by this kind of a reform are enormous.

I mentioned the vested interests of those who make scientific decisions today, but let me elaborate. When you're a scientist in Washington, as I happen to be, you're doing one of two things. You're giving advice, usually confidential advice, to government officials, or you're making a plea for research funds. Now scientists generally, and me in particular, do these things all the time. If it was anybody else, I think it would certainly be regarded as a conflict of interest, but thus far that point has usually not been made.

If we had an institutionalized method of getting scientific advice, if we moved toward a government of laws, as distinguished from a government of men, in the governance of science in its application to society, then, indeed, it would make life a little more difficult. Scientists in Washington would have to have a new method of operating. That's interest group number one, but there are others.

Interest group number two is industry. A science court would cause a big disturbance in the way industry operates, although I think that disturbance is coming anyway. But industry's natural tactic when faced with a disturbing report is very simple: play it very quietly; don't say anything and it will go away. The silent treatment is industry's standard tactic in dealing with any criticism. It usually works.

The third interest group consists of politicians who are able to use confusion as a political strategy with consummate skill. It enables them to get any reading of the facts they like. Modern politicians are really not constrained in the way King Canute was; he couldn't move the tides at all. Modern politicians can turn black into white very easily. They select the appropriate committee, which provides them with the factual statements they want.

And, finally, there is a small interest group that is important but not as important as the other three. It consists of radicals who don't want anything that will make the system work better.

Together, these four vested interests are enormously important, and to imagine, as I once did, that all you have to do is to suggest a better way to build a mousetrap and people will beat a path to your door is a naiveté that I still cherish.

I am persuaded, however, that in the course of time the necessity for due process in discussing scientific issues will be apparent to enough people so that the development of that process can seriously begin. Let me give three examples of past attempts.

The first attempt was made by the editor-in-chief of the *National Journal of Cancer,* who is an official of the National Institute of Health. He became upset at the practice of mass X-ray examination of women for breast cancer because he was persuaded that that process was doing more harm than good. He made that appeal to the American College of Radiology, but he couldn't attract their attention at all. Then he threatened them with the organization of a science court procedure to examine just that question: were they doing more harm than good? He says that the threat alone was enough to bring them to the negotiating table, in spite of all the cash flow that they have lost thereby. (Examining a hundred million women every year must produce pretty good cash flow.) He credits the very existence of the concept with making it possible to negotiate; now they have agreed not to screen women under fifty unless they have a special history.

The second case was in the Department of Energy, where the head of the division of magnetic fusion energy wanted to learn something about the merits of a series of inventions. He organized what he called science court procedures, got the inventor to be the advocate, and appointed critics and a panel of judges whom he certified as unprejudiced. He had the authority to do all this and he did it. At the end they all pronounced it an efficient system for finding the facts on a whole array of inventions.

The last case is really a very interesting one. In Minnesota a group of farmers got together to protest a power line being built across their lands. They didn't like the power line at all and they had various reasons, but prominent among those reasons was the evidence of two physiologists (Becker and Marino) at the Syracuse Veterans Hospital, who had been claiming for a number of years that the electromagnetic fields created by power lines have harmful effects.

A National Academy committee was appointed to examine their claims, which, if validated, would have enormous importance for all of us. We've got electromagnetic fields all around us, all the time. The Academy appointed a committee according to its procedures, which did not include Becker and Marino. They then refused to work with the Academy committee, claiming that there were members who had taken public positions against their work, but no members were favorable to their position. The Academy report was issued in due course, and at that time the Navy's Project Sanguine was involved, a project which used a low-frequency radio transmitter antenna designed to communicate with submarines to inform them that nuclear war was on, and that kind of significant information.

In spite of the fact that the Academy committee stated explicitly that there is no scientific indication of any harmful effects, the voters of Michigan found the Academy statement not sufficiently credible, so they voted this project down and, indeed, the Navy is still struggling to find a way to communicate with its submarines. That, as well as anything, I think, illustrates it.

In Minnesota these same physiologists came forward again, claiming that the Minnesota power line was going to be harmful to plants, to animals, and to humans. They had scientific statements on results drawn from their experiments which indicated that Governor Rudy Perpich was faced with a very serious question here. The utilities that wanted to construct these lines had gone through all the procedures required by Minnesota law, and the environmental agencies and such had approved the lines. They were through with all the legal processes. But the farmers were up in arms and the governor had to send state troopers to keep the farmers away from the construction crews.

The governor appealed to the American Arbitration Association, and it happened that one of the association's members was also a member of my committee, and he said, "Aha, this is great. Let's have a science court procedure." So the governor seized on this and we were going to have a science court procedure. I thought it was just lovely, and I was asked to help find the money for it, which I did. With support from the Ford Foundation, and with backup from NSF, we were going to do it.

Then the governor arranged for the farmers, on the one hand, and the utilities, on the other, to meet in his office—Camp David style—and he got them all to agree that they would go ahead with the science court procedure. The leaders of the farm organizations went back to their constituents and all of them—six farm organizations were involved—were kicked out of their leadership positions for endorsing the science court. The farmers then came out with a statement that if construction would stop during the science court proceeding, they would agree to it. The utilities responded with the obverse statement: they would go along if the farmers would stop protesting during the science court procedure.

Anyway, the farmers stopped discussing the health and safety issues after that and concentrated on the simple, clear, obviously valid statement that they just didn't want this power line across their land. That is where the matter stands.

These are the only three attempts that have come to my attention. I think that one must expect continued pressure to find some sort of due process for dealing with these very important issues, and when that process will seriously be begun I don't know. But it does demand a break from current practice, which depends essentially on a government of noblesse oblige in the administration of science.

I have, for those who are interested in the topic, three references from the law review literature. In the *Cornell Law Review* for April-May of 1977, Judge Bazelon wrote a paper in which he included a statement on the science court, in addition to a great many other things. Professor James Martin of the Michigan Law School published a paper at about the same time in the *Michigan Law Review*. A third paper, and the most illuminating one that I know of, is by Thibaut and Walker, and it appeared in the *California Law Review*, in May of 1978. They have made an analysis of legal practice that I found most illuminating. They distinguish between two types of processes that come before the law. One they call a distributive process: How do you distribute rewards and punishment? The other is cognitive: How do we get out of this forest that we're trapped in, where the conflicts that may exist are not conflicts in a distributive sense but only in the sense of knowledge? Thibaut and Walker say that the kinds of disputes that I call mixed disputes should be dealt with in a two-step process, as I have cited. They also discuss the degree of control that should be possessed by the advocates, on the one hand, and by the judges, on the other. Theirs is the most illuminating study I know on the subject.

DISCUSSION

Michael Olnick *(Institute for Research on Poverty, University of Wisconsin)*: I can understand the effectiveness of this procedure in addressing a problem for which the answer seems close at hand. But I don't understand how this procedure would help us if the level of uncertainty is extraordinarily high and will continue to be so for some time.

Arthur Kantrowitz: Just establishing that fact is a great contribution. To quote Socrates again, the beginning of wisdom is to realize what you don't know. We always will be disappointed in how little can really be said, but when that disappointment is met by a false assertion of certainty we can have the harmful consequences I think will be obvious to anyone. This is not a machine for manufacturing new knowledge. It's only a machine for preventing the partisan exploitation of scientific uncertainty.

Bernard Grofman *(University of California at Irvine)*: To the extent that in any advanced industrial society the way in which technology works is, as Arthur Clark puts it, indistinguishable from magic—

Kantrowitz: I don't know any scientists whom I would regard as magicians. I know how they work; they use trial and elimination of error. That's the way humanity works generally.

Grofman: But to lawyers, judges, laymen, the products of a study, whether conducted by the National Academy of Sciences or by a science court, are justified not in terms of the ability of those laymen to follow in detail the reasoning which gave rise to the conclusions, but by the aura of authority and expertise—

Kantrowitz: Magic.

Grofman: —and magic which backs them. The National Academy of Sciences, in one of the examples you gave, lacked sufficient mana or authority or magic to convince the voters of Michigan that their recommendations made sense. In what ways would you see a science court having the political magic that the very prestigious and elite National Academy of Sciences lacks?

Kantrowitz: I note that in controversial matters our society prefers the techniques of the laws to fighting in the streets. That isn't a very high recommendation, but it's an important difference. In the same way, I would say that our society will prefer a system that is adapted, that is, an adaptation from the system that we have developed for dealing with controversy, as superior to the system that's operative today, which is, as I said, the partisan exploitation of scientific uncertainty. The decisions are not made by going over the Academy report and finding it inadequate; they're made in the media by partisans.

Charles Baron *(Boston College Law School)*: Just to support your last statement, Thibaut and Walker conducted another study, described in a book called *Procedural Justice: A Psychological Analysis* (1975). It seems to indicate that people accept the decisions of judges partly because judges wear robes and sit in marble palaces. This has something to do with people's acceptance of their decisions, but it probably has more to do with the fact that people expect certain procedures to be followed in the courtroom. The judge is a judge; the advocates are advocates. You get an opportunity to hire your advocate and make whatever points you think should be made on your behalf. If you lose, at least you've had your day in court and it was a public proceeding. You were judged under law and not just by one man's opinion.

For the many people who think that fact and value can't be separated, your second and third points are all the more important. If you think that it's impossible for a judge not to make a value-ridden decision, at the very least you want him to hear arguments by advocates which may persuade him to abandon his values, and you want it to be done publicly.

Kantrowitz: I wouldn't accept any procedure that's based on the second and third rules without the first one. If you erected an institution which had the aura of magic that science has yet used a procedure that seemed credible, that would amount to an institution with tyrannical power. The only way to impose any control over it is to insist that, to the best of human ability, facts and values be separated.

Can you name an issue, and I would prefer one from the physical sciences, in which no value-free component can be found? I would be in your debt, if you could give me such an example.

Baron: I'm not a physicist but—

Kantrowitz: You don't have to be a physicist to give such an example. You know about nuclear war and all kinds of other high-value situations. Is there no fact component in these disputes that is substantially value-free? Philosophers of science have been arguing about the separation of facts and values since the beginning of time. The best treatment I know, incidentally, is in the introductory chapter of a book on social science called *Controversies and Decisions,* edited by Charles Frankel.

Many of the people who assert that facts and values cannot be separated do not want to separate them, for very good reasons. They want to be advocates and for advocates it is proper, but it is not proper for judges.

Robert Hallisey *(Superior Court of Massachusetts)*: I was just trying to imagine what the role of the science court judge would be in that Minnesota problem. Probably each side would present scientific data on the effect of electromagnetic fields on living creatures. One set of data would come out one way and the other would come out the other way. Then it might degenerate, if that's the proper term, into an argument over which statistical approach is more reliable. And I don't know that much about statistics.

Kantrowitz: That's the point, sir. There are people who can examine these experiments, can take them apart in detail. Then we can employ your engine of truth, the cross-examination procedure. We can learn from it and use it in the same powerful way that it is frequently used in the law.

Hallisey: Is the science of statistics that free from dispute that the judge can make a decision at the end?

Kantrowitz: The fundamental mathematical rules that govern statistical calculations are almost beyond dispute. They're ancient; I think the last great improvement was made in the nineteenth century. How those rules are used and the assumptions that underlie the statistical treatment can be contested. Those assumptions are the substance of what would go on in science, where those questions would be examined in all detail and by scientists cross-examining other scientists in the presence of scientist judges, people who would not be chosen for their knowledge of the law but for their knowledge of the relevant sciences. They would be subject to processes like voir dire to establish their lack of prejudice, to a degree, I mean, learning from how you people do it.

Peter Schuck *(Department of Health, Education, and Welfare)*: It seems to me that there may be some confusion of several related but distinct issues. One is the inclination of decision makers to use bad science to support decisions that they may want to make on somewhat different grounds. A separate issue, it seems to me, is the question of whether the public is being adequately informed as to the uncertainties with respect to particular issues and the quality of the science that underlies the debate. With respect to the former, a science court could do little to affect the incentives of decision makers to seek support for their positions that they will independently come to. As to the latter, politicians can almost always find support for any particular point of view; the question is how much support there is. Usually there are respectable bodies of opinion on both sides or most sides of a complex public policy issue. It seems to me we're observing total public confusion and perhaps a greater sense of uncertainty about important scientific issues than actually exists.

Kantrowitz: The science court could, after development, achieve a high enough credibility to make it difficult for a politician to "find support for any particular point of view." The science court could thus be helpful in reducing the "total public confusion" you referred to.

REFERENCES

Thibaut, John and Walker, Laurens. 1978. A Theory of Procedure. 66 *California Law Review* 541-66.

4

What Judges and Lawyers Need to Know About Applied Social Research

RICHARD LIGHT

CLARK C. ABT

KEN CARLSON

RICHARD LIGHT*

When I was asked to comment on what lawyers and judges should know about applied social research, I gave it some thought and decided that the two key issues are anesthesia and sex. So that is what I will be talking about for the next few minutes.

I am a statistician by training, not a lawyer. But from many conversations with my colleagues around Harvard and elsewhere my impression is that a crucial issue about evidence is often discussed and often becomes confused in reviewing evidence for cases. This issue is: At what level of aggregation should data be looked at? Rather than give an abstract discussion of aggregated versus disaggregated data and what is most useful for policy purposes, I will use two specific examples that I hope will illustrate the point.

The first example I call the anesthesia case. Table 1 presents some hypothetical data. Suppose they are from a survey that was done at Massachusetts General Hospital of 600 people who underwent surgical procedures last year. All 600 survived; 300 were given anesthesia A and 300 were given anesthesia B. For an outcome measure, the group was divided by fast versus slow recovery from the surgery. Notice that of those who received A, 220 had fast and 80 had slow recoveries; of those who received B, 200 had fast and 100 had slow recoveries.

TABLE 1.
Hypothetical Data for the Anesthesia Case

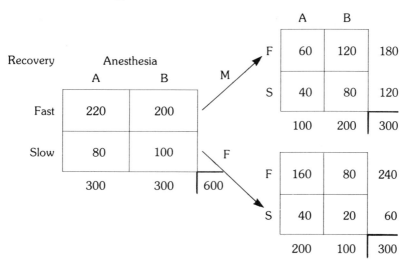

---

*Professor, Graduate School of Education and John F. Kennedy School of Government, Harvard University.

Which anesthesia would you request if you were shown these data and were going to have this sort of surgery done on you? I hope it is clear that A has a higher probability of a fast recovery rate.

Suppose you want to break these data down by the person's sex; that is, you want to know how males and females fare under these two types of anesthesia.

Notice the two arrows. The "M" arrow refers to males, and the "F" to females. The 600 people are divided into two subtables, each with 300 people.

Let's look at the males who received A: 60 out of 100 recovered fast. Of the 200 who received B, 120—that is, the same 60 percent—recovered fast. So if you are a male, it doesn't matter which anesthesia you receive.

It doesn't matter for women either: of the 200 women who received A, there were 160 fast recoveries, or 80 percent. Of the 100 who received B, 80 out of 100, also 80 percent, recovered fast.

To summarize, if you are a woman, it doesn't matter which anesthesia you receive, and if you're a man, it doesn't matter which you receive. But it is clear that A is better overall.

Now, which of these two conclusions is more useful for policy purposes, and which is right? The answer is that both are right. There is an imbalance in the numbers of men receiving A versus B and the numbers of women receiving A versus B. And at the same time women have higher recovery rates than men: 80 percent of women recover fast, regardless of which anesthesia they receive; 60 percent of men recover fast, regardless of which anesthesia they receive. But more men are given B than A, 200 to 100. More women are given A than B, 200 to 100.

What is the point? Is either data set wrong? No. They are both right. One is just at a more disaggregated level than the other. The grand two-by-two table with the 600 people is nothing more than a summary of the two small tables, each with 300 people.

I hope this example is clear. I think the statisticians have seen this; perhaps some of the lawyers have not. The key point is that the fingers have never left the hand. Notice that in the upper lefthand cell for men there is a 60. In the corresponding cell for women there is a 160. So the upper left cell altogether has 220. That appears as the 220 in the big table covering all 600 people.

If I were a judge and counsel for A said, "Your Honor, A is better; look at the numbers," I would nod and say, "That is clearly right." And if counsel for B said, "But, Your Honor, the data for men indicate no difference between A and B, and the data for women show the same thing," I would also nod and say, "That is clearly right." How would I make my decision?

I don't have a simple answer. But the crucial idea is that there are differential weightings for people who receive A and B and different recovery rates for men and women that would explain the data in the disaggregated table. The sex discrimination example is essentially the same idea carried one stage further in complexity. The data are presented in Table 2. Suppose a sex discrimination case has been filed by women at a university. There are 300

TABLE 2.
Hypothetical Data for the Sex Discrimination Case

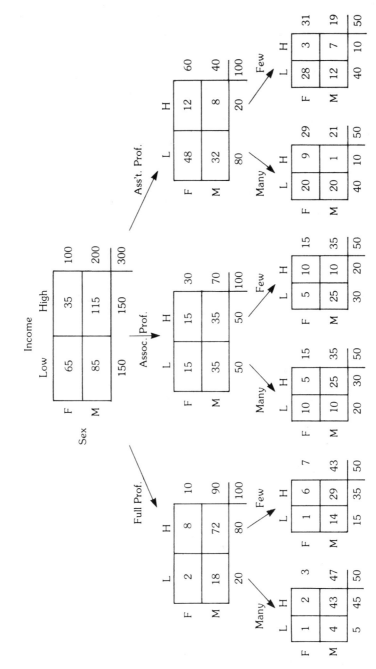

people altogether in the institution: 100 women and 200 men. The data on the 300 people has been disaggregated by median income: 150 receive low incomes and 150 receive high incomes.

It appears that indeed men are more likely to have high incomes. We see that of the 100 women, 65, or 65 percent, are low-income earners. Of the men, only 85 out of 200, less than half, are low-income earners. "Your Honor, the data show clearly that the women are discriminated against." "Yes, Mr. Light, that's right."

When we break out these data by rank, we find that assistant professors are primarily female. There are 60 female assistant professors and only 40 male assistant professors. But within that rank, notice that income and sex are independent. In other words, a female is just as likely to have a high income as a male, of the 60 females, 12, or one-fifth, have high incomes. Of the 40 males, eight, also one-fifth, have high incomes. So income here seems to be unrelated to sex. We conclude that within the assistant professor rank there is no discrimination and also that there are primarily females at this level. Perhaps that is because of recent Affirmative Action programs.

In the associate professor rank notice the independence again. Here there are more males than females, because females have only recently been hired to make up for past deficits. The data show that of the 30 female associate professors, half earn high incomes and half earn low; of the 70 males, half earn high incomes and half earn low. So there is clearly no sex discrimination in salary at this level.

Similarly, of the ten female full professors, eight, or 80 percent, have high incomes. Of the 90 males, 72 earn high incomes—also 80 percent. So the sex discrimination disappears entirely when we control for rank.

I hope it is clear that the three small tables add up to the big one. Take the upper lefthand cell in all three small tables. In the table of full professors, the upper lefthand cell has a 2: 2 full professors are female low earners; 15 associate professors are female low earners; and 48 assistant professors are female low earners. Those numbers add up to 65, which is the number in the upper left cell of the original big table. All I have done is break the big table down by rank.

These data indicate discrimination in the aggregate, but no discrimination when you disaggregate.

To take the example one last step, we can disaggregate even further. Suppose we argue that there is no evidence of discrimination at each salary level. But the other side claims we have ignored the key variable, which is productivity. Don't we want to reward people for being productive? Sure we do.

When we break down the data further according to whether people have published many papers or only a few, the relationship between sex and salary re-emerges. It differs depending on rank. In some ranks women are earning less than men. In other ranks men are earning less than women.

My point is simple. If I were a judge and three lawyers were presenting these sets of data—the first lawyer presenting the big two-by-two table, the next lawyer controlling for rank, and the third lawyer controlling for productivity—I think I would consider each set of data reasonable. But the different data sets lead to conflicting answers. So a judge needs enough familiarity with the concept of "controlling for third variables" to make some judgment about what level of disaggregation is useful. My judgment, for what it is worth, is that usually the more disaggregated the data, the better one can understand it.

We can keep disaggregating; we haven't controlled for age or number of children or teaching ratings or the prestige of the school that the Ph.D. was received from, and on and on and on. We can disaggregate until most of the cells become zero. So, if it is a tough question for statisticians, it will probably be even tougher for most judges. Yet this is precisely the sort of data that many judges will increasingly face.

CLARK C. ABT*

It may be important to distinguish between questions or issues on which social research has relevant and authoritative knowledge to offer and those on which it doesn't. That is not easy to do and requires a separate discussion. It is important to know when you have a social science problem.

The capabilities and limitations have to be applied to a distinction between facts and remedies, and they are differently applied. There has to be a distinction drawn between valid and invalid or good and bad social science, and the science court is one way to adjudicate conflicts among scientists concerning the validity of research.

Part of the problem in using expert testimony of social scientists is that they themselves are not always clear about when they are speaking as citizens, when they are speaking as scientists with an informed opinion on a matter, when they are speaking as scientists who have some evidence to present which is still controversial, and when they are speaking as scientists presenting scientifically confirmed knowledge about which there is little or no dispute. Furthermore, there is a spectrum of scientific validity of findings and methods, and it isn't useful to force scientific testimony into the extremes of that spectrum, classifying it as either fact or opinion.

I think it is useful for both judges and lawyers to know where the best applied social research and social science work is done and who does it. This is partly to be observed through the peer review process of selection of scientific reporting in the scholarly and scientific journals.

While one might argue with the quality standards, they do exist. And they do weed out the most obviously incompetent work. The mutual criticism published in those journals gives some idea of the relative quality of the work.

*President of Abt Associates Inc., Cambridge, Massachusetts.

Judges and lawyers need to know something of the costs of using applied social research and the constraints and uncertainties of using it. Costs include not only dollar costs but time costs and possible risks to various parties that could be damaged, in the form of violations of privacy or confidentiality that might be involved in primary data gathering.

The cost issue is important as a matter of equity, because much of the antitrust litigation that has used economic analysis has demonstrated that the people willing to spend the most money for econometric research are usually best able to prove their point. We may get to the point where the public treasury has to provide some sort of equalization of investment in research support to assure that the richest litigant doesn't win the case simply by virtue of being able to mobilize the most sophisticated scientific arguments.

Right now the costs of social science data vary enormously, depending on whether primary data have to be collected or secondary sources can be used. Data sources also tend to determine which discipline dominates. Economists use mainly secondary data sources—the national income accounts and nationally collected economic statistics. Sociologists and psychologists, except for education achievement statistics, are generally limited to primary data collection, which is much more expensive. Just to give an idea of the difference in cost, primary data collection costs about $100 per unit of data, whereas only a fraction of a penny is required to collect a unit of data from secondary sources.

The time required for data collection is important. The larger social experiments and evaluation research require at least a year and often several years for primary data collection.

This need not vitiate the use of primary data in the courts, although it is difficult to mobilize that kind of research effort for a particular case. But since, at least in civil cases, the waiting time is often several years, that delay is not necessarily inconsistent with the time to prepare the case.

Courts also need to know the sources of bias, not so much from the intentional aspect of introduction of the values of the scientist, but concerning the sources of accidental bias by weak methodology.

A classic book in the field, *Experimental and Quasi-Experimental Design,* by Campbell and Stanley (1960), presents in clear, nontechnical language, with only high school arithmetic required to understand most of it, various threats to the validity of scientific, particularly social science, evaluations and experiments and how they can be protected against such threats. It is certainly a book that any judge or lawyer could understand and apply as a defense against invalidly designed social science arguments.

Lawyers and judges also need to be able to select which particular social science specialty is most relevant to the particular case involved. Often these involve different disciplines. Perhaps the best way to select the appropriate ones, or at least to hear the arguments for selection, is to consult the leading social scientists in the field, and they can be identified through the professional journals and associations.

Concerning the duty to provide adverse information to a case being made and the question of ethics, it is important to point out that almost every social science professional association has rules of ethics and panels that discuss ethical issues. They call for the presentation of unfavorable data and of evidence supporting the counterhypotheses to a particular hypothesis that is being tested.

While as social scientists we can't claim that all social scientists adhere to these ethical principles, the best people in the field do follow them, and peer review is perfectly capable of identifying violations.

The gates to an understanding of the social sciences are not really guarded by mathematicians who require successful completion of advanced courses in higher mathematics, or years of laboring in a particular field of research. Much of the work is accessible to people who have not been trained in the social sciences, and it is all less frightening than has been made out. Through study and effort and the advice of leaders in a particular subfield, one can determine the difference between good-quality and bad-quality work, if not between truth and nontruth. The good-quality work in the field is not necessarily a guarantee of arriving at the truth. All we can modestly claim for the scientific methods used to obtain social data and attributions of causal realities in the social sciences is a more accurate, more reliable, more stable and objective way of finding those facts than pure judgment. We don't guarantee that we will provide the truth.

Truth in the physical sciences is also probabilistic and highly statistical in derivation, and what makes this hard to understand from the point of view of the layman is that the products of physical science clearly either do or do not work—airplanes fly or they crash; boats float or they sink. The reason is not that their design is based on a precise knowledge of the truth, but rather that they are all incredibly overdesigned. Designing a good airplane is much simpler than designing an efficacious social policy or program where we are still on the edge of effectiveness and often don't even reach that.

KEN CARLSON*

Dr. Abt's juxtaposition of truth and striving leads, I think, to a central and largely unaddressed issue: the evolution of mechanisms by which people who have not produced a scientific result and cannot do so can still assess the validity of the result. Until we have a science court or a social science court, we are stuck with the fact that those of us who are essentially outside the field have to be consumers of scientific and social-scientific truth, just as we have to be consumers of Volvos and Boeing aircraft. While to some extent we can get advice on rational consumerism from other sources, in the end we must use our own judgment about the competing claims advanced for different mod-

---

*Director of research in criminal justice at Abt Associates Inc., Cambridge, Massachusetts.

els. I think that the better informed our own lay judgment can be, the more effectively we can exercise it. What we need is a "consumer's guide" to the social sciences.

I would like to suggest one chapter in that consumer's guide. It deals with the difference between the way social scientists—and even physical scientists—deal with facts and uncertainty and the way in which those concepts are treated in the courts.

Partly because I like words in general and especially old words, I looked in *Black's Law Dictionary* to see what he thought a fact was, since we have a very broad scientific concept of what it might be. The definition was: "A thing done or a feat accomplished." Black cited in particular an Oregon court, which said that a fact was not something which might or might not have taken place (*Churchill v. Mead* 1919).

If we use that definition, it seems to me social scientists have very few facts to offer the world. What we have is not things that we know with confidence to have been the case, but assertions to which we can attach some probabilistic degree of certainty. It is the responsibility—the function really —of the professional social scientist not to assert that, for example, people in Amherst, Massachusetts, or in Atlanta, Georgia, change their opinions on the efficacy of capital punishment when confronted with different data, but to say *to what degree it is reasonable* to place confidence in an assertion of that kind.

We have in statistics two models of how to deal with facts that are known with less than perfect certainty. Game theorists have labeled these minimax and Bayesian approaches.

The basic notion of a minimax assessment of a fact is that one chooses the worst possible situation which might occur under the information available and proceeds on the assumption that that is what is going to happen. For instance, it is certainly possible that jurors in a small Georgia community would have views about capital punishment which are radically different from those espoused by people in Amherst, Massachusetts. Under a minimax approach, one is required to assume that the fact of the case is totally unknown and ranges anywhere from the best possible situation (which in this particular litigation would have been "All communities are alike") to the worst possible situation ("No community contains any information about the effect in any other community"). If you are a Georgia judge, apparently you act on the minimax strategy and choose the bottom end of that continuum and say "There is no information. The witness is excused."

The social science approach treats that range not as two points, but as a distribution of probabilities between those extremes and attempts to assess the degree of confidence that can be placed in the assertion that the fact lies at any point on that distribution. Until we as social scientists can present judges with that whole range, as opposed to the points, it seems to me that judges are going to continue to be justified in exercising the minimax simplification of the data.

Our ability as social scientists to deal with uncertainty is a strength that we can offer to the courts, which allows for better decision making than is made under the presumption that facts have to be things about which there is no doubt. It is also the case, however, that our restriction to statements of uncertainty is viewed as a weakness and may lead to adverse perceptions of the efficacy of social science. For instance, it is argued that if social science can't predict the effect of XYZ legislation with the accuracy with which George Gallup can predict the result of an election to be held next week, it is not fulfilling its purpose. There are two possible responses which social science often takes to this. One is to give up and not address the problem at all. The other is to produce an answer which in some situations is not very likely to be right and which then leads to a reputation for incompetence.

A particular example of a situation where I think social science is over-demanded is one in which social scientists are asked to predict the effects of policy. To take an example from Dr. Nagel, what is the effect of a policy of increased pretrial release on the net jail population? We have just completed a substantial study at the mandate of Congress to project prison and jail populations in the United States (Rutherford et al. 1977). The most significant finding for purposes of this conference is that social scientists are probably not prepared to predict the effects of the particular pretrial program under investigation in the context in which it was conducted, because the consequences depend on the decisions of so many actors. These decisions contain real information, in the sense of reducing prior uncertainty. They therefore are not merely natural science functions of past information. On the contrary, the effect of the policy can be whatever the policymakers choose to make it.

If social scientists announce to a court that the effect of a particular pretrial program will be a net decrease in the jail population of 37.4 percent, they will pay the price in credibility if the net decrease is actually zero percent (which is what it now is after seven or eight years of experience with such programs). The damage to credibility far exceeds any enlightenment on the part of the judge had the prediction been accurate.

If I were to draw one moral from these examples of social science in the courts, I think it would be that to make judges and lawyers more satisfied consumers of social science research, we need to present our findings in clearly probabilistic and tentative terms, even though we know that the end result has to be an affirmation or a denial of a decision.

DISCUSSION

Carol Werner *(University of Utah)*: I have the impression that what the courts are looking for is simple yes/no answers. What they lose is the complexity of our science. I see us as trying to present the conditions that will lead to a particular outcome. We can't give yes or no answers.

Stuart Nagel *(University of Illinois, Urbana-Champaign)*: I think that is where sensitivity analysis comes in, determining how results would be influenced by changing various parameters. The answer is always that it depends on what happens with regard to certain factors. On this matter of increasing the pretrial release rate in order to lower the jail population, it depends on what the prosecutor does with regard to further sweetening his offers to stop the decrease in guilty pleas; it depends on whether he is willing to dismiss more cases to stop the glut of trials; it depends on so many things.

Likewise, if you are talking about minimizing the sum of the weighted errors of convicting the innocent and acquitting the guilty, the optimum jury size depends on how many innocent people are going through the system. We don't know that and therefore can't give an answer to the question of optimum jury size. If we want to make an assumption that prosecutors are operating below the .95 level, then it sounds like twelve is the best size. If we want to assume that prosecutors are operating above the .95 level, then six is best.

What it really gets down to is values. I think people who have civil libertarian values assume that prosecutors are willing to prosecute more often than do people who have values favoring the prosecuting side of the legal process.

Werner: Do you find that the legal system is patient enough to listen to you say all that?

Nagel: I think the legal system is particularly willing to use social science in cases where it reinforces what the legal decision makers have already decided to do. One reason the Vera Foundation's recommendations of increased pretrial release were so popular is that they appealed to both conservative and liberal decision makers. Conservative decision makers liked the idea of saving the taxpayers money by reducing the jail population, while liberal decision makers liked the presumption of innocence and also the presumption that people will appear before the court. The same is true of flat sentencing: it is catching on because conservatives view it as harsher and liberals view it as more objective. With regard to research on optimum jury size, I think Justice Blackmun used it because it supported his view that a jury with fewer than six members was too small, but a size between twelve and six was all right.

If all we do is reinforce values, one could say that we are not doing much. On the other hand, if by reinforcing values we accelerate what seem to be socially desirable trends, such as increased pretrial release or more objective sentencing or a narrowing of the jury's role, one could say that we are doing something useful. But I don't think we can claim that we are changing people's minds; we are merely reinforcing what is already going to happen anyhow.

This is basically what the U.S. Supreme Court does, and it doesn't make the Supreme Court a feeble institution. The *Brown v. Board of Education* decision, for example, basically reinforced the trend toward integration or greater acceptance of blacks by white society.

REFERENCES

Campbell, D.T. and Stanley, J.C. 1960. *Experimental and Quasi-Experimental Design*. Chicago: Rand McNally.

Churchill v. Meade, 92 *Or.* 626, 182 *Pac.* 368 (1919).

Rutherford, A. et al. 1977. *Prison Populations and Policy Choices*. Washington, D.C.: National Institute of Law Enforcement and Criminal Justice.

5

What Researchers Need to Know About the Law and the Courts

STEPHEN BREYER

PAUL CHERNOFF

ORM W. KETCHAM

STEPHEN BREYER *

I will give one personal observation, speaking as a lawyer, and then I will try to make some distinctions.

I wrote a book with an economist and learned from that experience the difference in the way we are affected by our disciplines. I would say that he is judged by what he holds constant; what he doesn't hold constant he discusses in great depth and detail. And it isn't all that important that he hold certain things constant. What is important to him is that he deal well with what he chooses to deal with. I would call that a vertical approach to a problem.

A lawyer or a law school professor is held to a very different type of standard. It doesn't matter how badly we deal with each individual factor, but we had better deal with all of them, because if we leave one out and that one might have changed the result, we are open to criticism. We try to consider everything, even if our evidence on one factor is terrible, because it is better to have terrible evidence on one factor than to leave it out entirely.

It is difficult for people who are held to different standards to communicate intellectually. That is my personal observation. Now I will make a distinction that may be useful to you. In considering the usefulness of social science research in the courts, I would distinguish among at least three types of circumstances. In the first a social science study is used to prove a matter of fact. It is just one piece of evidence, like all sorts of evidence presented in the courts every day. In principle I don't think it is different from other difficult evidence. In the IBM antitrust case some jurors were asked, "Do you really understand what is going on?" It turned out they didn't, but they all thought they did. When asked, "What is a modem?" one of them said, "Oh, I know. That's the thing that goes between the interface and the module." There are lots of things that mix people up; social science is only one of them.

There also are always problems with experts. And how do you actually get the experts? Certain lawyers and judges may have a skeptical attitude. It's like the story of the man who every election day would call up the people who were running the voting booth and ask, "How many votes does Smith have?" And they would say, "Well, how many votes does he need?" There are social scientists on each side of the question. You tell me what you want to prove, and I will produce a social scientist to prove it.

In terms of using social research to prove a fact, what would worry me most is that somebody might present a study and the judge might feel that the opposite lawyer doesn't have the ability or the knowledge to attack this study. The judge doesn't know what is wrong with it, but he thinks something is wrong. For example, I ran some hearings on Civil Aeronautics Board (CAB) deregulation. The Air Transport Association (ATA), trying to prove that small communities will lose service if we deregulate, brought me into a large room, stacked with computer printout proving disaster if we have price competition.

I knew that the study was wrong. But I was very polite and thanked them for a wonderful study. I carted it all back to the office and sent copies to five

* Professor, Harvard Law School.

friends of mine in academic life. I asked them whether it was any good and if not what was wrong and why. They responded that the study proved nothing, and they had very good reasons for this conclusion. We then went back to the ATA, and it turned out the ATA study was totally wrong. We sent the study and evaluations to congressmen, and that rather disposed of the study.

But look at the resources that I had available to me which the judge doesn't have when somebody introduces a poor study. This is a possible problem at the district court level.

A second use of social science evidence is to determine a question of law. It is highly controversial whether this should ever be done, or if so, when. And it is rather unusual to do it. One of the cases in which it was done is desegregation. Should the right of the black child to go to an integrated school depend upon somebody's study about whether or not black children do better in integrated schools? Or should the Court simply have stated that segregation is wrong because of the stigma attached to sending children to segregated schools, regardless of what the social science studies show?

The Supreme Court chose a mixture, I think, in *Brown*. Maybe some of the problems we have gotten into reflect the difficulties that can exist when social science studies are used to determine questions of law, which is quite different from using them to determine questions of fact.

A third use of social science in the courts concerns administrative law. In an administrative law case, again and again the court is called upon to decide whether an action taken by an agency was reasonable. Sometimes the question is whether the action was supported by substantial evidence. The agency presents the judge with a record of studies, and the judge must decide, whether the action taken on the basis of those studies is reasonable or supported by substantial evidence.

The problem is not confined to social science, but exists whenever there are difficult technical areas which judges don't necessarily understand. How are they to say whether the decision is reasonable or not? It may be based on technology, hard science, or social science. Judges are having trouble making decisions in such cases. For example, the Occupational Safety and Health Administration (OSHA) announced that it intended to ban benzene, which is to say to reduce the standard for benzene from ten parts per million to one part per million. The industry claimed that OSHA would be imposing costs of $450 million without any evidence in the record that the reduced standard would save a single life. OSHA then came up with a set of extrapolations based upon animal studies that in fact showed much higher doses causing cancer. When the industry protested that these studies involved much higher doses of benzene, OSHA answered, "You can extrapolate down." But what kind of model do you use to extrapolate down? In this case the judge's decision wasn't that difficult, because OSHA didn't use any model.

The next time the subject comes up, I'm sure OSHA will have somebody in the hearing with some kind of a model which will indicate that the reduced standard is a reasonable extrapolation. Then Judge Leventhal or Judge Bazelon will have a difficult time deciding whether this is a totally crazy study or whether it means something.

Another example is saccharin. I know what the studies are because I was involved.

I think all human studies are inconclusive. Rat studies are also inconclusive, except for a few two-generation studies. In one such study rats were given 7.5 percent saccharin diets and they didn't develop tumors, but their male offspring developed bladder tumors. Now, does that show that saccharin should be banned? I don't know enough about how one extrapolates from rat studies to human beings. But I do know that scientists disagree about this. If I were reviewing such a study, I would want some help.

Should I turn to my new law clerk, who is a social scientist, or is there a panel, or a science court, or should I go to the library at night and read a book that Clark Abt suggests? This is a serious problem that the courts are now struggling with.

PAUL CHERNOFF*

As an administrator of a state correctional agency and more recently as a member of the judiciary, I have developed professional relationships with research personnel. I have seen firsthand the natural and perhaps healthy tensions between research and other interests within a department.

Problems often commence with data collection. During my tenure as chairman of the Massachusetts Parole Board, we attempted to reduce the paper flow, streamline reports, and improve casework management. Those employees who were dispatched to the regional field offices to collect data were perceived by the field staff as management spies, at worst, and as nonproductive staff members who carried no caseload, at best. It was only natural that field staff would feel threatened by working in close proximity with persons with whom they had little in common. One veteran parole officer told me that he felt he was being judged by someone who had never met a parole client or done casework in an urban community. Assurances from management that recidivism and casework studies would not form the basis of employee evaluation were not sufficient to insure total cooperation.

However, cooperation was eventually achieved through the formation of personal relationships. For example, the research staff developed a bona fide interest in the work of the field staff and, on their own time, accompanied parole officers during field assignments and into penal institutions. As an administrator I learned from the experience that both the line and research staffs must undergo a thorough orientation before the start of any data collection effort so that the sensitivities of each are made known to the other. Where the line staff engages in collective bargaining with management, research and basic data collection can be even more difficult as research invariably becomes a tool, if not a pawn, in employment negotiations over such

---

*Judge, Massachusetts District Court.

sensitive issues as caseload, overtime, advancement, merit evaluation, and salary and benefits.

The manner in which research is structured and its specific utilization by management can be the source of legitimate conflicts. For example, administrators of correctional agencies and project directors consider recidivism level a primary indicator of management and program success. The basic definition of a "recidivist" can color any program. In some jurisdictions a recidivist is defined as one who, within one year of release from a penal facility, is reincarcerated for a period of at least thirty days. Moderate variations in the length of the reincarceration period or the monitoring period can affect the success or failure rate by 50 percent or more.

Furlough studies may be even more revealing in this respect. Should the success rate be measured in terms of the percentage of successful furlough experiences or in terms of the percentage of inmates who have successfully completed furloughs? If ten inmates each experience nine successful furloughs and another ten inmates each fail on their first furlough, the success rate could be viewed as 90 percent or 50 percent. This reminds me of a traditional example of legal advocacy where the relevant appellate case law of precedential value consists of eight cases in California that go one way and one each in Massachusetts and Connecticut that go the other way. One lawyer argues that 80 percent of the case law supports his position while the other lawyer argues that two-thirds of the jurisdictions which have ruled on the issue are in accord with his position.

In a political world the administrators play the advocate role and attempt to fashion and use research as a tool of advocacy. This can create ethical problems for research which must be addressed from the inception of any effort. Administration and research must jointly resolve sensitive issues such as basic definitions, format of the final product, partial publication, and limitations on circulation.

The complaint of most researchers that only a few people have the interest to read and the inclination to understand a research product is well taken. The most important potential consumers do not have technical backgrounds. At the parole board research products were often simplified for consumption by legislative committees, since that which seemed technical was always suspect. The independence of the research staff adds much to the credibility of the research effort and in the long run the administration. I recall a study of the parole success rate of a certain class of released individuals that was rejected out of hand by a special legislative committee until it was learned that the agency's research director had been hired under the previous administration.

The past reticence on the part of courts to undergo the scrutiny of research on sentencing is currently placing the courts in a poor negotiating position with legislatures and governors, who are moving rapidly toward mandatory and presumptive sentencing. Only within recent years—or months in some jurisdictions—have courts agreed to participate in the type of sentencing studies which can suggest guidelines to address disparities in sentencing and thus offer a viable alternative to mandatory and presumptive sentencing.

What Researchers Need to Know

ORM W. KETCHAM*

As the only judge-in-residence at the National Center for State Courts, I get an awful lot of flak when I start asking what a megabit is or questioning a matrix or paradigms, and so forth. But I feel that I have a good scientific basis for such questions.

Some years ago when I was in the company of Dr. Karl Menninger I asked him why we couldn't get straight answers from the psychiatrists when we had mental health hearings. His answer was simple: "If you don't understand the answer, they are trying to hide something. Send it back and request that it come back to you so you can understand it."

There is more to that than a flip answer. This whole discussion suggests that we need to know each other's disciplines and activities much better than we do.

Certainly a good lawyer does not go to see a client or question a witness without considerable preparation in advance. I think that sometimes social scientists bring their findngs into court believing that they are the scientific truth, and they are rather shocked that they don't get the deference that they would like to receive.

In courts we are not in the business of seeking scientific truth; we are in the business of resolving disputes between individuals. I think you need to know more about what our business is, know more about courts; and conversely we need to know more about megabits.

When Pontius Pilate questioned Jesus, Jesus said that he was not a king but a witness for the truth. And Pilate's answer was, "What is the truth?" So there you have your first expert witness, and you can see what Roman justice did to him.

Don't be dismayed. You are probably not going to be crucified literally, but you may have a hard time if your research does not stand up, or if you feel that just because you say it is so and it is your opinion, that should be enough. You are going to be questioned, and there will be others, in all probability, who feel differently than you do about what scientific truth is.

It is a fact to say that the Supreme Court of the United States has decided that separate but equal educational facilities are constitutional, and I quote *Plessy v. Ferguson*. A good lawyer, however, will not stop there but will want to know who wrote the opinion and when. In fact, that case was decided in 1897. You have got to put these things in context if you are to understand fully the materials that come before a court.

Again, most trial judges do not feel that they are in the business of finding the ultimate truth. I recognize that I have difficulty in putting into that context class action litigation and other cases resulting in decisions that affect all of us. I think that most trial judges are very uncomfortable with that kind of decision making. And I don't know exactly what I would suggest for such cases. Perhaps we should have special courts to make those all-important decisions.

---

*Senior staff attorney, National Center for State Courts.

But in the day-to-day business of automobile accidents and misdemeanor cases, judges are not seeking the ultimate truth; they are resolving disputes.

I have tried to think of ways in which I have been involved in areas in which social science research has come into my own experience. I think they illustrate my point that we are not in the business of seeking scientific truth. But you may think otherwise.

The first experience I had with social science research presented in court was *United States of America v. E.I du Pont de Nemours & Co.* (1956), in which du Pont was sued by the U.S. Department of Justice's Antitrust Division. After several other associates and myself made a fairly thorough study of just what the government could prove, and in fact had it put into a 157-page brief and showed it to the du Pont Company, we were all convinced that we could not prove that the du Pont Company did not have a monopoly on cellophane. Since we couldn't get the right answer, we decided to change the question. We went about the process, with the aid of Heller Associates from Cleveland, for a $5 million fee, to determine just what people used to wrap everyday products. We were able to persuade the U.S. District Court, the U.S. Court of Appeals, and finally the Supreme Court of the United States that the field was wrapping and not cellophane, and that in the wrapping field the du Pont Company was not in violation of the monopoly laws.

A second case that I recall, *Bridoux v. Eastern Airlines, Inc.* (1954) is somewhat more personal. In 1949 the worst air disaster in the United States up to that time occurred in Washington, D.C. A World War II surplus P-38 was being tested by a Bolivian pilot to see whether the Bolivian government wanted to buy a group of P-38s. It crashed into an Eastern Airlines plane off National Airport and killed all fifty-five of the people in the Eastern Airlines plane. I think there were two congressmen aboard; Helen Hokinson was aboard. For those who are old enough to remember her cartoons, that was a great loss. And we were brought into the case.

Well, the whole issue so far as that case was concerned depended on one small fact, not social but physical, and that was whether the plane crash occurred in Virginia or the District of Columbia. Virginia was under the Lord Campbell's Act statute in those days, and the maximum recovery was $10,000 per decedent, which wasn't worth the litigation. If the plane crashed over the District of Columbia, it meant that we could recover whatever the jury would award for wrongful death.

So we went to the Forrestal Laboratories in Princeton, New Jersey, and with their help we were able to prove that the crash occurred over a little estuary of the Potomac River, and all of the Potomac to the high water mark on the Virginia side belongs to the District of Columbia. Eventually, that fact went to the Supreme Court and was accepted. Thus, we used scientific research and won the case.

But these are not examples of a search for truth. They represent an effort by attorneys to win litigation.

At the National Center for State Courts we are about to start a study called Gault Revisited. The *Gault* decision, written by Abe Fortas in May of

1967, is replete with many footnotes and much information that seems to support the conclusions (*In re Gault* 1967). In fact, I think it does. But I give you an interesting vignette about these social data.

In December of 1966 Monrad Paulsen and I had almost completed a casebook on juvenile court law (Ketcham and Paulsen 1967). I heard the argument in the Gault case in the Supreme Court and I called up Monrad and said, "We can't go to print until this one is out." So we persuaded Foundation Press to hold off publishing as long as they could and still make the law school market in the fall. In May the decision came out. But before that, in March, I got a call from the librarian of the Supreme Court. She said, "I can't tell you who, but one of the justices understands that you have a book that is about to come out. Could he see the page proofs?" We sent the proofs to the Supreme Court, and the materials in our book are rather liberally quoted in the opinion, which was then printed in our book.

These things are human and they are real. Don't think of yourselves as scientists up in some great tower where you are going to get deference. It is a human process. It can and does have its effect. There is a great need for more interaction and for social scientists to know more about how the courts actually operate.

One of the things I tell all the students I teach in law schools is "Don't tell me that the Supreme Court decided something. Tell me who wrote the opinion and who was in the majority, who was in the minority, and when it was written." This is a world of people, and social scientists need to know the courts. Every lawyer who is worth his salt wants to know what judge he is going before.

Researchers need to know the operations of the court and the people in it. They need to persuade the judges that what they have to offer is useful to the courts. Judges, in turn, need to come to sessions like this more than they do to learn how researchers operate and what they can produce, as well as what is not available. In the courts we don't usually think of social science research as the ultimate truth, but we do use it.

REFERENCES

Bridoux v. Eastern Airlines, Inc., 348 *U.S.* 821, 75 *S.Ct.* 33, 99 *L.Ed.* 647 (1954).

In re Gault, 387 *U.S.* 1, 87 *S.Ct.* 1428, 18 *L.Ed.* 2d 527 (1967).

Ketcham, Orman W. and Paulsen, Monrad G. 1967. *Cases and Materials Relating to Juvenile Courts*. Mineola, N.Y.: Foundation Press.

United States of America v. E.I. du Pont de Nemours & Co., 351 *U.S.* 377, 76 *S.Ct.* 994, 100 *L.Ed.* 1264 (1956).

6

Case Histories

DAVID C. BALDUS

SHARI SEIDMAN DIAMOND

PETER ROSSI

JOSEPH MITCHELL

STUART S. NAGEL

STEPHAN MICHELSON

GEORGE MICHAELS

BERNARD GROFMAN AND HOWARD SCARROW

QUANTITATIVE METHODS FOR
JUDGING THE COMPARATIVE
EXCESSIVENESS OF DEATH SENTENCES

DAVID C. BALDUS[*]

I am concerned with the methodology used by courts, primarily appellate courts, in determining whether a death sentence given in a murder case is excessive in comparison with sentences of other "similarly situated" defendants who have been sentenced for murder.

At the moment, this is an area in which applied social science is not used in the courts; they normally treat this issue in an intuitive and unsystematic manner. The purpose of my paper is to suggest possible quantitative methods that might be used to facilitate the analysis of excessiveness issues. I will recommend some possible measures for this purpose, and will illustrate their utility with the results of a pilot study I recently did with colleagues at the University of Iowa.[1] The data set for the pilot consisted of the files of 239 California murder cases in which a convicted murderer was sentenced by a jury between 1958 and 1966.[2]

The Concept of Excessiveness

The concept of excessiveness has different meanings in the law. However, in the context of capital sentencing for murder an excessive death sentence is one given in a case which in terms of the circumstances of the offender and the offense cannot be meaningfully distinguished from numerous other cases in which the defendant received a life sentence. If a defendant sentenced to death can show that there is a very low probability, say .10, that similarly situated defendants would receive a death sentence, the defendant has a potential claim that the death sentence is excessive. The legal support for such a claim may be the Eighth Amendment of the United States Constitution or a state statute which prohibits the imposition of "excessive and disproportionate" death sentences. To date, the courts have not specified the level of probability at which a defendant's death penalty becomes legally excessive, but the lower the probability that similarly situated defendants would be sentenced to death, the stronger the claim of excessiveness.

I would like to distinguish this concept of excessiveness from the idea that certain punishments are inherently inappropriate and excessive for certain kinds of crimes, for example, the death penalty for theft. Although community sentencing practices provide an important background for such judgments, they are primarily based on moral and philosophical grounds.

*Professor, College of Law, University of Iowa.

I would also like to distinguish excessiveness from invidious discrimination, which refers to the influence of illegitimate factors, such as race, in the decisions of sentencing authorities. Discrimination can result in excessiveness if racial minorities frequently receive death sentences while most similarly situated majority group defendants receive life sentences. Moreover, the methodology with which we propose to measure excessiveness will generally uncover evidence of invidious discrimination if it exists in sentencing; the system can, however, be perfectly even-handed with regard to race and still impose a substantial number of excessive sentences.

Why is excessiveness of interest to courts? In 1972 the Supreme Court in *Furman v. Georgia* held that all death penalty statutes as they were being administered in the United States at the time were unconstitutional because they did not provide sufficient procedural protections against excessive and discriminatory sentences. The Court likened the administration of the death penalty to a lightning bolt or a lottery. Out of hundreds of indistinguishable defendants, only a handful were executed. From *Furman* emerged the concept of a constitutionally excessive death sentence. The Supreme Court's more recent death penalty cases have made even more explicit the Eighth Amendment's prohibition of "excessive" death sentences. Furthermore, since *Furman*, over thirty states have adopted new death penalty statutes, many of which provide for appellate review of each death sentence to ensure that it is not excessive or disproportionate. Thus, in each of these jurisdictions an individual can also claim under state law that the death sentence is disproportionate or excessive.

The Current Judicial Approach to Excessiveness

The current judicial approach to excessiveness is best illustrated by the procedures currently employed by the Georgia Supreme Court. The usual procedure in Georgia is to compare the case under review with five to twenty "similar" cases listed in an appendix to the court's opinion. These "similar" cases are selected from a universe of all murder convictions appealed to the Georgia Supreme Court since 1970. In recent years, however, the universe of potentially relevant cases appears to have been limited to murder cases appealed since 1973. As of June 1978 this list included approximately 325 cases. Although a death sentence was given in only 20 percent of these cases, in almost all the cases listed as similar by the Georgia Supreme Court in the appendices to their excessiveness review opinions the defendant was sentenced to death. Therefore, it is not surprising that between June 1973 and June 1978 the Georgia court found only one out of forty-seven death sentences to be excessive.

In its opinions the Georgia Supreme Court sometimes describes those facts of the case under scrutiny which it considers most relevant when selecting similar cases, for example, torture or killing a witness to a robbery. Normally, however, a discussion of the facts used to select the similar cases is omitted, and the court simply states its conclusion that the death sentence in the case at bar "is neither excessive nor disproportionate to sentences imposed in similar cases."

The long-run objective of our current project is to analyze a series of death sentence cases in Georgia and elsewhere to see how well the appellate courts are evaluating comparative excessiveness. Without further systematic investigation we simply have no way of knowing, for example, whether there was only one excessive sentence in Georgia between June 1973 and June 1978. And without answers to these questions, we are unable to assess the validity of the Supreme Court's assumption in *Gregg v. Georgia* (1976) that procedural reforms of the type adopted in Georgia (especially appellate review of excessiveness) will reduce excessiveness to a tolerable level.

In a pilot study I conducted with colleagues at the University of Iowa, we developed three quantitative measures of excessiveness and reanalyzed several death sentences from a study of 239 murder convictions given by California juries from 1958 to 1966. For each of the 239 defendants, of whom 42 percent received a death sentence, we had data on over 150 variables.

Constructing Quantitative Measures

We were guided by six principles in the construction of our quantitative measures. First, keep it simple. If possible, use intuitively grasped measures; avoid procedures that turn on hard-to-verify assumptions from complex models.

Second, build on approaches that the courts are already using. Make the changes incremental, if possible.

Third, use generally accepted statistical procedures. Give the court only an interpretative question about the meaning of the results; try to avoid questions about the validity of the underlying procedure.

Fourth, recognize explicitly the threats to the validity of the results so that the judge has a clear picture of what the dangers are, particularly threats related to sample size and the failure of assumptions in the statistical models used.

Fifth, recognize the limits of the statistical proof. Be aware that a single measure normally focuses on only one aspect of the issue and that multiple measures may be necessary to present a complete quantitative analysis.

Sixth, recognize that it may not be possible to quantify all relevant aspects of the problem. Sentencing decisions often hinge on unquantifiable subtleties of fact and value. One cannot expect a numerical analysis to resolve the ultimate question. In recognition of this fact, we believe the statistics should serve only a threshold, burden-shifting function, somewhat analogous to their function in a Title VII classwide discrimination case. When the numerical measures of excessiveness cross the threshold, they should trigger a presumption that the death sentence under review is excessive, and the burden should shift to the government to rebut that assumption, on the basis of either additional quantitative evidence or nonquantitative evidence.

The Salient Features Measure. The first measure, which we call the salient features measure, expands only slightly on the current judicial approach. It requires identification of the factors of the case under review that are most relevant to the sentencing decision. To illustrate, Table 1 lists in order of importance the features of case C from the California data that a jury would be expected to find most relevant to the question of whether the convicted murderer should live or die.

TABLE 1.
Salient Features of Case C, California Data

Factor Number	Factor Name
1	Defendant killed one person.
2	Defendant had a criminal record.
3	Defendant lured or ambushed his victim.
4	The murder was premeditated.
5	Defendant had a record of violent crimes.
6	The killing involved a violent fight.
7	The killing was bloody.

To apply this measure one needs to (1) identify in the pool of potentially similar cases those which match the case under review on one or more salient features, and (2) calculate the proportion of those similarly situated defendants who received a death sentence. Table 2 presents the results when this measure was applied to case C in the California data, with all 239 cases in the universe reviewed as potentially similar cases. As indicated in column C, five cases possessed all seven of case C's salient features (match 1), seven cases possessed each of the first six features (match 2), eighteen cases had each of the first five features in common (match 3), and so on.

Column C of Table 2 indicates the proportion of death sentences within each of the subgroups of similar cases, and column D presents a 95 percent confidence interval around each of these proportions. Except for match 7, which matched on only one factor, more than 50 percent of all defendants similar to the defendant on this measure received a death sentence.

The salient features measure produces easily comprehended, fact-specific matches whose validity does not rest on hard-to-verify assumptions about the nature of the underlying data. Another strength of the procedure is that it gives great discretion to the reviewing court in its selection of the factors on which the matches will be made. With this discretion, the court can identify and match cases on the basis of subtle and unusual nuances in the case before it.

However, this measure has two important weaknesses which result from the large role that intuition can play in the court's selection of the salient fea-

TABLE 2.
Salient Features Measure Applied to Case C, California Data

A	B	C	D
		Proportion of Death Sentences Within Subgroup	
Match	Factors Matched*	(death cases/ total cases)	Confidence Interval for Estimate in Column C**
1	1 through 7	.60 (3/5)	.15 to .95
2	1 through 6	.71 (5/7)	.29 to .97
3	1 through 5	.72 (13/18)	.42 to .86
4	1 through 4	.66 (19/29)	.44 to .82
5	1 through 3	.67 (22/34)	.47 to .80
6	1 and 2	.57 (74/129)	.46 to .64
7	1	.49 (81/166)	.42 to .58

*The salient features matched are:
1. Defendant killed one person.
2. Defendant had a criminal record.
3. Defendant lured or ambushed his victim.
4. The murder was premeditated.
5. Defendant had a record of violent crimes.
6. The killing involved a violent fight.
7. The killing was bloody.
**Likely range at the 95 percent level of probability that similarly situated defendants will receive the death penalty.

tures used to identify similar cases. The first weakness is the risk of inconsistency in the selection of salient features in similar cases. The second weakness is the risk that important factors will be overlooked. Evidence from our reanalysis of the California data and elsewhere suggests that there are many factors influencing the capital sentencing decisions made by juries; that is, many circumstances increase and decrease the probability that defendants will receive a death sentence. The difficulty with the salient features measure is that in practice it may tend to isolate only a few factors for matching and overlook important determinants in the sentencing process, especially mitigating factors. Even if the effect of each overlooked factor is relatively small, the combined effect can be substantial if the number of ignored factors is large.

Main Determinants Measures. To overcome the weaknesses of the salient features measure we have developed two measures which match cases on the basis of the main determinants of the sentencing system under analysis. The main determinants are identified with a "logit" multiple-regression analysis, which isolates each factor that appears to be influential with sentencing juries and assigns it a weight or point score indicating its relative importance in jury deliberations. Table 3 lists the thirteen factors which a regression analysis suggested were important in the sentencing decisions of California juries from 1958 to 1966.

TABLE 3.
Main Determinants and Culpability Coefficients,
Case C, California Data

A	B	A	B
	Points (culpability-coefficient)*		Points (culpability-coefficient)
Main Determinants		Main Determinants	
1. Victims killed by defendant:		7. Alcohol consumption	
None	0	Heavy to moderate	0
One	5.7	None or light	1.8
Two or more	8.0	8. History of drug use	
2. Defendant had criminal record		Yes	0
No	0	No	1.5
Yes	2.2	9. Murder weapon	
3. Contemporaneous felony		Gun	1.3
No	0	Other	0
Kidnap	2.4	10. Premeditation	
Any other	1.2	Less than 5 minutes	0
4. Motive		5 minutes or more	1.9**
Sex	3.5	11. Defendant unemployed at time of crime	
Revenge	0	No	0
Any other	1.4	Yes	1.2***
5. Mitigating circumstances		12. Defendant resisted arrest	
Yes	0	No	0
No	1.4	Yes	1.2†
6. Persons wounded by coperpetrator(s)		13. Unstable job history	
None	0	No	0
One or more	3.4	Yes	.7†

*Culpability coefficients are statistically significant beyond the .01 level unless otherwise indicated. The constant in the equation was −15.9.
**Statistically significant at the .02 level.
***Statistically significant at the .05 level.
†Significant at the .10 level.

Column A identifies the thirteen main determinants and column B lists the "culpability coefficient" (culpability score) for each factor. For example, main determinant 2 indicates that if a defendant had a criminal record, his culpability score would on average be 2.2 points higher than if he did not have a record.

The calculation of an overall culpability score for an individual defendant, which takes into account each of the main determinants in Table 3, is a straightforward matter once one knows the defendant's characteristics for each main determinant.

Table 4 shows the procedure for the defendant in case C from the California data. Column B indicates his characteristics for each main determinant, and column C indicates the culpability points he receives for each characteristic. The total of these points—his overall culpability score—gives a picture of his culpability after accounting for all important aggravating and mitigating factors.

The overall culpability measure compares the defendant in the case under review with a group of defendants whose overall culpability scores are close to his. For the California data this required the calculation of a net culpability measure for each of the 238 potentially similar defendants. From this group we selected the 29 cases in which the culpability scores were closest to case C. Of the 15 "near neighbors" with higher scores and 14 with lower scores, 5, or 17 percent, received a death sentence. This figure contrasts sharply with the results obtained from the salient features measure, which found more than 50 percent of similarly situated defendants receiving a death sentence.

The overall culpability measure also has strengths and weaknesses. Its greatest strength is that the main determinants used to identify similarly situated defendants have a solid empirical foundation. We are fairly confident that the regression analysis underlying this procedure accurately identified the factors that were most influential with California's sentencing juries. In general, we have much more confidence in matches based on the main determinants of a regression analysis than we do in matches based on intuitively selected salient features. Also, the overall culpability approach takes into account the relative importance of the different factors matched. Moreover, when sample sizes are limited, the overall culpability measure allows one to match simultaneously on many more individual characteristics than is possible with the salient feature approach.

The major weakness of the net culpability approach is that it can overlook important circumstances of the case, because multiple regression analysis is insensitive to any factor that does not occur with sufficient frequency to be picked up in the statistical model. This is an important limitation on the utility of the measure whenever a unique or unusual circumstance of a case appears to have been an important factor in the sentencing decision.

Another problem with the overall culpability measure is that it is not fact-specific. It is based on an index which reduces many dimensions (thirteen in the California data) to one dimension (the overall culpability score). As a consequence, very near neighbors on the culpability scale can be quite distinct factually from the case under review. A final weakness of the net culpability approach is its reliance on a multiple regression model which is complicated and difficult to understand. Moreover, the accuracy of the results depends upon the validity of hard-to-verify assumptions about the data used to estimate the regression model.

TABLE 4.
Main Determinant Characteristics and
Culpability Score, Case C, California Data

A	B	C
Main Determinants	Characteristic	Culpability Score
1. Victims		
(none, one, two or more)	one	5.7
2. Criminal record		
(no, yes)	yes	2.2
3. Contemporaneous felony	yes,	
(no, kidnap, other)	other	1.2
4. Motive		
(sex, revenge, other)	revenge	0
5. Mitigating circumstances		
(yes, no)	yes	0
6. Persons wounded		
by coperpetrator(s)		
(none, one or more)	none	0
7. Alcohol consumption		
(heavy to moderate, none or	none or	
light)	light	1.8
8. History of drug use		
(yes, no)	no	1.5
9. Murder weapon		
(gun, other)	other	0
10. Premeditation		
(less than 5 minutes, 5		
minutes or more)	yes	1.9
11. Defendant unemployed at time		
of crime		
(no, yes)	no	0
12. Defendant resisted arrest		
(no, yes)	no	0
13. Unstable job history		
(no, yes)	yes	.7
Overall culpability score		15.0

To compensate for some of these weaknesses, we developed a measure which makes fact-specific matches using the most important main determinants. The measure identifies the proportion of defendants with main determinant characteristics identical to the defendant in the case under review who received the death penalty. Table 5 shows the results of four matches on the first to the fifth most important main determinants in case C from the California data.

TABLE 5.
Results from the Fact-Specific Main Determinants
Measure, Case C, California Data

A	B	C	D
		Proportion of Death Sentences	*Confidence Interval for Estimate*
Match Number	*Main Determinants Matched**	*Within Subgroup (death cases/total cases)*	*in Column C***
1	1 through 5	.40 (2/5)	.05 to .85
2	1 through 4	.33 (2/6)	.04 to .78
3	1 through 3	.56 (48/85)	.45 to .65
4	1 and 2	.58 (74/127)	.48 to .68

*Main determinants matched are:
  1. Number of victims;
  2. Prior criminal record;
  3. Contemporaneous felony;
  4. Motive;
  5. Mitigating circumstances.
**Likely range at the 95 percent level of probability that similarly situated defendants will receive the death penalty.

For example, match 2 indicates that six defendants matched case C on the first four most important main determinants and 2, or 33 percent, of those defendants received a death sentence.

The strength of the fact-specific main determinant measure is that it is more straightforward and easier to understand than the measure based on overall culpability scores. It also insures that similarly situated defendants will be factually similar. Nevertheless, because the measure matches only main determinants, it remains insensitive to factors that do not occur with sufficient frequency to appear in the regression model.

Our current answer to this problem is to combine the salient features and overall culpability measures. Cases are sorted by applying the salient features measure to smaller and smaller clusters of cases on the overall culpability scale. Table 6 demonstrates the procedure for case C from the California data. It presents the results when the salient features measure is applied to all of the cases regardless of their overall culpability scores, and when it is applied to subgroups of cases in proximity to case C on the overall culpability scale. One obvious result is a reduction in the number of similar cases for each match. In addition, as the universe of potentially similar cases is more circumscribed in terms of overall culpability, the proportion of death sentences begins to approximate the results obtained with the main determinants measures. Because this combined approach allows us to match simultaneously on the basis of salient features and main determinants, we consider it a particularly probative measure, and when sample sizes are large enough to allow reasonably valid estimates, we believe it should be given greater weight than the other measures.

TABLE 6.
Salient Features Measure Applied to Subgroups
of Cases, Case C, California Data

	Salient Features Simultaneously Matched*						
	1	2	3	4	5	6	7
Salient Features Measure Applied to:							
100 percent of cases on culpability scale			.65 (22/34)	.66 (19/29)	.72 (13/18)	.71 (5/7)	.60 (3/5)
Nearest 50 percent of cases on culpability scale			.42 (8/19)	.33 (5/15)	.43 (3/7)		
Nearest 25 percent of cases on culpability scale			.44 (4/9)	.38 (3/8)	.40 (2/5)		
Nearest 10 percent of cases on culpability scale	.00 (1/6)	.08 (1/12)					

*Salient features matched are:
1. Defendant killed one person.
2. Defendant had a criminal record.
3. Defendant lured or ambushed his victim.
4. The murder was premeditated.
5. Defendant had a record of violent crimes.
6. The killing involved a violent fight.
7. The killing was bloody.

Interpretation

We recommend that quantitative arguments in an excessiveness review proceeding establish a threshold and perform a burden-shifting function. If the numbers in the aggregate suggest that similarly situated defendants receive a death sentence less than a certain percentage of the time, say 50 percent, then the burden of proof on the excessiveness issue should shift to the state, which can rebut the inference with either qualitative evidence or further quantitative proof. Probably a common rebuttal by the state would emphasize the unique factors in the case which the numbers could not capture.

For example, assume that case C of the California data is under review in a jurisdiction which shifts the burden of proof, in the manner suggested, upon presentation of quantitative evidence indicating that fewer than 50 percent of similarly situated murderers are likely to receive a death sentence. The following is a summary of the quantitative proof:

Overall culpability measure—.14.

Fact-specific main determinants measure—from .40, matching on 5 factors, to .58, matching on 3 factors.

Salient features measure—from .60 to .72 when applied to 100 percent of the cases and from .33 to .44 when applied to the closest 50 percent and the closest 25 percent of the cases on the overall culpability index.

We believe these data would probably support a weak prima facie case that the death sentence in case C is excessive. The .17 estimate from the salient features measure is quite low, but it is not clearly echoed in the results from the overall culpability measure, which range from .33 to .58. Furthermore, when one applies the salient features measure to 100 percent of the cases, it yields consistently high probabilities of a death sentence (.60 to .72) on the basis of deep matches (up to seven factors) and reasonable sample sizes (five to thirty-four cases). On the other hand, when one limits the application of the salient features measure to more proximate subgroups on the overall culpability index, the estimated probability of receiving a death sentence falls to around .40.

The difference between the results when the cases are sorted solely on the basis of salient features and the results when they are also matched on the bases of the main determinants poses an interesting legal question as to the relative weight that should be given the results from the two measures. For the reasons noted earlier, we believe that the firm empirical basis of the main determinants measures gives greater validity to the probability estimates which they yield. If one were to accept this preference as a matter of law and rely primarily on the results of the salient features (.17) and on the results of the main determinants measure when applied to 50 percent or less of the cases on the culpability index (.33 to .44), one could reasonably estimate that the probability of a jury sentence of death in a case similar to case C is less than .50. The inference is not strong, however. Moreover, if equal or greater credit were given to the results of the salient features measure applied to all cases (.60 to .72), one could reasonably conclude that similarly situated defendants had a greater than .50 chance of receiving a death sentence and on this ground reject the claim of excessiveness.

Conclusion

The Supreme Court's recent Eighth Amendment adjudications have focused attention on the validity of the Court's assumption that recent procedural reforms in the states have considerably reduced excessiveness in capital sentencing. We hope that our research will contribute to the debate about how this assumption and others like it can be systematically and empirically tested with the tools of applied social science.

SHARI SEIDMAN DIAMOND*

In evaluating the role suggested for these excessiveness measures, it is important to note that the courts would retain the important standard-setting functions. Mr. Baldus is not suggesting, despite the normative tone of the term "excessiveness," that social researchers provide value judgments, based on number manipulations that will replace judicial and jury discretion. In order to arrive at the presumptive sentence in a potential death penalty case, the legal system would have to decide (1) how close in culpability score cases must be in order to be considered similar, (2) how many salient factors must be matched for a case to be considered similar, and (3) what percentage of prior death penalty impositions among similar cases would warrant a death penalty in the given case. Moreover, the culpability score itself would have to be derived from past sentencing patterns by the court, and salient factors would be identified by the court. What Mr. Baldus is suggesting is not a usurpation of power, but a tool that can systematize the comparison approach that courts currently, albeit less formally, engage in.

The approach is intriguing, but there are a number of assumptions underlying the measures that need to be spelled out. All the measures assume that comparative cases will be identified by scores on the culpability index. The similar cases are ordered along the continuum of the culpability index, and the cases that come close to the same value are the ones that are used for comparison. Therefore, if the culpability index value is used to reflect similarity, it is very important that it actually represent the qualities that jurors are using and are entitled to use in making their decisions. It also means that the sample used to develop the culpability index must be an appropriate one. Both conditions are necessary for the viability of the measures, and there is reason to be concerned about whether both can be met.

The culpability index presents certain problems. First, the index in the sample Mr. Baldus used was able to explain a little over 50 percent of the variance. This figure is comparable to that obtained in other studies attempting to

*Associate professor in the Departments of Criminal Justice and Psychology, University of Illinois, Chicago Circle.

explain sentencing variability. Almost 50 percent of the variation thus remained unexplained. We do not know exactly what caused the unexplained variation, and it is possible that cases with similar culpability scores were actually quite different.

The second potential problem is the distribution of death penalty cases in the sample used to develop the index. In Mr. Baldus's California sample 42 percent of the defendants received the death sentence. This, however, need not be true of future samples, and if a death sentence is received by a very small percentage of defendants in a sample, it is extremely difficult to avoid a conclusion of excessiveness. Most of the death penalty cases are going to be in the category of one out of five, one out of ten, or two out of eleven, unless decision making has been successfully directed at a particular cluster of cases. While the outcome of many "excessiveness" judgments may please those who are opposed to the death penalty, it is unlikely that a system with growing interest in its adoption will be content with this pattern. Alternatively, if the sample distribution contains a majority of death penalty cases, the reverse will be true: few cases will be judged excessive.

Another problem with the culpability index is that the same culpability level may result from very different configurations of variables. Similarity of culpability assumes that, however different those combinations are, if they add up to the same level of culpability, they will be accepted as similar. Although social scientists may be comfortable with the assumption, the courts may find it less satisfactory.

This leads me to say a few words about the salient features measure, in defense of that stepchild, because I know that Mr. Baldus prefers his main determinants measures. But the salient features measure has a number of advantages. Based on the idea that cases sharing particular characteristics are similar, this measure makes clear what factors have been considered in comparing cases. As a result, there is a much greater opportunity for legislative action to follow application of the salient features method. Explicit standards can be adopted for imposing the death penalty if one knows what salient factors are being included. I do not think the logit-derived model is as amenable to that kind of process.

In addition, I would like to suggest two ways in which the salient features measure might be improved. One way would be to give the judges in an appellate court reviewing these cases, for example, in Georgia, an opportunity to sit down at a terminal and plug in what they consider to be the salient features. They could then look at the distribution of cases sharing these features and see how many of the defendants received the death penalty. The terminal input by the judges would enable a social scientist to see what salient features judges wish to include in their decisions. Those features might then be incorporated into guidelines or legislation for future sentencing.

Another possibility, and one that is perhaps more difficult to implement, would be to have the salient features selected by members of the jury pool. This might be an appropriate strategy in view of the fact that the courts have ruled that jury discretion should be preserved in these areas. Mandatory death sentences have been deemed impermissible because they impose constraints on juries that the courts have found unacceptable. If we are concerned with jury discretion in these instances, perhaps it is more appropriate for juries rather than judges to be selecting the salient features.

A few policy issues concerning implementation also deserve mention. One issue concerns a time frame. Until some consistency is achieved, there is no reference sample group. Without consistency in past sentencing and a record of less than 50 percent death sentences among eligible cases, nearly every new recommendation for death is going to be excessive. We need a reference sample group with some consistency so that we can say, "Yes, we know the death penalty was given with some frequency in particular kinds of cases."

I also think that if we consider jury discretion an important element, we have to talk about evolution, because standards may change over time. We have certainly seen them change in the recent past, as public opinion has come to favor the death penalty. We have to think about building into such a procedure an opportunity for this evolution. Once we use this kind of system, we reinforce those decisions that compare with past decisions and solidify the standard that has been used in the past. Even if there is pressure to change that standard, this procedure will freeze it and make it a little more rigid.

There is also the question of whether the regressions would be expected to differ across jurisdictions and, if so, what to do about it.

In general I find the procedures suggested by Mr. Baldus most attractive, and I think that we might even be a little less modest in talking about when they could be used: this attempt to structure jury discretion in capital cases through systematic review has the larger implication that discretion can be structured in other areas by setting up guidelines in advance and reviewing the coherence of past decisions. I will talk briefly about two areas in which I think the approach might be worth pursuing.

One area is ratification of plea bargains. Suppose that a plea bargain is presented as the appropriate sentence. A judge might decide that it is way out of line for similar cases and that therefore he will not accept it. He could use this kind of standard information to justify a decision not to accept a particular plea bargain.

The other area is structuring of all sentences. I think the appropriate reference here is to research that Professor Wilkins of the State University of New York at Albany has been doing. He has incorporated something like a salient factor—what he calls a salient factor score—in sentencing and in parole board decisions where a judge is provided with guidelines based on a summary of past practice in the particular court. If one of the evils of discretion is variation that cannot be explained by the particular characteristics of the case, then the procedures that Wilkins and Baldus suggest should be at least partial solutions.

DISCUSSION

Phillip Finney *(Southeast Missouri State University)*: Wouldn't this procedure take us almost back to square one? If you had a case and it was found that one case out of ten ends up with the death penalty, wouldn't the jury or judge have to say, "Well, we can't give the death penalty to this person," and in another case, where maybe four out of five received the death penalty, they end up saying, "Well, we have to give the guy the death penalty here"? And we are back to no discretion.

David Baldus: Well, in the latter case if four-fifths of the similarly situated people get it, no one is saying that you have to give it. It is just saying we aren't going to overturn the decision of the jury. That is what the procedure is here, a matter of reviewing what the jury did.

In a jurisdiction, for example, that has very few death penalty decisions given, you are reduced to the problem of working with a very small sample. So you would have to look at just the special features, and the court is going to have to go on its intuition.

Finney: The jury, then, wouldn't know about these statistics ahead of time?

Baldus: Well, that's another question, as to whether or not you would want to present numbers like this to a jury. And substantial risks are associated with it, especially if anybody like your defendant has ever gotten the death penalty, it seems to me.

Stuart Nagel *(University of Illinois)*: I think at the end Shari made a point that nicely distinguishes traditional social science research from the kind of optimizing perspective that I advocate; namely, that if one really wants to get at the extent to which the death penalty should be invoked or the extent to which long sentences ought to be invoked, what we should definitely not be doing is codifying what has been done previously.

A social scientist attempting to account for the variance with regard to who gets the death penalty and who doesn't get the death penalty might use race as one of the independent variables because it might have very high predictive value. But we don't want that included as a salient factor. You might respond by saying you didn't include it, but you may have done so by including, say, prior arrests, which tend to correlate very much with race.

What I would like to suggest as an alternative is to devise some way of determining an optimum level of invoking the death penalty. It would be analogous to the notion of optimum flat sentences, taking as your dependent variable not the extent to which the death penalty has been invoked but some goal variable, like trying to maximize deterrence. You get data, say, from all fifty states, in order to determine not what the relationship is between the death penalty and homicide, but what the relationship is between different situations in which the death penalty is used and a reduction in homicides. Maybe the death penalty does reduce homicide in certain types of cases and not in others. This method would take as a dependent variable or a goal variable maximizing homicide deterrence to come up with some notion of when the death penalty should be invoked, rather than merely codifying all the previous racism and other arbitrary values that may be implicitly in your model.

MARKET RESEARCH DATA IN DECEPTIVE ADVERTISING CASES

PETER ROSSI*

I am going to discuss the role that I played as an expert witness in several cases before the Federal Trade Commission (FTC) Administrative Law Courts. The cases all involve deceptive advertising. The Federal Trade Commission staff brought complaints against Wonder Bread in one case; Listerine in another; and analgesics (Anacin, Excedrin, Bufferin, and the like) in a third.

The cases concern two questions. First, is the product exactly as advertised? In the Wonder Bread case the advertising in question claimed that Wonder Bread gave "eight wonderful ways to grow," that is, the product was effective for the growth of young children. A large number of experts, whose testimony I never read, stated that such was not the case; Wonder Bread in fact was no different in these respects from almost any other bread. Indeed, Wonder Bread Bakeries often supplied the bread that appeared under other labels as competitive brands. Wonder Bread was not noticeably different in any significant respect and certainly did not contribute to more effective growth.

Since Wonder Bread had advertised this theme for a long period of time, the second question was whether the advertising had any effect upon consumers. Did the consumers believe that Wonder Bread was different or that Listerine actually was effective against colds?

A related question that the FTC staff posed in regard to these three cases was whether there should be some counteradvertising if deleterious effects were found.

This case was first argued against Wonder Bread in 1972 and 1973. I was called on by the Federal Trade Commission law staff to help them look over market research subpoenaed from Wonder Bread. The tactic was to examine this evidence and possibly conduct secondary analyses of it to see to what extent consumers actually had an image of Wonder Bread that was distinctively different from their images of other brands of bread which were advertised, and whether the image of Listerine as an effective cold remedy was different from that of other mouth washes. Also, was there any evidence that these images, if they did exist, had some solidity to them, that is to say, resisted decay over time?

Other social science experts also testified. For example, there were experts on advertising who could look at the advertising and assess what that material was intended to do. Since I know little about advertising in a techni-

---

*Professor of sociology, University of Massachusetts.

cal sense, I could not make such assessments. My particular task was to look at the survey material and characterize the patterns of consumer opinions concerning Wonder Bread or Listerine or Anacin as similar to or different from the patterns of opinions concerning competing brands.

The presentation I made in the Wonder Bread case in front of the administrative law judge was a disaster. I tried to explain multiple regression to the judge. And the law firm defending Wonder Bread, with several experts behind them, had an enormously good time making fun of me, a process which I probably aided.

I was disappointed not to be able to use effectively the didactic methods which I ordinarily use in courses in elementary statistics to get across the point that the end result of a linear regression is to run a "best fitting" least-squares regression line through an ellipsoid distribution of points. I had enormous difficulty (as those of you who have ever tried to do it also may have experienced) explaining the intercept.

When the administrative judge rendered an opinion upon the case, he characterized my testimony as "a leap over the chasm of conjecture toward insubstantial and speculative conclusions." That was case number one.

In case number two, the Listerine case, both sides were a little more sophisticated. The experts who were marshalled on the side of the Listerine company, Warner-Lambert, were better than in the previous case. The administrative law judge was a little more sympathetic to this sort of evidence, and I had a much easier time presenting what was in effect a time series analysis of the consumers' image of Listerine as effective against colds. Warner-Lambert's market research constituted a nice time series of studies over about fifteen years. Trends in the series were sensitive to the amount of dollars used to advertise that theme.

I also was able to find in the subpoenaed material (after my eyes wore out from the ninth-order copies that were supplied to me), a study of a test market in California, where Listerine stopped advertising "effective for colds" for a period of two years. I could use that study to estimate the decay function of the advertising. The basis of my testimony was that, lo and behold, the image of Listerine as effective against colds was extraordinarily different from images of other mouth wash products, and the Listerine image was sensitive to the amount of money poured into such advertising by Warner-Lambert. Furthermore, the decay curve indicated that the effect of advertising could not possibly drop to zero in two or three years. The end result was that the FTC lawyers were able to make a convincing case not only to the administrative law judge, but to the Federal Trade Commission, and through appeals. The courts have ordered corrective advertising, partially based upon my testimony.

In the more recent Anacin case, everyone was even more sophisticated. Not only did the lawyers on the other side, American Home, have better expert witnesses than in either of the other two cases, but the chief lawyer who was defending the case for Anacin took an advanced course in multivariate analysis so that he could question me more sharply and directly.

This development of sophistication on the part of attorneys is interesting. One of the major problems in presenting this material before a court of this sort, even though an administrative law court is very informal, is that it is very difficult to present all the evidence that one may have. The evidence is brought forth in questioning. If a lawyer who is questioning a witness doesn't know what questions to ask, he is at an extreme disadvantage in bringing out what may be either the strengths or weaknesses of a case. I had some doubts about how strong the evidence was, since the data involved were not collected specifically to illuminate the issues in the cases; indeed, the data had some serious defects in them. In the earlier cases some of the strengths of the data and interpretations were also lost in the testimony; neither the FTC nor the company lawyers knew how to bring out through direct or cross-examination the richnesses and weaknesses of the data. The Anacin case was different. A battery of econometricians who sat behind the Anacin lawyer sent a steady flow of yellow slips of paper toward him. The lawyer's preparation in this case enabled him to ask the right questions. As a result, Anacin gave me a very hard time on the stand for about three days.

Nevertheless, the administrative law judge ruled that corrective advertising on the part of Anacin would be necessary. It will probably take about four or five years before the case gets through the entire appeal process.

These FTC cases have been my major experiences with the courts. My experiences have some interesting implications, I think, for the role of a social scientist in the legal process. I was very nervous the first time I testified; having been influenced by television, I expected a rapid cross-fire examination. In fact, the process of direct and cross-examination is incredibly slow, a characteristic that is very good for a slow thinker. You can formulate answers much better in the court than you can in the classroom, possibly because the lawyers want to think before they ask questions, which may not be the case for students.

Second, it is somewhat difficult to give a balanced testimony. Despite the fact that a witness is supposed to be impartial, that is not really the case. A witness is presented as one side's witness; since the other side treats that witness like an adversary, it is easy to become identified with the friendly lawyer. Because of that identity sometimes one may not volunteer a full answer but withhold some information or even stress particular points rather than others. The truth may not be told fully. My answers to questions in class often involve complex qualifications. Answers given in court tend to be a little more crisp than those given in class.

Another difficulty in remaining balanced is that the other side, in order to bring out a possible uneasiness you might have with a particular piece of evidence, must know how to reveal it by asking the right questions. And that is relatively difficult without some expertise; the evidence that I gave contained relatively sophisticated—that is to say, second-year graduate—statistics and sociology.

There are also peculiar reactions on the part of the court and the lawyers to the question of plausibility and likelihood. "It is not likely that that finding could occur by chance" is a statement which one side or the other doesn't like and the judge doesn't like. It is very difficult, I think, to state things probabilistically.

JOSEPH MITCHELL*

I think that something that can be learned from our previous speaker's case study is that before an administrative body—which usually has a lot more expertise than a court does—and especially before a court, communication is extremely important. If you mention multiple regression analysis to state court judges, they will think you are talking about Chinese script; they have no understanding of the kinds of concepts that you generally deal with. Therefore, it is most important that before appearing before any of these bodies, you prepare a simple analysis that will communicate your ideas to the person who has to understand them, whether it is a judge or a jury or an administrative judge.

I believe that more and more of you will be having the opportunity to testify in court, because not only are the federal government and the Federal Trade Commission in the business of market analysis, but all of our states now have consumer protection laws which will require market analysis on the part of both the attorneys general who are protecting the consumers and the defense lawyers.

As Peter Rossi suggested, in many instances you are going to have to educate your lawyer before you even get to the point of educating a judge or jury. You will have to tell him what questions he must ask in order to bring out the information that is necessary to present in the particular case, because he will not have had the training necessary to know the right questions.

I would also suggest that you present the judge with a simple written summary of your evidence so that he will know what you are talking about. While you are on the stand, you can use all the long and big words that you want, but at least the judge or jury will have the written summary to digest and understand. I think that if you do all of these things, you might win your case.

DISCUSSION

Teb Marvell *(National Center for State Courts)*: I once was told by a federal judge that in every patent case he had all the attorneys and all the expert witnesses meet with him in chambers for a day or two, or even longer,

---

*Judge, Superior Court of Massachusetts.

until he was absolutely sure he understood what was going to come out in court. That might be a good procedure to use when social scientists testify about complicated matters.

Joseph Mitchell: I think that is an excellent idea. And if your lawyer doesn't make the suggestion, maybe you ought to ask the lawyer to have a pre-trial orientation for the judge.

George Michaels *(Private practice attorney)*: Professor Rossi, were you told by counsel in advance what to expect in the direct examination and what to anticipate on cross-examination?

Peter Rossi: Yes. I should have mentioned that one of the more annoying parts of the whole experience was the many days of advance preparation in which it seemed to me the lawyers were going over and over the same point in questioning me and learning how to question me to bring out only the pertinent points.

Up to two eight-hour days would be devoted to preparation before the presentation. And the cases are prepared over a period of about two years. So I would say I spent about twenty to thirty days preparing for each one of the cases.

Michaels: Did the lawyers ask the same questions in the trial itself?

Rossi: Yes. They had a script in front of them.

I was also told that it would be inadvisable to bring notes to the stand because the notes could be subpoenaed or my work papers; anything that I did on the material in my testimony could be subpoenaed by the adverse side. Anything that I put on the papers I might have to explain.

Michaels: Were you prepared for cross-examination as well?

Rossi: Yes. I got to be quite expert at it; I could tell what was going to be cross-examined by knowing the expert witnesses on the other side and what their specialities were. They had quite an array of well-known text-book writers.

Michaels: And you aided your own counsel in questioning them?

Rossi: That's right.

Clark Abt *(Abt Associates Inc.)*: It was argued earlier that social scientists may not feel the ethical need to present fairly both sides of the question on which they have information and analysis.

Assume that a social scientist wants to present a balanced view of both sides of a question but in effect is not permitted to do so because of the sequence of questions asked. Do you think both from the social scientist's point of view, Professor Rossi, and from the court's point of view, Judge Mitchell, that it would help if as a matter of regular procedure expert witnesses were allowed a brief period of time, without interruption or cross-examination, to give their own interpretation of both sides of the question that they were being asked to testify on?

Mitchell: It is a good idea, but it wouldn't work because we have rules of evidence, especially in court, and you have to do it question by question so the other side has an opportunity to object. What the witness might be saying might not be admissible under our rules of evidence. And the other party must have that opportunity to preserve their rights in the case.

Rossi: In my first case, when the lawyer on the other side asked the wrong question, I said, "I can't answer that question, but I know the question you should ask." The judge was quite upset by that. You see, the lawyer was on the verge of asking a very important question which I think would have cut the ground out of much of my testimony. He should have had the right to ask that question, but it just didn't work.

Geoffrey Peters *(National Center for State Courts)*: The purpose of Dr. Rossi's testimony was not to prove any ultimate truth about Anacin or Listerine or anything else. The purpose was to adduce evidence which his lawyer wished to present to the court for the court's consideration.

If the lawyers are properly prepared and if the expert witness is properly prepared, the lawyers should be able to ask the right kinds of questions in the right way, even without the prompting of the expert witness. That should be sufficient to present the evidence that the court needs in order to make a decision.

Your question to Dr. Rossi about whether or not the evidence was adduced on both sides is more properly addressed to him in his role as a social scientist than in his role as an expert witness. When he publishes his findings in a journal, they are reviewed by his peers, and the way in which he does his research is elucidated not in a simple fashion that can be understood by the court, but in a fashion that can be understood by fellow social scientists.

Too often we confuse the roles that we play because we are one person. But when we are an expert witness, that role is a very different role from the role of a social scientist qua social scientist.

Stuart Nagel *(University of Illinois)*: Peter, with regard to your role as a social scientist, one reason a lot of social scientists don't participate in that kind of litigation is that the research required for it doesn't lend itself to publication. In the reward system you don't get much credit for having testified in an administrative proceeding.

In the typical testimony on survey evidence the social scientist says, "I drew my sample and asked questions in the following way; 70 percent of the people said yes to this question and 30 percent said no." There is nothing of any theoretical significance in this type of research; there is no causal analysis.

But the implication in what you were reporting was that you were concerned with accounting for some kind of variance, otherwise you wouldn't have done a regression analysis. What was the variation you were trying to account for?

Rossi: I was trying to determine whether, in the opinion of consumers, both users and nonusers, the product appeared different to them from other brands. Such information is usually indexed by what the market research people call image data. They have a long check list of adjectives describing the product, and they ask, "Is Wonder Bread this, that, or the other?" The question is whether there is a significant difference in the image data associated with a particular brand. Is Anacin looked at differently than the store brand of aspirin? It is very easy to show that in fact they are quite different.

Nagel: And you might include as your independent variables economic class of the consumer, race, and so forth?

Rossi: Yes. What you do then is to show that the image held by a consumer of a particular brand is a function of exposure to the advertising.

These are heterogeneous, messy data. And I like to think of this kind of work as artistic data dredging. Of course, it does not appear in professional journals, because it is irrelevant to professional interest.

Elton Klibanoff (*Abt Associates Inc.*): I think I hear from you, Clark, that you are bothered by the fact that not all the information is revealed. I think there is a way for social scientists to deal with that ethical problem. As more and more of them become involved in the court system and concerned about it, as citizens they can put political pressure on the court system to change or to open up; even the rules of evidence can be changed under public pressure.

Rossi: I think that would drive the good money out with the bad. If a social scientist insists that the lawyer let him say exactly what he wants, the lawyer will simply find another social scientist.

Klibanoff: Right.

Rossi: And that is what the lawyer should do, because he is trying to defend a particular person or party in the litigation. This may seem self-serving or at least self-excusing, but I thought that the role I could play as an expert witness was to answer every question precisely and accurately; I did not feel obliged to say everything that I knew. This is a distinction between judgment calls, fudging, and faking. Faking is bad, fudging is phtt, and judgment calls are okay.

Alan Paller (*Applied Urbanetics Inc.*): It seems to me that after you have done a few cases they get boring, they are not on the cutting edge of your research, and they are not publishable. You have to spend thirty days doing work that any good graduate student could do but that you don't dare give to him because you are going to have to testify to it. Is it something you will only do a little of and then quit?

Rossi: That is very insightful. I have quit. The Anacin case was just the last pill. There are three more cases coming up, and I don't want to do them. Now I'm in trouble, however, because the other side is going to subpoena me as a witness for them. So I am embroiled in this endlessly.

Marvell: I have one more word on the ethics question. There is an enormous difference between legislative facts and adjudicative facts. Adjudicative facts were involved in the FTC hearings. Social scientists are simply plugged into the adversary system, and they have to move with it. But when it comes to legislative facts, by and large the judges are free, though they often don't know this, to lay aside the rules of evidence and accept any testimony. Also, social scientists can submit an amicus brief; they don't need to go through the lawyers. So they have plenty of chances to present the full story if it is legislative law-making information. And that is the most important information before the court.

Arthur Konopka *(National Science Foundation)*: Picking up on a point Stuart Nagel made about the reward system, the best or the most prevalent rule of law right now is that expert witnesses may not participate in cases on a contingent fee basis. So the reward structure is not the same as it is for lawyers.

Presumably, the reason for that rule is that if expert witnesses were allowed to participate on a contingent fee basis, it would in some way manipulate their expert findings. This overlooks the fact that lawyers go searching for expert witnesses who are willing to take positions which represent their case.

I wonder if the panel would express itself on whether that is a realistic rule. Highly qualified people like Dr. Rossi might be enticed into testifying in these cases if they had some commensurate economic gain, something similar to that of the lawyers who have to invest their time in the preparation of the case. When we prohibit the expert witness from participating in a contingent fee are we preserving something which is of real value?

Rossi: Well, I want to assure you, this is no way to make a living. The work isn't steady, for one thing. And it's seasonal and very hazardous.

Konopka: That's what they said about antitrust when it started.

Rossi: I don't know what the contingency fee arrangement would be. Remember, I am not the only expert witness. There can be as many as sixty in a case over a period of two years. The percentage involved would necessarily drop quite rapidly.

Mitchell: I think the rule is a good one. When you put an expert witness on a contingency fee basis, you are going to destroy his effectiveness. The other side will question him about his fee, and he will have to admit that he is getting one-third of whatever the poor victim recovers and that is why he is testifying the way he is. It is not the best way to seek truth. Under the current rule, even though the expert is called by one side, at least he can have some semblance of being detached from the case.

Shari Diamond *(University of Illinois)*: I had an experience which might be relevant. In Illinois I testified on probabilities of various systems for assigning ballot position on the assumption that if you had less of an opportunity for a particular ballot position, it might affect your chances of being elected. The only preparation that the attorney who was conducting the

105

direct examination gave me was to set the fee in advance and to instruct me that if I was asked what fee I was receiving, I was to say I was being paid for my time, not for my testimony.

Stephen Wasby *(State University of New York at Albany)*: It might be interesting to test empirically whether the contingent fee results in more bias than the flat fee.

Abt: I have a question for David on the death penalty. Judge Hallisey has suggested that one of the problems with the death penalty, and particularly the mandatory death penalty, is that it would influence the self-selection of judges. He questioned whether we ought to have judges who would feel comfortable handing out death penalties.

My question to Mr. Baldus is, have you looked at the impact of the death penalty meted out by judges on their subsequent behavior?

It would seem to me that there could be significant long-term impacts—admittedly difficult to research—that might shed some light on the desirability of that process.

David Baldus *(University of Iowa)*: I think it is an interesting idea, but I haven't investigated it.

Stephan Michelson *(Econometric Research Inc.)*: Three quick comments. First of all, I just want to go on record to say that I think contingency fees are unethical. I am amazed that it would even be considered as a topic.

Second, I put every case, once it has been reported, on my résumé. I don't understand that discussion either. I grant that the academic profession hasn't given me great rewards, but there are rewards elsewhere. For instance, the legal system thinks I am experienced.

The third comment goes back to the death penalty thing. Shari Diamond suggested that a judge could sit at a terminal and request data on various matches—and perhaps inadvertently also be giving data by typing in a particular request. I think that is a nifty idea.

VALUE REINFORCEMENT AS A KEY TO POLICY RESEARCH UTILIZATION

STUART S. NAGEL*

I have been asked to comment on the use by the U.S. Supreme Court of my policy analysis research model in deciding that five-person juries are unconstitutional. My general reaction is pleasure at being cited by the Supreme Court,

*Professor of political science, University of Illinois, Urbana-Champaign.

but slight disappointment at the apparently selective use of the analysis to support what may be preconceived values. The experience adds to the notion that some policy research, including policy analysis in the criminal justice field, is used especially by policymakers because it reinforces their values.

The case involved is *Ballew v. Georgia* (1978). Justice Blackmun, writing for the Supreme Court, says that states can have criminal juries with fewer than twelve members but not fewer than six. He bases his statement in part on an operations research approach which says too few jurors result in too many type 1 errors of convicting the innocent, and too many jurors result in too many type 2 errors of not convicting the guilty.[3]

The quantity of type 1 errors (E1) is equal to the probability of convicting an innocent defendant associated with various jury sizes (P1), multiplied by the number of truly innocent defendants subjected to jury trials out of every 100 defendants (D1). Likewise, the quantity of type 2 errors (E2) is equal to the probability of not convicting a guilty defendant associated with various jury sizes (P2), multiplied by the number of truly guilty defendants subjected to jury trials out of every 100 defendants (D2).

The optimum jury size is thus the number of jurors for which the sum of type 1 plus type 2 errors is minimized, with the type 1 errors weighted more heavily than the type 2 errors. A weight of ten was tentatively used because William Blackstone says it is ten times as bad to convict an innocent defendant as it is to acquit a guilty defendant. Figure 1 summarizes some of the relationships.

According to the analysis, seven is the optimum jury size in light of the above definition of optimum. To deduce that conclusion involves a combination of normative and partly empirical premises. The key normative premise is the above-mentioned 10-to-1 trade-off ratio. The optimum jury size, however, is not sensitive to reasonable changes in that ratio from a 5-to-1 up to a 15-to-1 trade-off.

FIGURE 1.
Graphing the Number of Errors for Various Jury Sizes

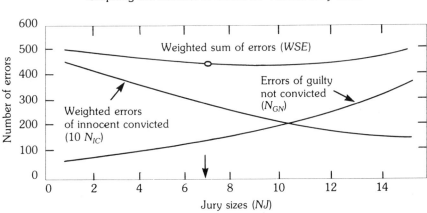

One key empirical premise relates to the probability of a twelve-person jury convicting a truly innocent defendant or a truly guilty defendant. The optimum jury size is also not sensitive to reasonable changes in those probabilities from about .20 to .70. The optimum is, however, quite sensitive to the second empirical premise—how many truly innocent defendants are tried out of every 100 defendants—and the complement of that figure for the number of truly guilty defendants.

Judge Blackmun used the analysis selectively when he dwelt on the meaningfulness of the normative premise and concluded that the model makes sense, but ignored the empirical premise to which the model is so sensitive. The model tentatively works with the idea that 5 out of 100 defendants are truly innocent, assuming prosecutors are operating at a .95 confidence level in bringing defendants to trial. If, however, one does not trust prosecutors and feels they may be operating at a .90 confidence level, then larger juries are needed to protect those additional innocent defendants from being convicted. On the other hand, if one is more trusting of prosecutors and feels they may be operating at a .99 confidence level, then smaller juries are needed to convict those guilty defendants. The level of confidence on which prosecutors are actually operating is unknowable, and one's perception of the level is basically a value judgment.

The real value of the model is thus not in deducing an optimum jury size, but in clarifying the kinds of information one needs to know in order to arrive at an optimum jury size. Regardless of its real or intended value, the model did serve a useful purpose of providing partial support for stopping the slide of the Supreme Court toward allowing smaller juries in criminal cases. That stopping was supported by both liberals and conservatives on the Court. The liberals do not like smaller juries because they may increase the chances of an innocent person being convicted. Conservatives are willing to go below twelve but not below six, possibly because five-person juries seem too much of a deviation from tradition and precedent.

Thus, we have here a situation in which liberals and conservatives agree on a policy or decision but for substantially different reasons. Whenever that kind of situation occurs, evidence from social science or operations research that is supportive of the policy or decision is much more likely to be utilized than evidence supporting only one side of a criminal justice controversy.

Other examples of that phenomenon can be given. The pretrial release studies in the 1960s, for example, tended to show that one could release many more defendants than were being released without jeopardizing the appearance rate by having more selectivity in releasing, some supervision during the pretrial period, and notification just before the trial. Those studies were widely cited and used by policymakers, although the methodology was frequently flawed. However, the results appealed to both liberals and conservatives. Liberals like the idea of releasing more defendants out of respect for the presumption of innocence and lack of respect for the class bias represented by pretrial detention based on a money bond. Conservatives like the idea of releasing more defendants in order to save taxpayers the high expense of pretrial detention, lost GNP, and the welfare costs of families of detainees.

Another example is the rehabilitation studies of the 1970s which show that rehabilitation does not work and that more emphasis should be placed on deterrence and determinate sentencing. Those studies that totally reject rehabilitation may be even more methodologically flawed, but their implications also appeal to both liberals and conservatives. Liberals like determinate sentencing because it removes some of the arbitrary discretion which parole boards and judges otherwise exercise. Conservatives like determinate sentencing because they view it as harsher than the more discretionary sentencing, especially if one emphasizes the required minimum rather than the maximum aspects of determinate sentencing.

Policy analysis research may thus tend to be most utilized not necessarily when it is brilliant, but when it fits preconceived liberal and conservative values. Researchers should, however, be pleased if their research is able to trigger or accelerate governmental reforms. It may be overly presumptuous to think one's research is going to change people's values. If one's research is to be adopted, one might try to show how the policies recommended promote widely held values more than previous policies. One should thus not be disappointed that value reinforcement is often a key to use of policy analysis, at least in cases where the values being reinforced lead to "socially desirable" results.[4]

STATISTICAL DETERMINATION IN EMPLOYMENT DISCRIMINATION ISSUES

STEPHAN MICHELSON[*]

First, there were some comments or questions raised earlier about comments that Judge Skelly Wright made in the *Hobson v. Hansen* (1971) decision concerning the usefulness of the social science presentation. I would like to make it clear that I am completely in agreement with Skelly Wright; I think it was a brilliant decision. A judge should always make a decision on the basis of the prima facie case, if he can, for many reasons.

---

[*]President, Econometric Research Inc., Washington, D.C.

Consider a school system in which 95 percent of the students are black and 5 percent are white. If the per-pupil expenditure for whites is $100 more than that for blacks, and you take that $100 away from the whites and distribute it to the 95 percent black population, each black student will receive $5.25. You took a lot away from a white kid and gave little to a black kid. It may not have any educational effect, but that's hardly a reason not to do it; it should be done.

There's a problem, though, with what's been taken up as Skelly Wright's view. I see nothing either moral or constitutional about arithmetic, it's just more understandable to more people.

By the way, there are tremendous numbers of discrimination cases that are white collar and that disturbs some of the people who are working in the field. It's not the most important social issue if somebody's making $19,000 as opposed to $21,000, but these are the people who gain access to the courts. There's a larger social problem of who has access and who understands what kinds of facilities are available to them.

In *Presseisen v. Swarthmore* (1974) the judge didn't say, "I'm going to decide this on the basis of moral and constitutional arithmetic." He said, "I think the statistical experts on both sides have done a really good job in destroying the presentations of the other side and have done a really lousy job of resuscitating their own. So go away; I won't deal with it." He dismissed the case or found for Swarthmore, if you will, which may have been the correct finding. If you read the Skelly Wright opinion you'll realize that he was very much influenced by the social science presentations, whereas the judge in *Presseisen* was not. A case that I was involved in between January and April of 1977, *EEOC v. Tufts,* has not been decided yet. Once Judge Murray in Boston reads this *Presseisen* decision, he'll say, "That's the answer—just tell these people to go away."

So the big problem in presenting statistical evidence in discrimination cases is that the judges have an out when they decide that the evidence is not convincing. When the experts on each side find errors in the other side's presentation, and the judge concludes that both sides have destroyed each other, you haven't put social science into the courts. That's possibly what's going to happen for a while, and though it may look to some people like Skelly Wright's handling of the evidence, it isn't.

The essence of the Hobson decision was really formulated in *Green v. McDonnell Douglas* in 1972, that is, the procedural essence. I guess it wasn't anything new but people nowadays refer to *McDonnell Douglas* as the procedure you use in court. The plaintiff must make a prima facie case and then the defendant may have other explanations for the data presented in the prima facie case. Then you can come back conceptually and reconstitute, rebut the rebuttal, as it were, and reconstitute the prima facie case. That sequence is called burden shifting.

There is a phenomenal case in the First Circuit called *Blizard v. Fielding* (1978) in which the plaintiff clearly wasn't going to win anything, but it was reversed anyway because the judge's opinion didn't make it clear whether he

110

felt she had made a prima facie case that was rebutted, or whether she hadn't made a prima facie case at all. The conclusion was the same thing; she didn't have a case. I'm sure the reversal is going to infuriate the district judge, who will write an opinion saying she didn't have a prima facie case; case dismissed. But it's a very serious issue, the presentation of data in this burden-shifting manner: What is a prima facie case and what isn't? Unfortunately, nobody knows. I will make only one prediction: it is going to be harder and harder to make a prima facie case.

Consider the issue of wage discrimination on the basis of sex. Traditionally, you can make a prima facie case based on evidence that the average woman's salary is $8,000 and the average man's salary is $14,000. Then the defendant explains, "Well, the average woman is a clerical worker with a high school diploma, and the average man is a draftsman." And the rebuttal might be, "Actually, half of those female clerical workers have draftsman degrees but you just wouldn't give them that job." That's the kind of argument you might have.

But there's probably no firm in the country that you can go to—except possibly the Women's Bank on K Street, although I'm told it's not even true there—in which the average woman's salary isn't going to be substantially below the average man's salary. This means that if you accept that comparison as a prima facie case, you could take any firm in the country to court. Many of them might have explanations but they'd have to give them in court. So you've got to expect that the judges are not going to accept that kind of prima facie case much more in the future.

I know I'm supposed to present case studies and I haven't given you a case yet. It is hard to know what case to talk about. Let me give you a problem I see in the law and a case that looks very much like *Hobson*.

One of the most powerful decisions that's come down is the *Castaneda v. Partida* (1977) decision. Footnote 17 in *Castaneda* should be added to the literature of footnote 11 in *Brown*. You no longer have to reference the case. You say footnote 11 and everybody knows what case it is; you say footnote 17 and everybody knows what case it is. Footnote 17 in *Castaneda* is the two or three standard deviation rule. The judges don't understand how far away three standard deviations is from two but they have finally set out a rule.

The rule pertains to representation on grand jury lists. For example, a certain percentage of Mexican Americans live in Hidalgo County, Texas, but a smaller percentage of Mexican Americans are on the grand jury lists. What we need is a rule to tell us how much discrepancy in the percentages would be so unlikely that some explanation other than the luck of the draw would be needed. The court aggregated eleven years' worth of data, which is a strong position to take. They learned that the expected standard deviation from a random selection process, which is a measure of the expected variation, could be calculated from the binomial distribution. Having done that in footnote 17, they found that the proportion of Mexican Americans on the grand jury list is many standard deviations below what you'd expect it to be—so many that it's unlikely that the discrepancy could be attributed to chance.

So they decided that that was strong enough evidence that chance didn't produce the finding, and therefore the sheriff did. A lot of other things were involved, like the key man system. The sheriff found a couple of people and told them to round up a jury. The sheriff's friends and those people's friends, as you might expect, weren't Mexican Americans.

This decision has had an astounding impact on the profession because now there's a rule. You see complaint after complaint filed in federal district court mentioning two standard deviations. They give some data and say, two standard deviations below what you'd expect and, therefore, prima facie case, shift the burden, let the defendant explain why this is happening.

One of the cases in which this was done in the district court was the *Board of Education of the City of New York v. Califano.* This is a case in which Emergency School Assistance Act funds were denied the City of New York because of a misallocation of black teachers. It was an employment discrimination case, even though it was under Title VI of the Civil Rights Act, not Title VII. The government claimed it has the right not to grant monies appropriated for the Emergency School Assistance Act, which is for desegregation, if there are discriminatory employment practices.

The Board of Education, of course, sued saying, "We don't have discriminatory employment practices. You have to prove that we do. If you don't prove it, you can't deny us the money." The United States Attorneys are the defenders of government agencies, and so it became the U.S. Attorney's job to prove that the City of New York was discriminating.

The Office of Civil Rights in the Department of Health, Education, and Welfare had developed the evidence before it went to the U.S. Attorney; the evidence led to a letter informing the City of New York that it wasn't going to get this money because it discriminated. The Office of Civil Rights basically used a *Castaneda* approach. It picked out a school where the percentage of blacks on the faculty was more than two standard deviations below the percentage of black faculty in the system, and on this basis claimed discrimination at this school. Each school was assessed in this manner. The office found a total of ten schools with percentages of black faculty that were two or more standard deviations below the citywide average.

There were eighty-seven academic high schools in the city at that time. The *Castaneda* rule doesn't apply when you look at eighty-seven schools. It's just wrong statistics. The question no longer is, can you find one of eighty-seven observations with two or more standard deviations? Instead, the question is, do you find *too many* of them? So it's conceptually wrong to pick a school out and say it discriminates.

In fact, of eighty-seven schools you'd expect to find on the average two in which there are too few black teachers and, therefore, you don't know which schools have the discriminatory practices. There is no conceptual way to name a school and say there is discrimination at that school. The proof has to be how many schools there are.

Unfortunately, at the district court level the judge simply gave the case to the U.S. Attorney before he had a chance to put in any evidence. The judge turned to the U.S. Attorney and said, "Why don't you make a motion for summary judgment?" The U.S. Attorney, being no fool, said, "I move for summary judgment," and the judge said, "Granted." That was it. Thus, the attorney never got to put supporting evidence in the record.

So I wrote a couple of paragraphs of the appeals court brief under the pretext that the data were in the record and this was manipulation of it; this was part of the lawyer's brief. I argued that a better analysis would compare the distribution of black teachers among high schools in the City of New York to the Poisson Distribution—which is what it would look like, approximately, if the names of schools were drawn from a hat.

There's a more precise way to do this with something called the hypergeometric, but neither you nor I nor anyone else I know wants to use it with 500 or so teachers. Poisson is quite good. We didn't put all of this into the brief, but since then I've written it up more completely. I compared the distribution of black teachers in the school system to the Poisson Distribution by means of a chi square test and I got a chi square of about 400 for 11 degrees of freedom. You can't write the number of zeros it takes to get to the probability level. This is just not going to be found unless something other than the random model posited as the null hypothesis is at work.

That, to me, was really convincing evidence of half the argument, namely, that there was some nonrandom distribution. You'd then have to add the argument that the excess blacks were found in the schools that had excess black pupils. That was the essence of the discrimination—putting black teachers in black schools.

There are all sorts of reasons why that happens in New York and, like any other kind of case, it's not really all that simple. Also, the federal government has changed its rules recently, and that doesn't help very much. I remember a few years ago the idea of the role model was popular—the idea that it was good to put black teachers in black schools. Suddenly the government changed its mind and said, "We'll take your money away, if you don't accord to our current standards."

There's a lot wrong with the way in which these things are regulated, but there is also really no question of the statistical conclusion, as in *Castaneda*. Even though no adjustment was made for age of jurors, the *Castaneda* finding is tremendously robust. There's no manipulation I can do that suggests the Supreme Court was wrong.

The same thing is true in New York, and we got a unanimous decision from the Second Circuit Court. They picked out Lafayette High School as an example of a school that was more than two standard deviations below the expected value for blacks and that, therefore, there was discrimination.

I conclude from that two things. First, they're wrong; we don't know whether there's any discrimination at Lafayette High School. It's actually one of thirteen schools, whereas the expected number is two. The probability of finding thirteen with very few blacks when you expect two is infinitesimally small. But you do expect two and Lafayette could have been one of them.

There are two problems here. One is that in a case involving a rule of the Supreme Court, other courts are not likely to bother with any other argument. If they can write their opinion based on this high school that is two standard deviations or more below the expected value, they don't care that it's conceptually wrong.

It's tremendously difficult to try to change the Supreme Court's conception of this rule. I have utter sympathy for the circuit court. They have a rule; they have a particular way of writing the case. It's not going to be appealed to the Supreme Court. It looks like *Castaneda,* and it's going to stand.

The second problem is that as reviews of discrimination are mechanized, this little issue in the case in New York is going to become a big issue. Before Hidalgo County was selected as the place in which there were too few Mexican Americans on the grand jury, suppose some government body reviewed 1,000 counties and systematically put through the computer the percentage of Mexican Americans on the grand jury lists in each county. Suppose in five the percentage was more than two standard deviations below the expected value, and these five counties were brought to court. The court would consider five counties a highly unexpected finding from a random draw, whereas in fact it's a very predictable finding, if you look at 1,000 counties.

Thus, a big problem is the way cases are brought to court and the way the statistics are used as if you only looked once. That's probably okay for many employment discrimination cases because an interesting aspect of Title VII is the plaintiff being the motive force. It's the individual who complains and it's the enforcing agency, in most Title VII cases, and most Title VII cases are not EEOC cases; they're individual plaintiffs who get a letter from EEOC saying, "We're too busy, you go ahead and sue."

The *Castaneda* approach makes a lot of sense if the plaintiff has only looked once at his or her particular circumstances, but it does not make sense for review agencies. A relatively unknown agency which is enforcing Title VII kinds of law is the Office of Federal Contract Compliance Programs (OFCCP). It supports executive orders, not laws. The history of these orders goes back to President Roosevelt. The one that is in force now is Executive Order 11246, promulgated by Lyndon Johnson in 1965, which says, "I, as the administrator of U.S. government affairs, have the right to set the rules about the kinds of contracts we will have. One rule is that the federal government will not contract with firms above a given size which discriminate in employment."

There's no penalty. You don't go to jail, you just don't get your contract. This is big business for a lot of people, so they pay attention. OFCCP employs field agents who do systematic screening by means of desk audits. They will find the cases which will simply occur by chance. I'm not saying there's no discrimination out there and it's all chance, but I am saying that the model we use to prove it has a major fallacy when you start getting into systematic selection. Add to that the fact that there is an agency of the United States government whose job is filtering through lots of observations, picking out some of them, and claiming back damages (back pay for the affected workers), and I don't know how to deal with it.

I'll just end on one other possibility, which goes back to the court as a legislature rather than a fact finder. It could be that the Supreme Court is saying, "As a matter of social policy, we don't like to see big disparities in society. If you're more than two standard deviations away from the expected value in employment of minorities, men's and women's salaries, and so forth, we don't want to see it; fix it up." It's not really a statistical case.

I started by saying I think the *Hobson* case has been misunderstood. The real issue in *Hobson* is the appearance of the system to the children. It is not a question of the educational outcome of $5 more per black child or $100 less per white child. It is a question of the validity of the system of educational expenditure as seen by children. The test of the redistribution is not in child reading, but in behavior as adults of minority children who grow up in a *fair* system, as opposed to their behavior if they grow up in an *unfair* system.

The concept of fairness—a social concept, not a legal one—may get us out of the dilemma produced by the misuse of statistical tests, particularly when defendants are found by a screening process. If the two-three standard deviation rule is taken as a precept of social policy, then many potential disputes about the legitimacy of one or another test fade away. Even though a random assignment system might produce two New York schools with very few black teachers, society might want to impose a nonrandom solution. It might want to eliminate the disparate schools and disparate firms and other public agencies, as a matter of policy.

Obviously these problems are not yet even seen within the judicial system. Therefore, I can close with this point: we are in a period of adjustment. The Court has accepted the concept of statistical proof, opening the gates to many seemingly similar arguments. As statistics, some of these arguments are simply incorrect. Others may be questioned, depending on how the data were generated. All raise the question: are we really judging behavior by an inference from the outcomes, or do we have a social policy concerning the outcomes themselves? I hope some of the attention paid to the use of statistics in the law will focus on that issue.

GEORGE MICHAELS[*]

I've been involved in a couple of dozen Equal Employment Opportunity Commission (EEOC) cases and I don't know how to deal with them either. The law is so weighted in favor of the government that it's practically impossible for any lawyer doing a decent job to represent his client in a reasonable manner, so far as his client and the economics of the situation are concerned.

---

[*]Attorney in private practice, Boston, Massachusetts.

Let me tell you about one situation. The case was filed in 1974. It was filed before the state agency, as it is in almost every state in the United States. In Washington, D.C., it's called the Human Rights Division, I believe. In Massachusetts it's called the Massachusetts Commission Against Discrimination (MCAD). At the same time, the complainant files his case with the Equal Employment Opportunity Commission under Title VII.

The EEOC doesn't take any action until such time as the state agency produces its findings, which generally takes two or three years. A case that's filed in 1974 may not be resolved until 1977, at which point the state agency, having spent hundreds of hours going through all of the records, using your client's time as well as its own, comes to the conclusion that there is no case and dismisses the action.

Within ninety days you receive a letter from the EEOC stating that the case has been in a position of hiatus while it was being determined by the state agency and the EEOC is now going to examine this case for the first time. Will you please send all the material over that you sent over to the state agency? They want to take a look at it. So you do that.

There are interrogatories and maybe another year goes by, and you take a look at the liability of your client. Dr. Michelson says that it's no great shakes really insofar as the world is concerned whether a person is earning $19,000 or $21,000 a year. But suppose 200 women who are earning $19,000 should have been earning $21,000. Under Title VII the damages go back to three years prior to the time of filing—to 1971. If my arithmetic is correct, we're talking about $400,000 a year over a period of seven years, which is almost $3 million.

Now you're dealing with an examiner at a very low level of EEOC and he or she is going to make a determination. Generally that person does not have the education and the background that people who have been speaking from this stand have had, and she looks at it or he looks at it from a very classical point of view and says, "Yes, it seems to be a prima facie case here, women are making less." The examiner is not very much interested in variables or what-have-you, and he or she will tell you, "I'm going to make a decision against this company." You turn white and you remember that next month you have to report to the bank. It's the end of the fiscal year of the company and there'll be a footnote in the financial records of the company that there is a contingent liability of $4 million. This company may have a net worth of $1 million, who knows? And after the bank receives that footnote, the bank officer is going to call you up and you say, "Well, this is a very low level and we haven't gone into court and the Justice Department hasn't even decided that it's going to take the case into court," and the bank officer says, "Yes, but why don't you try to pay us off next month?"

This is the kind of real-life situation that lawyers have to deal with. My experience has been that, once litigation begins, you get a fair deal from the judges and they will very often summarily dismiss many of these complaints. I think the EEOC sees its job as negotiator. If the examiner knows that you're prepared to go into court and do everything you have to do in order to support your client's case, he or she will say, "There probably was discrimination. If you will agree not to discriminate anymore and you agree to take this section of your employees and increase their pay by x number of dollars per week and you agree to pay $25,000, we will settle the case."

In a criminal court that's known as plea bargaining and that's exactly what they do at EEOC. I think that that is somewhat less than fair.

Earlier we were talking about fairness and what trial lawyers do in cross-examination. Dr. Rossi's account of his terrible treatment by counsel reminded me of a story. A number of years ago I represented the Massachusetts District Commission (MDC) and the question was whether or not certain prestressed concrete pipe, which was made by Lockjoint Company in New Jersey and which was specified by the MDC, was better than regular reinforced pipe. I found the one man in the world who knew more about prestressed concrete pipe than anybody else. He turned out to be an Israeli and I found him in New York, of all places.

I went to New York and spoke with him and he said, "Yes, there's no question, the prestressed concrete pipe was better than reinforced concrete pipe, and I will testify for you." I brought him up to Boston and went through two days of preparation. At the end of that preparation I said, "This is an important case, $15 million is involved, and there are five lawyers on the other side who are going to cross-examine you. Remember, English is not your first language, so whenever you're asked a question and you want to think about the answer, just ask them to repeat the question."

We went through two days of direct examination; he was well prepared for it. The direct examination could not have been better.

Lou Weinstein, who started the cross-examination, was a very good trial lawyer in Massachusetts. He asked the first question, which was a neutral question, and the witness said, "Could you repeat that, please?" Lou repeated it, and the engineer thought about it and said, "Could you repeat that, please?"

Well, after three days of that, Lou said, "That's all I want from this witness." He turned around and said under his breath, "You dirty son-of-a-bitch." The witness yelled out, "I'm not a dirty son-of-a-bitch. You're a dirty son-of-a-bitch."

MATHEMATICS, SOCIAL SCIENCE, AND THE LAW

BERNARD GROFMAN AND HOWARD SCARROW*

Let me begin by stating some summary generalizations based on my reaction to the earlier presentations and on the lessons I've gleaned reviewing both Supreme Court cases on jury decision making and New York cases on representation involving weighted voting electoral systems.[5]

*Presented by Bernard Grofman, associate professor of political science and social psychology, University of California at Irvine. Coauthored by Howard Scarrow, professor of political science, State University of New York at Stony Brook.

I would propose that the social scientist who wants to do research which will have an influence on court decisions should do four things.

First, publish in law journals.

Second, explain, preferably in words of one syllable, exactly what the research consists of and how it is relevant to potential legal decisions that courts might be expected to confront. As social scientists, we are accustomed to presenting our research in terms of which theories are rebutted and which supported. If we are going to write for the courts, we have to explain ourselves in terms of relevance to the legal issues on which courts must decide.

Third, use a self-promotion strategy; in other words, send a copy of one's published research to the judges that one expects will be concerned with it (or to their law clerks, if it's the U.S. Supreme Court) as well as to those lawyers who might make some use of it or who might cite it in their law journal articles. (Be careful, however, to make it available to all parties to any legal dispute.)

Finally, and most importantly, recommend something which the judges already want to do, because it will then be used by the courts to provide a rationale for a decision which was actually reached on other grounds, but one will be able to claim that one's work was influential.

With these observations out of the way, let me turn to some actual cases on jury decision making and on equal representation. Because of time limitations I will state conclusions without being able to substantiate them fully. For details see Grofman (1974, 1976, 1980a, 1980b, 1980c) and Grofman and Scarrow (1979a, 1979b, 1980).

Let me summarize in advance my main points. First, with the important exception of the Blackmun opinion in *Ballew v. Georgia,* a 1978 case in which the U.S. Supreme Court held that five-member juries are constitutionally impermissible, the recent Supreme Court rulings on jury size and jury unanimity requirements represent the *misuse* of social science by the courts.

Second, the New York state courts' rulings on the constitutionality of weighted voting (in particular, the rather obscure New York Court of Appeals case that I'm going to concentrate on, *Iannuci v. Board of Supervisors of the County of Washington* [1967]) provide intriguing and important examples of the *use* (indeed whole-hog acceptance) of social science by the courts.

Finally, since the conference deals with use, misuse, and nonuse, let me also mention briefly an area which seems to exemplify perfectly the *nonuse* of social science by the court, and that is *Buckley v. Valeo* (1976), a recent Supreme Court case in which the Court dealt with the constitutionality of limits on campaign contributions and expenditures, and with public financing of election campaigns. In my view, had the Supreme Court been willing, social science could have played a major role in resolving the complex issues in this case by addressing certain important factual questions which the Court dismissed as irrelevant to its decision making because it claimed they had no known answers.

The Jury Cases

As I look at the jury decision-making cases, I think of the opening lines of *A Tale of Two Cities*. For me the jury cases offer a view of the U.S. Supreme Court in which the Court makes use of the best of reasons and of the worst of reasons. The use of social science by the Court ranged from *abysmal* in the first of the jury cases, *Williams v. Florida* (1970), to remarkably *sophisticated* in the Blackmun opinion in the fourth of these cases, *Ballew v. Georgia* (1978), to *nonexistent* in the most recent of the jury cases, *Burch and Wrestle v. Louisiana* (1979).

I want to present an overview of the jury cases in terms of a variety of approaches which the Supreme Court has taken to the use of social science. I call the first of these the "Kris Kringle" approach, in honor of *Miracle on 34th Street*. In that approach the Court appears to be unwilling or unable to distinguish between speculation and social science.

In the first of the jury cases, *Williams*, the Court listed a variety of studies which purported to say something about whether or not six-member juries were likely to be discernibly different from twelve-member juries. As a number of scholars (including Shari Diamond and Michael Saks) have pointed out, these "studies" were in fact not studies at all; they were unsupported opinions. The Court's reliance on such evidence is akin to the strategy that proved that Kris Kringle was really Santa Claus in *Miracle on 34th Street*.

You may remember that in that movie the proof comes when the post office delivers to Kris Kringle dozens and dozens of stacks of mail addressed to Santa Claus. The fact that Kris Kringle has been given stacks of mail by people who happen to think that Kris Kringle is Santa Claus does not really prove that Kris Kringle is Santa Claus. Similarly, the fact that the Supreme Court was able to find some number of lawyers and judges who happen to think that six-member and twelve-member juries would not arrive at different verdicts does not really prove that there will be no discernible verdict differences between six-member and twelve-member juries.

A second approach of the Court is the "Lice-in-the-New-Hebrides" approach, which is a term I will use to refer to the Court's inability (an inability often shared by social scientists) to distinguish between methodologically sound and methodologically flawed research. We may describe the Lice-in-the-New-Hebrides approach as follows. A scientist interested in how one can improve the health of the New Hebrides citizens goes to the New Hebrides, examines healthy and unhealthy people, and discovers that the healthy people have lice and the unhealthy people do not. The scientist concludes, in good Millsian fashion, that if one wishes to improve the health of the citizens of the New Hebrides, one should import lice.

In the third of the jury cases, *Colgrove v. Battin* (1973), the Court claims that four empirical studies provide convincing empirical evidence that there is "no discernible difference" in verdicts between six-member and twelve-member juries. These four studies have been devastatingly critiqued and appropriately demolished in work by Zeisel and Diamond (1974) and Saks (1977). It is fair to say that, after one has listed all of the methodological flaws of these studies, even though confusion of cause and effect is not among them, it would still be a presumptuous social scientist indeed who would claim that these studies proved either singly or in toto anything at all about the existence or nonexistence of differences in verdict outcomes between six-member and twelve-member juries.

A third difficulty with Supreme Court uses of social science in the jury case is that the Court is generally prepared to exaggerate or distort available social science evidence and theory in order to buttress the intuitions of justices. I think of this as the "It-Always-Snows-on-Christmas" approach. That is to say, when courts and judges look at social science, they eliminate the hedges, the buts, the ifs, the ands, the maybes, and the ceteris paribus clauses which make social science social science.

In *Ballew v. Georgia* (1978), Justice Blackmun cites a study by Nagel and Neef (1975) which purports, at least as summarized by Justice Blackmun, to show that it is indeed permissible to draw the line at six jury members but not at five. However (as Stuart Nagel pointed out in his earlier presentation), it was improper by social science standards (and I think by legal standards) to use the Nagel and Neef piece to support the claim that the optimum jury size is between six and eight members, because that conclusion rested on a series of assumptions, at least some of which are questionable and at least one of which is in fact impossible to verify directly.[6] Furthermore, Nagel and Neef (1975) themselves were quite careful to point out the "if-then" nature of their results.

Fourth, the Court has shown itself willing to ignore evidence unfavorable to its views and, in fact, to "Bury the Evidence in the Footnotes," a common strategy among lawyers who are drawing up contracts. This occurred in *Williams* (1970), in which several important studies were cited but their findings were not discussed, because their conclusions ran counter to the assertions made by the Court majority.

Fifth, the Court has followed a strategy which I would call "Sticking to the Yellow Brick Road," by which I mean that if an article is not to be found in the *Index to Legal Periodicals,* it is unlikely to be found in Court opinions. With rare exceptions lawyers simply are unwilling (or perhaps uninterested or unable) to search out potentially relevant nonlegal references that are not referenced in the legal literature. Hence, as mentioned earlier, if one wants one's research to influence courts, one really has to publish it in ways that will make it accessible; in other words, it should appear in the periodicals that lawyers read.[7]

Sixth, even when it has relied heavily on social science evidence, the Court has been unwilling, in my view, to acknowledge the overwhelming implications of that evidence, when to do so would entail a politically unpleasant task for the justices, namely, reversing previous decisions. I think of this as the "Wrapped-in-the-Bosom-of-Abraham" mentality of judges, although this is perhaps an unfair way of characterizing *stare decisis*. The Court has thus been unwilling to take social science where it leads, especially if it leads to the reversal of decisions made by judges still sitting on the bench.

Hans Zeisel has said that *Ballew* (1978) represents the first case in which social science has moved out of the footnotes of U.S. Supreme Court decisions into the body of the text. Those who are familiar with the case know that Blackmun's opinion reads like a social science article, citing both empirical and theoretical studies. Moreover, not only is Blackmun's opinion in *Ballew* social science, it is, by and large, *good* social science. Nevertheless, in *Ballew* (in which the Court rejected five-member juries as unconstitutional) social science evidence in my view should have led the Court to a reversal of *Williams V. Florida* (1970) (in which the Court accepted the constitutionality of six-member juries). The empirical studies that the Court (or at least Justice Blackmun) relied upon in *Ballew* to declare *five*-member juries unconstitutional were in fact studies which compared *six*-member juries and *twelve*-member juries. Justice Blackmun accepted the fact that the studies cited in *Williams* and *Colgrove*, which previously had been used to support six-member juries, were methodologically flawed, and he cited favorably a variety of studies which condemned six-member juries relative to twelve-member juries. For Justice Blackmun to then come out in opposition to five-member juries and to reaffirm his support for six-member juries seems, to put it mildly, to have been disingenuous.

Seventh, reaction to Blackmun's opinion in *Ballew* reveals that at least some justices of the Supreme Court think of social science as "That Old Black Magic" and are resolved that "That Old Black Magic" will never get them under its spell. In *Ballew* Justice Powell (joined by Justices Burger and Rehnquist) refers to social science research as "numerology" and condemns Blackmun for his reliance on it.[8]

Equal Voting Representation and Weighted Voting at the County Level in New York

Recent Supreme Court cases have stressed the requirement that apportionment and electoral systems at all levels of government approach the ideal of "one person, one vote." In the 1960s and thereafter unequally populated, single-member legislative districts were more or less eliminated due to court and legislative action. Also eliminated have been so-called unit voting systems, which provided for one representative from each political subunit, regardless of the population of that unit.

In order to preserve traditional political boundaries and the traditional political power of Republican machines in the smaller counties, many county governments in New York responded to these one-person, one-vote decisions either by shifting over to a combination of single- and multiple-member districting in which smaller townships became single-member districts and larger townships were divided into multimember districts, or (in twenty-three counties) by following the example of Nassau County, which since 1917 had made use of weighted voting. (In a weighted voting system, rather than having, say, one representative for every 10,000 people, a representative has, say, one vote for every 10,000 people represented.) Thus, in New York county legislatures, one township with 20,000 people may have a representative with 10 votes, while a township with 200,000 people has a representative with 100 votes.

In 1967 the New York courts were confronted with the issue of whether or not weighted voting could pass constitutional muster as satisfying one-person, one-vote standards. In *Iannuci v. Board of Supervisors of the County of Washington* (1967), a state court held that an argument put forward by a lawyer, John Banzhaf III (Banzhaf 1965), was to set the standard which would govern whether or not systems of weighted voting apportionment would be held constitutional.

As an example of how Banzhaf's standard works, imagine that we have three districts with 200, 200, and 100 voters. If we allocated 2 votes to the districts with 200 voters and 1 vote to the district with 100 voters, we would have a weighted voting system with 3 representatives having 2 votes, 2 votes, and 1 vote, respectively. The relative proportions of these weights might seem to satisfy the one-person, one-vote guidelines; that is to say, a legislator representing 200 of the 500 voters, or two-fifths of the total voters, would have 2 votes out of 5, seemingly two-fifths of the total power.

Banzhaf argued that rather than look at the proportion of weights, we should consider the likelihood that a legislator would cast a *decisive* vote. In this example if 3 votes are needed for passage, the representatives with 2 votes are not more powerful than the representative with 1 vote, because *any* 2 legislators, by combining their votes, are able to insure passage. Moreover, if either changes his mind, the position is reversed. Thus, in Banzhaf terms, all 3 legislators have equal power because each has equal ability to affect the outcome.

Banzhaf (1965) argued that the appropriate criterion for one-person, one-vote standards in legislatures using weighted voting is whether the power held by a legislator is proportionate to the population that that legislator represents. In the 2-2-1 example we would violate the Banzhaf criterion, because legislators representing two-fifths of the population would have only one-third of the power and legislators representing one-fifth of the population would also have one-third of the power.

Through *Iannuci* it is now law in New York that all twenty-four counties which make use of weighted votes have their proposed weighted voting system subjected to the test of the Banzhaf doctrine. In order to calculate Banzhaf indices, we must look at the number of possible combinations of votes. For larger legislatures it is necessary to do a computer calculation to determine whether or not a proposed apportionment scheme in fact satisfies the Banzhaf criterion.

Iannuci is a remarkable example of the whole-hog acceptance of social science notions in the law. But as we look at the response by New York courts to applications of this mathematical notion of power as a measure of fair representation, we discover some interesting facts suggesting an inability to apply well in practice what has been wholeheartedly adopted in theory.

First, we discover that what the New York courts have adopted with relish the U.S. Supreme Court has looked upon with dismay. The U.S. Supreme Court, when it was confronted with an argument inspired by Banzhaf (1966) against the constitutionality of a mixed, single- and multiple-member district system, rejected the argument. According to the majority opinion in *Whitcomb v. Chavis* (1970), "while we have no fault to find with the defendant's mathematics, we find his reasoning irrelevant to the constitutional issues before the court, . . . because it neglects 'political realities'."[9] In *Whitcomb* the Court rejected the argument of Banzhaf (1966). In *Iannuci* (1967) the New York Court of Appeals embraced the closely related argument of Banzhaf (1965); but the New York courts never reconsidered the *Iannuci* decision in the light of *Whitcomb*, despite the fact that a dictum in *Whitcomb* suggested the Supreme Court has no more appreciation for Banzhaf (1965), the Banzhaf analysis relied on in *Iannuci*, than the Court did for Banzhaf (1966), the Banzhaf argument rejected by the Court in *Whitcomb*.

Second and relatedly, no New York court has ever seen the applicability of the Banzhaf measure envisaged in *Iannuci* to mixed single- and multiple-member districting systems. Yet in a system where representatives are elected from the same constituency by the same electorate and, hence, given the realities of party politics, those representatives tend to vote alike, a system involving mixed single- and multiple-member districts is mathematically identical to a system of weighted voting. Thus, the same standards which are applicable to weighted voting apportionments ought to be applicable to mixed single- and multi-member districts, at least if one believes, as I do, that bloc voting of district representatives is the political reality. The New York courts have simply failed to recognize this.

Third, the New York courts have been inconsistent in operationalizing the extent of deviation allowed from the Banzhaf criterion. Because the measurement of deviation involved a percentage standard in some cases and a percentage *point* standard in others, weighted voting schemes held permissible under prevailing guidelines by some courts would have been held impermissible by others, and vice versa. For example, if a township has 2 percent of the weight and 1 percent of the population, some courts have treated this as a 1 percentage point discrepancy, while others have treated it as a 100 percent discrepancy. Moreover, in cases where one subunit (for example, a township) has more than 50 percent of the county population, the attempts by New York courts to reconcile the Banzhaf criterion with one-person, one-vote standards have been ingenious but specious (see especially the recent Nassau cases *Franklin v. Krause* [1973] and *Franklin v. Mandeville* [1970]).

Finally, no court, whether state or federal, has ever really fully understood the reasoning underlying the mathematical arguments in Banzhaf (1965, 1966); or successfully distinguished among what, upon careful analysis, turns out to be the three *different* criteria suggested by Banzhaf in one or the other of these articles;[10] or realized that while these three criteria coincide for single-member district systems, for other systems (especially weighted voting systems) the three criteria may lead to different policy recommendations.[11]

To sum up, New York courts have adopted a Banzhaf criterion for fair apportionment without ever recognizing that Banzhaf enunciated more than one such criterion, without being consistent in judging deviations from that standard, and without ever really understanding what Banzhaf (1965, 1966) meant. Thus, the New York weighted voting case represents an extensive application of social science ideas, but in a badly flawed way.

NOTES

1. My colleagues on this project are Charles Pulaski of the University of Iowa College of Law; George Woodworth, University of Iowa, Department of Statistics; and Frederick Kyle, Seattle, Washington.

2. The data used in the pilot study were collected by the editors of the *Stanford Law Review* and provided to us through their courtesy. An earlier analysis of the same data can be found in "A Study of the California Penalty Jury in First Degree Murder Cases" (1969).

3. For further details on the deductive model briefly described in this paper, see S. Nagel and M. Neef, *Legal Policy Analysis: Finding an Optimum Level or Mix* (1977, pp. 75-162). For a shorter version, see Nagel and Neef, "Deductive Modeling to Determine an Optimum Jury Size and Fraction Required to Convict" (1975, pp. 933-78).

4. For further discussion of what variables, besides value reinforcement, lead to research utilization by the courts and other policymakers, see Weiss (1977) and Rosen (1972).

5. See Grofman (1980a), Grofman and Scarrow (1979a), and Grofman (1980b).

6. For example, Nagel and Neef (1975) give alternative assumptions as to the percentage of individuals brought to trial who are "truly" guilty. Exactly which assumption is chosen has a tremendous impact on the results.

7. This was particularly unfortunate in *Ballew*, since Justice Blackmun remained in ignorance of the best work done on modeling jury decision making, that of Alan Gelfand and Herbert Solomon. Their articles appeared in the *Journal of the American Statistical Association* in 1973, 1974, and 1975.

8. I should, however, point out that the studies which Blackmun made use of in *Ballew* were not published in refereed social science journals. So Powell's attack on social science "numerology" is not quite as much of a slam against social science as one might think. In fact, it turns out really to be much more of an attack against the reliability of articles published in law journals!

9. Of course, as Justice Harlan points out in a brilliant and quite scathing opinion in *Whitcomb*, if one is to chastise anyone for neglecting political realities, the chastisement is at least equally relevant to the Court itself in its decisions in *Wesberry v. Sanders* and later cases in which strict population equality standards were held as the only legitimate test of fair equal representation. As Harlan says, to equate strict district

population equality with equal representation is to "neglect political reality," and the question is, in Harlan's felicitous phrase, whether one prefers "higher mathematics" (Banzhaf) to "sixth grade arithmetic" (the Court).

It's also interesting to note that the U.S. Supreme Court disliked the Banzhaf measure because of its political unreality, yet it is this characteristic which appealed to the New York court in *Iannuci*. The New York court praised the Banzhaf measure because it is abstract and divorced of political realities and, therefore, results in calculations which do not need to be revised with each new set of election returns.

10. The task had, however, been complicated by Banzhaf's own failure to label these three criteria. See Grofman and Scarrow (1980).

11. In practice two of the three criteria usually give rise to virtually identical results even for weighted voting systems. See Grofman and Scarrow (1980) for further details.

REFERENCES

Ballew v. Georgia, 198 *Sup. Ct. Rev.* 1029 (1978).

Banzhaf, John III. 1965. Weighted Voting Doesn't Work: A Mathematical Analysis. 19 *Rutgers Law Review*, 317-43.

_____ . 1966. Multi-Member Electoral Districts—Do They Violate the "One-Man, One-Vote" Principle? 75 *Yale Law Review* 1309-38.

Blizard v. Fielding, 1st Cir. 17 *F.E.P. Cases* 149 (1978).

Buckley v. Valeo, 424 *U.S.* 1 (1976).

Burch and Wrestle v. Louisiana, 99 *S. Ct.* 1623 (1979).

Castaneda v. Partida, 430 *U.S.* 482 (1977).

Colgrove v. Battin, 413 *U.S.* 149 (1973).

Franklin v. Krause, 344 *N.Y.S. 2d* 885 (1973).

Franklin v. Mandeville, 308 *N.Y.S. 2d* 375 (1970).

Furman v. Georgia, 408 *U.S.* 238, 92 *S. Ct.* 2726 (1972).

Gelfand, Alan A. and Solomon, Herbert. 1973. A Study of Poisson's Models for Jury Verdicts in Criminal and Civil Trials. 68 *Journal of American Statistical Association* (June) 271-8.

_____ . 1974. Modelling Jury Verdicts in the American Legal System. 69 *Journal of American Statistical Association* (March) 32-7.

_____ . 1975. Analyzing the Decision-Making Process of the American Jury. 70 *Journal of the American Statistical Association* (June) 305-10.

CASE HISTORIES

Gregg v. Georgia, 428 *U.S.* 153, 96 *S. Ct.* 2909 (1976).

Green v. McDonnell Douglas, 411 *U.S.* (1972).

Grofman, Bernard N. 1974. Mathematics and Politics: Mathematical Reasoning and Optimal Jury Rules. Paper presented at the Cornell-Aspen Colloquium on Choice and Decision. Aspen, Colorado, June.

_____ . 1976. Not Necessarily Twelve and Not Necessarily Unanimous: Evaluating the Impact of *Williams v. Florida* and *Johnson v. Louisiana.* In *Psychology and the Law: Research Frontiers,* Gordon Bermant, Charlan Nemeth, and Neil Vidmar, eds. Lexington, Mass.: D. C. Heath, pp. 149-68.

_____ . 1980a (forthcoming). Mathematical Modeling of Jury/Juror Decision Making. In *Perspectives in Law and Psychology,* Vol. III: *The Jury, Judicial, and Trial Processes,* Bruce Sales, ed. New York: Plenum.

_____ . 1980b (forthcoming). Jury Decision-Making Models and the Supreme Court: The Jury Cases from *Williams v. Florida* to *Ballew v. Georgia. Policy Studies Journal.*

_____ . 1980c. The Slippery Slope: Jury Size and Jury Verdict Requirements. Unpublished manuscript.

_____ . 1980d. Preliminary Models of Jury Decision-Making. In *Frontiers of Economics,* vol. 3, Gordon Tullock, ed. Blacksburg, Va.: Center for Study of Public Choice.

Grofman, Bernard and Scarrow, Howard. 1979a. Iannuci and Its Aftermath: The Application of the Banzhaf Criterion to Weighted Voting Systems in the State of New York. In *Applied Game Theory,* Steven Brams, Andrew Schotter, and Gerhard Schwodiauer, eds. Vienna: Physica-Verlag.

_____ . 1979b. Computerized Weighted Voting in New York County Government. Paper presented at the annual meeting of the Operations Research Society of America, October.

_____ . 1980 (forthcoming). The Riddle of Apportionment: Equality of What? *National Municipal Review.*

Hobson v. Hansen, 327 *F. Supp.* 824 (USDC D.C. 1971).

Iannuci v. Board of Supervisors of the County of Washington, 282 *N.Y.S. 2d* 502 (1967).

Nagel, S. and Neef, M. 1975. Deductive Modeling to Determine an Optimum Jury Size and Fraction Required to Convict. *1975 Washington University Law Quarterly* 933-78.

_____ . 1977. *Legal Policy Analysis: Finding an Optimum Level or Mix.* Cambridge, Mass.: Lexington-Heath.

126

Presseisen v. Swarthmore, 386 *F. Supp.* 1337 (1974).

Rosen, Paul. 1972. *The Supreme Court and Social Science*. Urbana, Ill.: Univ. of Illinois Press.

Saks, Michael. 1977. *Jury Verdicts: The Role of Group Size and Social Decision Rule*. Lexington, Mass.: D.C. Heath.

A Study of the California Penalty Jury in First Degree Murder Cases. 1969. 21 *Stanford Law Review* 1297-497.

Weiss, Carol. 1977. *Using Social Research in Public Policy-Making*. Cambridge, Mass.: Lexington-Heath.

Wesberry v. Sanders, 376 *U.S.* 1 (1964).

Whitcomb v. Chavis, 403 *U.S.* 143 (1970).

Williams v. Florida, 399 *U.S.* 78 (1970).

Zeisel, Hans and Diamond, Shari S. 1974. Convincing Empirical Evidence on the Six-Member Jury. 41 *University of Chicago Law Review* 281-95.

7

Applied Social Research as Evidence in Litigation

ARTHUR F. KONOPKA

ROBERT J. HALLISEY

JAMES COLEMAN

ARTHUR F. KONOPKA*

I'm interested in how the sort of thing we have been talking about, highly complex scientific information, reaches the court to be used there in some way in decision making. In the first instance we are interested in where that information comes from, and in the second, what rules allow it to come before the court.

Finally, I'm going to mention some of the mechanisms which the courts have at their disposal for handling complex scientific information. We tend to treat an idea like the science court as if it were the only way of handling highly complex scientific questions when, in fact, the courts have over the years designed various strategies for attempting this. Most of these are not used, which is an interesting problem itself.

I'm in a difficult position when talking about these things because I do not have an empirical study to back up what I am suggesting to you. In short, most of my comments are based on intuition. The empirical studies (with the possible exception of Vic Rosenblum's, which hasn't been published yet) simply are not available.

I think there are three things that we're looking for when we talk about scientific information in the courts. I state them in the following three questions:

1. Does reasonable science get introduced in these cases? Would an impartial panel of scientists recognize the testimony of adversarially presented expert witnesses as at least state of the art?
2. If reasonable science is presented, is it understood with sufficient clarity by the finder of fact to form the basis for a conclusion?
3. If such science is presented and understood by the decision maker, what role does it play in the mixed fact/policy decision which is involved in the litigation?

To my thinking we have not been able to adequately address these questions, although they are particularly important if we're going to talk about the benefits or the validity of using scientific information in judicial decision making.

I think that we are involved in an evolution of sorts which causes us to be even more concerned with these questions. The real impetus for introducing highly complex scientific information in litigation came with the New Deal and the growth of administrative agencies which oversaw various segments of the national economy and society. And with this growth came antitrust and price and wage stabilization cases, as well as the various 1930s and 40s labor cases.

A large bureaucracy of federal agencies was created which hired social and physical scientists who prepared government rules and regulations. Sub-

---

*Director of the National Science Foundation's Law, Science, and Technology Program.

sequently, their rules and regulations were challenged in court. And when these agencies went to court they brought their administrative findings and their administrative expertise with them. As a result, the federal courts started hearing cases with federal attorneys and federal expert witnesses, and litigants had to prepare themselves in the same fashion to be able to countervail those forces. With the tremendous growth of the administrative process in government came a substantial increase in the filing of scientifically complex cases. During the war years there was a substantial amount of litigation involving large contracting efforts for research and development, as well as production. Contract cases with very strong references to engineering, physics, chemistry, and the like became common. Then after the war years, we moved into an era of civil rights litigation.

Civil rights litigation brought with it all sorts of scientific, particularly social scientific, information which formed the basis of these cases. One of the strategies used by government lawyers, you may remember, was the creation of backup centers which helped lawyers prepare cases using social science data. Handbooks were even prepared for this purpose and were so successful in teaching the lawyers how to use social science data that an imbalance was created in the courts. In fact, when the Legal Service Corporation was formed subsequently, the backup centers were prohibited by the law for several years. What these centers contributed, more than anything else, was that they gave lawyers the ability to use social science information, a skill they had not possessed before.

Finally, we moved from the civil rights cases to the environmental ones. Environmental cases tend to make very heavy use of biological and social sciences. However, it isn't as though we're evolving, passing from one stage in litigation to another, starting out in the 1930s with terribly complex antitrust cases and their economic evidence; those cases are still with us.

Just start counting the cases that are in the federal district courts. Judge Bazelon did, informally, the other day, and found that at least two-thirds of his cases have a major scientific element in them, which makes him uncomfortable because he feels he can't adequately understand that information.

At any rate, we're in this business and we ought to pay some routine and regularized attention to it, which is something we haven't done very well up to this point.

I was interested to note an August newspaper article which stated that a New York federal judge, in considering an antitrust case before a jury, dismissed the lawsuit on a motion for mistrial. The motion was brought and granted on the basis that the testimony was so complex that no jury would be able to decide the case reasonably.

I have no idea what the fallout of that case will be, but it's extremely provocative that a judge could dismiss a case because of the scientifically complex testimony presented by the litigants.

Let me move very quickly on to the rules of evidence. Most of the people here are acquainted with the courts and know that there are a great number of courts, many of them with their own rules of evidence.

The *Federal Rules of Civil Procedure* and the *Federal Rules of Evidence* are often regarded as leaders in the development of court procedures and the admission of scientific evidence.

The four rules that I'm particularly interested in are the *Federal Rules of Evidence* series, Rules 702, 703, 704, and 705. They deal with the introduction of expert testimony, the basis of opinion testimony, the admissibility of opinion testimony on the ultimate issue, and the disclosure of underlying facts.

There are two major concerns that the courts consider when they make these rules on the introduction of expert testimony, and we should not lose sight of what the courts are attempting to guard against by instituting them.

First, they are anxious that special consideration be given to expert testimony under applicable rules, particularly with regard to the hearsay exclusion. The courts recognize the need for expert testimony and are also aware that the normal application of their evidentiary rules, especially those concerning hearsay, might exclude it. So an exception is made to the normal rules. Second, the exceptions having been made, the courts are concerned that the parties in the litigation have adequate access to the expert and the information which has led him or her to a particular conclusion.

The first rule we consider, 702, states, "If scientific, technical, or other specialized knowledge will assist the trier of fact to understand the evidence or to determine a fact in issue, a witness qualified as an expert by knowledge, skill, experience, training, or other education may testify thereto in the form of an opinion or otherwise."

Two essential elements that you'll recognize are contained in this rule. First, it describes an expert as someone who has specialized knowledge. He or she does not have to have a degree, nor does such a person have to be certified. For example, an expert can be someone as pedestrian as a tenant who can testify about paying rents or conditions in a building, or a police sergeant who will testify about the practices of pickpockets. In fact, those are actual cases which you will find in the annotations on admissibility. There have been only a few instances where folk have been excluded because they were not considered to be true experts.

The second point is that one can bring in opinions. Opinions which would otherwise be inadmissible as evidence. This is extremely important to the social and behavioral scientists who almost always deal in opinion and who would not care to characterize their findings as scientific or legal fact.

Rule 703 deals with the basis of opinion testimony by experts, that is, the facts on which the information is derived. The rule says, "The facts or data in a particular case upon which an expert bases an opinion or inference may be those perceived by or made known to him at or before the hearing if of a type reasonably relied upon by experts in the particular field in forming opinions or inferences upon the subject. The facts or data need not be admissible in evidence."

This rule is relevant to the scientist and in particular to the social scientist. The primary purpose of the rule was to allow the expert to testify as to what his or her expertise suggests happened in the event being discussed. Ordinarily, a witness may testify only to the facts which he or she has observed. However, in all likelihood the expert did not observe the event under litigation. But by reason of this rule, the expert is allowed to refer to the issue in controversy while deriving his or her information and opinion from sources other than the direct observation of the event.

Thus, a metallurgist can testify as to what happens to wing structures made from a specified grade of aluminum when they are subjected to certain temperatures and stresses, and can give an opinion as to the cause of an airplane crash without having seen the accident.

This rule is particularly interesting to the social scientist because most of the sources of information from which a social scientist derives an opinion would be inadmissible as evidence. Surveys, census data, and regression analyses all violate the hearsay and relevance rules of evidence, but because of the wording of this rule, they may be relied upon by an expert. (Furthermore, in conjunction with Rule 705, those otherwise tainted data sources may be introduced into the trial.)

The third rule is 704, opinion testimony on the ultimate issue. In earlier times it was feared that if an expert, cloaked in the authority and mystique of education or high position, were to testify before the jury on precisely the question the jury was to answer, then it would be overwhelmingly difficult for the jury to find a result different from that recommended by the expert. To avoid such a situation testimony on the ultimate issue was prohibited. This prohibition was usually avoided by asking the expert to comment on elaborate hypothetical situations which would just skirt the issue before the jury. When it became clear that the hypothetical situations were becoming more ridiculous and the juries more reasonable, the exclusion rule was abandoned. Rule 704 states, "Testimony in the form of an opinion or inference otherwise admissible is not objectionable because it embraces an ultimate issue to be decided by the trier of fact."

Rule 705 deals with the disclosure of facts or data underlying expert opinions. It states, "The expert may testify in terms of opinion or inference and give his reasons therefor without prior disclosure of the underlying facts or data, unless the court requires otherwise. The expert may, in any event, be required to disclose the underlying facts or data on cross-examination."

This rule is somewhat discomforting because an expert witness may be required by the judge or the opposing party to disclose the data which he or she relied upon in forming an opinion. This could conceivably lead to a demand for information which the researcher regards as confidential. Since the expert can have no guarantee that neither the judge nor the opposing side will demand to see the background data, the researcher is taking some risk since his or her files may be opened. There has been some litigation on this point but none of it appears definitive, and we should anticipate further developments.

I will move on to what I have identified as six different ways in which the court can take in scientific information on its own. Underneath the rules I have outlined are these mechanisms, and I will briefly touch on each one.

Court-Appointed Experts

It is within the province of a judge to hire an expert who can come before the court to advise him or her and testify on information which is brought before the court in a highly complex case. In some of the cases that we were talking about earlier it was noted that judges had hired this kind of help to get them through a case. It's within their authority, but it's not looked upon too favorably in many quarters of the bar because the expert is someone who owes allegiance to no party. Further, he or she may not develop the case in the way the parties would like. Parties have a right to develop the case, that is, agree out of court upon certain issues which they don't want raised in court. A court-appointed expert may go after those issues because he or she is not privy to their agreements, thus disrupting normal litigation strategies.

The court-appointed expert is usually thought of as someone who is put on the stand and is, therefore, available for cross-examination by the parties, so the role is, at least, less onerous to the bar than that of the court advisor.

Judicial Notice of Scientific Fact or Method

The court can take judicial notice of scientific facts, such as when the sun rises, how long people can expect to live, and that sort of thing.

Another mechanism, which I include here, is the agreed upon text. If there is a text, for example, a table or an economic theory, which the parties will agree upon, the judge may admit it for use by the parties in the court.

Reference to a Special Master

Rule 53 of the Rules of Civil Procedure allows for reference to a special master. This person is usually used in extremely complicated cases such as bankruptcy. There the court may refer to a master who is a certified public accountant to handle the very difficult accounting questions. His or her report to the court, which is read to the jury, or to the judge if it is a nonjury trial, is usually binding on the court. That's the rule under which it operates and it can be overturned only in the face of gross negligence or error.

Court Advisors

The use of court advisors is not popular with attorneys. This advisor is hired by the court to explain difficult questions. The problem is that the advisor's communications with the court are generally *ex parte*, that is, he or she sits in the judge's chamber and tells the judge what he or she thinks about the testimony. While the judge may need some help to understand, what is offensive to attorneys is that an outside advisor only has contact with the judge; the parties have no chance to hear and comment on his or her remarks. Nevertheless, the use of court advisors is allowed by the *Federal Rules*.

Advisory Jury

The Federal Rule of Civil Procedure 39 C provides that in all actions not triable of right by a jury, the court may, upon motion of its own initiative, try any issue with an advisory jury. The advisory jury can be made up of all sorts of people, such as a panel composed entirely of scientists, and is not selected from the normal jury rolls. It's simply a jury which is empanelled to be advisory to the judge.

The use of advisory juries appears to have fallen into nonuse since World War II. We don't have court records of the use of an advisory jury in recent years, yet Rule 39-C still stands. So the sort of thing that Arthur Kantrowitz was talking about, empanelling a group of impartial scientific experts who would have knowledge of an area but no particular axe to grind in it, is entirely permissible in the federal courts; we may not have to create a separate institution.

Specialized Courts

Finally, within the courts themselves are specialized courts which could handle highly specific kinds of cases. One of these courts is the Court of Customs and Patent Appeals. It is an interesting kind of science court in itself because most of its judges are also engineers. They also have two kinds of clerks—law clerks and engineering clerks who are knowledgeable in patent matters.

The thing that makes the engineering clerk not so onerous to the legal profession is that the judge is usually a qualified patent engineer and attorney; therefore, he or she is in a position to judge the information received from both the law clerk and the engineering clerk because of a legal and engineering background.

Another specialized court, created for a specific and difficult purpose, was the Railroad Reorganization Court. They simply went to Judge John Minor Wisdom, Judge Friendly from the Second Circuit, and Judge Roszel Thomsen from the D.C. Circuit and created a court which, in a sense, acquired expertise in railroad reorganization so it could knowledgeably handle those cases and save time.

Let me leave you with one thought and perhaps the only intellectual contribution that I have to make here. It's something which I have only been tinkering with recently and, if you find it interesting, you can tinker with it yourself.

I was looking through some of the writings of Professor Lawrence Friedman and others about Max Weber. In particular I was interested in the process of legitimation. Weber identifies three factors which cause the public to grant authority or legitimacy to rules, namely, tradition, charisma, and bureaucracy. Certain leaders, religious and political, are followed because of their charisma. Support for the rules of the executive and legislative branches is developed and maintained through the continued, extensive contacts between their bureaus and the people. Science, too, maintains support through a relatively open-access, bureaucratized system of state and private educational institutions, government research support, and private scholarship funding. The judicial branch, however, seems to maintain authority by tradition. But the courts are increasingly asked to perform nontraditional functions, such as deciding cases grounded in highly complex scientific evidence.

I suggest that many of these decisions produce no real satisfaction for either the litigants or the public. In substance, the court ruling on, let's say, a claimed environmental peril is questionable because the scientific controversy remains unresolved and, perhaps, cannot be resolved by scientists and other interested parties. By asking the court to rule on very tough scientific or scientifically laden issues, we may be causing the deterioration of confidence in the courts and in science, and the legitimacy of both may be questioned. I see little to gain in encouraging a process that seems uniquely ill-suited to both interests at hand. We need either to find another place to resolve these controversies or to develop more suitably designed procedures for use in existing institutions.

ROBERT J. HALLISEY*

I think that perhaps the best I can do is try to explain why the courts may be a little reluctant to embrace all social science studies instantaneously. I'm not a legal historian, but I do think that the courts look back with regret and sadness on dispute resolution processes now viewed as misguided. We no longer think much of trial by ordeal or torture or combat.

There was a time in England when cases were decided by what were called oath helpers. Whichever side could bring in a greater number of people to say that they were truthful people would win the case. We still admit reputation testimony, which isn't awfully far off the mark, but we recognize that that was a bad idea.

In the first jury trials jurors had to be from the community in which the problem had arisen; and they had to know the people and know the facts. That still goes on in places like Nantucket. I understand our judges arrive at Nantucket and they think they're going to preside over trials and that decisions are going to then be made. But, as a practical matter, everybody on Nantucket knows all about the case, including all the jurors, and the trial is really just a rubber stamp of what the community has already decided.

The theory now is that you present the case to jurors who are completely ignorant and indifferent about the particular problem. And the problem is presented in an adversary system, with rules of evidence designed to present the

---

*Justice of the Superior Court of Massachusetts.

jury with the most reliable evidence, not secondhand but eyewitness, to the extent possible, with confrontation of the witness under cross-examination, which has been described as the greatest engine for the discovery of truth.

This is the process and I think it works pretty well. It certainly works well in the rather simple cases of who got to the intersection first, who pulled the knife first, and so forth.

Another trend in the history of the courts is the shift from specialization to generalization in judge and jury. At one time in England there was an institution known as the Elder Brethren of Trinity House. The members were old, retired sailors and shipmasters who decided ship collision cases. They knew what they were talking about. But jury specialization fell into disuse—I suspect for the same reason that some federal administrative agencies in Washington are in somewhat bad aroma: they begin to become captives of the very industry that they're supposed to be judging.

Probably the pendulum swings back and forth, and we're now at that end of the swing where we favor generalization and seek impartial jurors. We educate them as best we can and rely on their good will and honesty to come up with the right decision.

There are exceptions. In Massachusetts we have a housing court which specializes in housing problems; we have a land court which deals with technical problems of land title; and we have a medical malpractice tribunal in which a judge, a doctor, and a lawyer decide whether or not a medical malpractice case has enough merit to continue down the assembly line.

I wonder about that. I wonder why we don't have a cabdrivers' court and a plumbers' court and a landlords' court. If we keep this up, pretty soon we'll have a special court for every imaginable kind of litigant. Then people will complain that the courts are too specialized, and we'll go back the other way again.

Right now we have the jury system and I must say I think it works. Most of the judges I know think it works. Most lawyers I know, even when they've lost cases, think it works.

Turning to the experts, there again I think we get nervous. The idea is that the main event is supposed to go on in the courtroom in front of the jury, not somewhere else.

I think that social research has been somewhat guilty of two extremes in the past. One is ponderously documenting the obvious. In a seminar on criminology I read a very thick book that, after pages of statistics, suggested that if you were born in the darkest ghetto slum and your father was doing life at the state prison for murder and your mother was a madam and all your brothers and sisters were dope pushers, there was a substantial chance you were going to get into trouble before you turned fifteen.

It didn't seem to me that it required so much effort to prove that proposition. That's one extreme that bothers us.

The other extreme is the Ripley-Believe-It-Or-Not type of study designed for *Reader's Digest.*

Massachusetts still feels guilty about the witch trials, and I noticed a reference that in 1655 a Dr. Brown testified in Salem that anybody who displayed certain characteristics was a witch.

Also, regrettably, I think, we have developed skepticism about the hired guns. You can always find doctors to say the fellow is going to be okay, in a year he'll be dancing at the discotheque like a madman; others will say he'll probably be paralyzed and drag himself around the rest of his life. People trained in the same field, given the same evidence, shouldn't differ that widely.

I just finished a case of land taking, eminent domain, where two equally qualified experts used the same types of techniques that social scientists use. They compared sales of real estate to find out the value of the parcel that was taken and they used capitalization of income techniques. The expert for the defense placed the value of the land at $4,400; the expert for the plaintiff placed it at $27,900. Now, I leave it to the statisticians to decide whether that disparity is due to chance. We get suspicious.

Psychiatrists, too, worry us. I had a case where I was supposed to be getting some input on contemporary community standards on obscenity and so somebody fashioned a poll. It was obvious to me that somebody had rigged it, because one question asked, "What do you think is more important: stamping out inflation or dealing with pornography?"

The courts have always been suspicious of out-of-court experiments. I had a high school physics teacher who would try to do something in class and it would never work. He'd say, I'm sorry; it worked beautifully yesterday afternoon, but something's gone wrong today. I think judges suspect that something like this may go on sometimes, that the experiment is run out of court until it works and then that's all you hear about.

Massachusetts is not in the forefront in the area of evidentiary laws, but we are moving along. I think we are in the forefront in admitting testimony from a roentgenologist in a terrible murder case where all they found was bones (*Commonwealth v. Gilbert* 1974). He was permitted to testify that in his experience no two adults had exactly the same bone structure anymore than they have the same fingerprints, though that probably is an act of faith, as I think fingerprints are.

I think we are probably in the forefront in admitting voiceprints in a case (*Commonwealth v. Lykus* 1975). A recent case encouraged the use of polls in the obscenity area (*Commonwealth v. Mascolo* 1979), although the particular evidence was held properly excluded because it wasn't done scientifically. It was just a random chat with neighbors.

We use the breathalizer test in Massachusetts and that, of course, is in the realm of physical science. There are cases in which physical science is the whole answer; we welcome it in these cases because the experts are of tremendous help. But in the social sciences we encounter this problem of how much the jurors know. We credit them with a lot of knowledge and I submit to you that they have a lot of knowledge.

I would think Dr. Kantrowitz, who is obviously a wise man, would agree with me that uneducated people sometimes know a lot. I think it takes a while to appreciate that. But we tell them to use their common sense and their experience in life and to consider the opportunities to observe and the bias and the interests and most of those things that are appropriate in deciding where the truth lies and what weight should be given to testimony.

As a footnote, some of that is working into the law now. I think that's where you help us: we read your works and you refine the problem more than we have time to do. You cut it up into smaller pieces, which is helpful, and you can ascribe weights to those elements, which we are not equipped to do and probably can do only in a rough fashion. And that works its way into the law.

The *Manson* case (1975), as I remember it, spells out several criteria about the circumstances of eyewitness observation: whether there was a good oral description early on that matches the defendant, whether there were mistakes in identification, length of time, and certainty of the identification. These things, I'm sure, emerged out of the eyewitness identification work that you folks did.

I didn't tell you about our court. Our court is the General Trial Court of Massachusetts. We handle all kinds of cases, criminal and civil. We travel all over the state. We don't get the major social issue cases; the desegregation case, which has torn up Boston for years, went into the federal court finally.

My own experience has been more in the rather routine kind of case and the effect of social research on it.

The first case I had was a question of interpreting a zoning by-law in Cambridge which allowed only a drive-in restaurant in a zone. One side presented a professor of linguistics, who tried to convince me that I didn't really know what a drive-in restaurant was and that the meaning of that term had changed in the five years since the zoning by-law had been passed. He told me that this was based on a survey that he'd done in his class at Harvard and also at a few cocktail parties. When the lawyers had finished I said, "Professor, have you had any courses in statistics?"

"No."

"In poll-taking?"

"No."

"In probabilities?"

"No."

"Thank you very much." That was put in a footnote.

Another case involving social science evidence was an eyewitness identification case, in which a white girl claimed to have been robbed by a black man. A fellow came over from Harvard with a big bundle of literature on eyewitness testimony, and I heard him, again, out of the hearing of the jury. As I'm very interested in this, I read all his material, but there were things in there I just couldn't swallow. One study said that the ability of whites to recognize blacks is worse among white students attending a university that is predominantly black than it is among white students going to all-white universities. Now, I don't know statistics, but I do know that's wrong.

When Stephan Michaelson talked about the Poisson Distribution, I thought Poisson meant fish and that it was some sort of a fishing technique. It reminded me of the summer I spent as a mate on a Boston Harbor excursion fishing boat. I didn't know anything about fish when I went out, but by the end of that summer I could identify at a glance codfish, halibut, hake, and cusk. If someone told me that a summer's experience on a fishing boat would not help me recognize the different types of fish, I would say they were crazy.

This fellow was not willing just to testify about the factors that play a part in reliability of identification. He wanted to give his opinion that the identification by the victim was worthless. The federal rules say you can do that, but I really don't like it. It cuts across the whole jury theory. If it's that easy, let's not pay the twelve jurors every day; let them stay home and do what they want to and we'll have a social scientist come in.

I've had other cases where I've had to wing it on my own. I had a name confusion on Cape Cod. Somebody opened an outfit they called The Lighthouse Boatel about three miles away from the Lighthouse Inn, which actually had a lighthouse as part of it and had been there for 100 years. I had to decide whether there'd be enough confusion of names to make it unfair. I based my decision on what I knew about the geography of the Cape. I took a ride around and looked at the two places. I knew them anyway and I knew the routes. I decided there was a substantial risk that somebody who didn't have good directions to the Lighthouse Inn would mistake the Lighthouse Boatel for it.

There's an interesting evolution in Massachusetts in the use of the polygraph, which I think falls in the area of social science. In *Commonwealth v. Fatalo* (1963) the judge excluded it and was affirmed. Then in *Commonwealth v. A Juvenile* (1974) the court said it could be admitted. With some preliminary findings to be made by the judge and an agreement by the defendant that the results would be admitted whether he passed or flunked, they reviewed all the literature, particularly Skolnick's article in the *Yale Law Journal*.

In *Commonwealth v. Vitello* (1978), with two new judges on the court, the decision reflects a shift to the earlier position. The judges cite Skolnick (1961), but they also cite several other articles written since the *Juvenile* case, including articles by Axelrod (1977) in the *National Journal of Criminal Defense* and others in sociological publications. They say what I've been saying: they don't want the battle to move out of the courtroom. They find out on closer analysis that much of the polygraph testing really is a judgment call by the examiner before he even starts to test and that there are lots of holes in it.

Thanks to the *Vitello* decision, polygraph results can be used on cross-examination or during the prosecutor's rebuttal case, only after the defendant has testified in the first place. But they talk about confusion, the mystic infallability, popular misconceptions, and so on. Here's a footnote:

> Public confidence in the omniscience of science [is] greater than the trust medieval men placed in torture as a method of eliciting truth.
>
> There can hardly be any doubt that as soon as expert testimony as to the result of psychological tests is in principle admitted the weight of procedure will shift from the courtroom to the testing laboratory. The psychiatrist will become the real judge. Moreover, like torture, psychological testing cannot be conducted in public. Where the issues are decided in a laboratory, the institution of public trial is obviously a farce.

JAMES COLEMAN*

I would like to address three questions concerning the use of social science data in school desegregation cases in the courts: Who uses it? What kind of use has been made of it? Under what conditions is it used? I won't answer any of these questions conclusively; I'll simply give some examples with regard to each of them and try to derive some weak generalizations from those examples.

First, who uses social science data? If we look at school desegregation, the 1954 *Brown* decision represents a striking use of social science evidence on the psychological effects of segregation. There is dispute over the weight of that evidence in the decision itself, but the evidence was introduced by the plaintiffs, by the NAACP, and accepted by the Supreme Court. It has been hailed as a prominent use of social science data.

A second body of data used in school desegregation cases was of a very different sort. Like the data cited in the *Brown* decision, it was used between about 1968 and 1973 by the NAACP and others who were plaintiffs in school desegregation cases. The question to which the data were addressed was this: What are the cognitive effects—that is, the effects on learning—of racial segregation in schools? The data were primarily from *Equality of Educational Opportunity*, a study carried out in the U.S. Office of Education.

Since I know that study with some degree of intimacy, I have been interested in who used it and why they used it. One of the things that was striking to me was that the U.S. Office of Education never used it. It was conducted for and within that office when John Gardner was Secretary of the Department of Health, Education, and Welfare and Harold Howe was Commissioner of Education. Because these men were enlightened about the use of social science data and not averse to its use, one can ask why it was that the executive agencies did not use it.

*Professor of sociology, University of Chicago.

An administrative agency gains its legitimacy from the very fact of authority, that is, either from its formal position or, as an elected official, from the implicit mandate from constituents. Officials can authoritatively dictate a policy. The legitimacy that arises from social science research is different. It purports to be based on objective facts and not upon the position of the agency which might use it.

Thus social science data are often neither necessary nor helpful to an authoritative agency. One might argue, in fact, that such data are less useful to authorities than to opponents of authorities. To put it another way, research provides a window into an area of social policy, in this case education, for those who are otherwise shut out from the knowledge that would allow criticism of that policy.

In fact, I believe that research results in education will be more widely used by those without decision-making authority than by those with such authority. What I am suggesting is that the very conduct of research will on the whole favor outsiders rather than insiders. It will be used more often by plaintiffs in court cases than by defendants.

Second, what kind of social science data are used? In the 1954 *Brown* decision data on the psychological effects of school segregation were used. In the late 1960s and early 1970s, data on achievement were used to determine the effect of segregated schools on the academic performance of students in those schools. In addition to this research, the courts have used another kind of social science information: demographically descriptive data, that is, the proportion of blacks and whites in each school.

Notice that the first two kinds of social science evidence—psychological and achievement data—were related to difficult questions about effects. The third kind concerns matters of fact: What are the statistical distributions? I think these data began to come into use in the courts when basically conservative southern courts grew unhappy with local school districts attempting in one way or another to minimize the impact of school desegregation on their schools. The courts finally began to use the distribution of children in these schools as the sole criterion of district desegregation.

Such distributional questions can come to be rather complex. For example, in a school desegregation case in Tucson a major issue was whether segregation should be looked at as segregation between two groups, that is, whites versus blacks and Hispanics, or whether the degree of segregation should be described in terms of three ethnic groups. Another question had nothing to do with effects, but was concerned only with statistical distributions: Are schools more segregated than residences in Tucson? It turns out that this last question is not easy to answer. Evidence which looks straightforward at the outset—the statistical distribution of students in schools—is not really straightforward.

Another kind of research, which has only recently begun to play a part in court proceedings, concerns the demographic effects of desegregation, commonly termed "white flight": Does within-district desegregation bring about segregation between districts? There has been a good deal of discussion and dispute about this. It's been used in the courts to some degree but not widely.

Third, under what conditions is research used? Many social scientists are concerned that their research is never used. On the other hand, there are examples of research results being used extensively.

I think one can trace a number of cases—the *Equality of Educational Opportunity* research and Kenneth Clark's research that was used in *Brown*, among others—in which research is not designed to be used for desegregation policy but comes to be used when it is considered relevant to the interests of one of the parties in a legal dispute. That is, research is used when one of the parties to a court case sees some evidence in it that can aid his case.

It turns out that in 1954 conflict emerged which had lain dormant since *Plessy v. Ferguson*. The plaintiffs looked for all the evidence they might find that could aid their case. So it's not a question of generating social science research which is going to be used; it's a question of conflicts generating the interest to look for research results which might be useful to one of the parties.

This leads to another tentative generalization: research results will be more widely used and have more impact when there is a conflict between those in authority and those without authority than when no such conflict exists. Obviously, conflicts are what courts are all about, so that the generalization is not a profound one. Nevertheless, it does suggest that research is often not used because it does not fit the three criteria: that someone's interests are at stake, that the data are useful in aiding those interests, and that the party whose interests can be aided is one of the parties to the conflict.

DISCUSSION

Jeanne Katz *(Legal Times of Washington)*: I wanted to ask why some of you are so threatened by social scientists. You keep talking about how they are going to destroy the jury system, and I don't see where you get that from.

And I'd like to ask the social scientists why, if they are unhappy with the way the courts have used their studies, they don't submit amicus briefs to the court?

Robert Hallisey: I excluded my proffered expert who wanted to say that the eyewitness identification was valueless, because I thought that really was up to the jury. I think now I would permit a properly qualified expert to testify as to the factors involved in the reliability of eyewitness testimony and possibly the weight that each bears. But I think that's really all that should be said.

I'm not in sympathy with those who believe the expert should be free to give a full answer. I think then the jury deliberations, instead of analyzing the evidence carefully and weighing it, might degenerate into a battle over which expert should be believed, and that leads to the belief that you can go off on irrational considerations, such as who's the most attractive, who's the most articulate, where he comes from, rather than how good his opinion is.

Michael Saks *(National Center for State Courts)*: I might just mention that it has taken at least two psychology professors several years of conversations with Judge Hallisey to get him to be willing to allow that much in.

Hallisey: Also, you help the judge through this cross-fertilization. During my charge I now go into more detail on the factors. I don't go into the weighting of them because I don't understand that enough, but it has helped me to cut it up in smaller pieces, so I charge the jury to consider these things.

James Coleman: I'd like to respond to the question about amicus briefs. They are filed by interested parties, but not by the principally interested parties. The social scientist is not an interested party. The social scientist's principal interest is staying out of these things as much as possible, so why should he be filing amicus briefs?

Katz: People can file objectively.

James Coleman: A person can do so if he feels very strongly that somehow injustice is being done, but most amicus briefs are not filed for that reason. They're filed by interested parties who stand on one or another side of the issue.

Paul Rosen *(Carleton University)*: I'd like to address my comments and questions to Professor Coleman. You mentioned the use of social science in the *Brown* case. Very little research on that particular problem had been conducted before 1954, and several of the citations applied only in a very general sense at best. I wonder if you would care to comment on the value of manufactured research for particular instances of litigation, and what do you think about the contribution of such research not to the litigation but to social science in general?

Coleman: With regard to the first question, my own opinion is that the *Brown* case was not really affected by those social science data. As a graduate student in one of my seminars noted, the data were simply used to add weight to the decision.

I think it was unfortunate that the information was used at all, because it obscured the strong constitutionality of the decision itself. Suppose all the research results that were cited had come out the opposite, would one then argue that the decision should have been reversed? Obviously not. The constitutional issue stood apart from the social science result. It seems to me we often lose sight of that. It was lost sight of in the use of the Equality of Educational Opportunity survey results on cognitive effects. Here again there was confusion about whether or not this was a constitutional issue.

Rosen: My question was about research which is manufactured for a particular instance of litigation. I wonder what kind of validity or value that particular research has for social science, aside from its legal applicability?

Coleman: First of all, I don't think much research is manufactured for that purpose, because most research takes too long to do. Instead, plaintiffs or defendants search for research results which aid their case and, as a consequence, I don't think court cases generate original research very often.

Clark Abt *(Abt Associates Inc.)*: A grave current intervention in social policy by the courts is the decision by some courts to order busing and by others to consider other alternatives. Professor Coleman has conducted significant research on the possible impact of busing. The use of that research in the courts where remedies are being considered for school desegregation is controversial right now because there is not complete agreement in the social science community about that research. Some courts have actually used social scientists to support their remedy of busing, social scientists who take the position that white flight to the suburbs and resegregation are not induced by busing. Other courts have used different research findings suggesting that between-district segregation is actually encouraged by this attempt to desegregate schools within districts, as Professor Coleman has found.

This poses a dilemma for the judge who wants to propose and enforce both an equitable and an effective remedy to the problem of school integration and even residential integration. Faced with this conflict in the social research community, what should that judge do to gain access to the available social science knowledge and make sure that it is the best available research to address the issue in both an equitable and effective way?

Coleman: I don't know. I think it puts the judge in a very difficult position; it's not as bad as the testimony of two psychiatrists, but it's a little bit like that. I'm very taken by some of the things that Arthur Konopka mentioned. He mentioned that the advisory jury is in disuse, but it seems to me that would be an interesting possibility in such a case. I think the development of such institutions could be extremely useful in resolving this kind of disagreement over facts.

Hallisey: I think that the courts are badly equipped to deal with these sorts of ongoing problems. The legislatures are far better equipped to deal with them, but the executive and legislative branches don't want to touch controversial social issues, so they develop into constitutional problems and are tossed at us.

We don't have large staffs to do studies and administer programs over a long period of time. The classic function of the court is to listen to two sides and decide which is right, based on an already-developed record.

I don't know what I'd do in that instance. I think I'd get the experts in; I would hope there were good lawyers on both sides who would cross-examine the hell out of them, and whatever they didn't do I'd do. If I was still on dead center, I'd fall back and try to use some of these devices. Meanwhile, I'd be cursing in the lobby that the legislature hadn't handled this long before.

Coleman: One thing that I didn't mention earlier and I am reminded of by what you said is that cross-examination by lawyers can be extremely valuable to a judge. One of the major sources of misuse of social science data in the courts is inadequate cross-examination.

Eleanor Wolf, who is a professor of sociology at Wayne State University, has written about the Detroit school desegregation case. Having looked through all the testimony in the case, she claims that there was a misuse of social science data. It seems to me that the principal misuse was not by the plaintiffs themselves; although they overstated the case in many instances, it was in their interest to do so. It was in the interest of the defendants to cross-examine appropriately, and I think that was the cause of the misuse.

Arthur Konopka: Let me make just one comment in direct answer to that. One strategy the courts have within the provisions of their rules that they didn't use because it didn't really bear on adjudication is the use of the magistrate as a special master. In the case of *Hart v. The Commonwealth School Board of Brooklyn, School District No. 21*, in fact, the court reorganized the school districts under its own injunction, because the school board wasn't able to do so to the court's satisfaction. The judge used a master who was particularly qualified to undertake reorganization of the districts. That isn't part of the adjudicatory process, but the judge has the authority to hire someone who has special expertise.

Stephen Wasby *(State University of New York at Albany)*: I don't think we are likely to find the development of privileges for social scientists on cross-examination; the trend is against developing new privileges. In the *Popkin* case a social scientist was held in contempt of court in an Ellsberg-related matter for refusing to reveal his sources. The law is still there. That case was not overturned.

Art mentioned the Yankelovich study, particularly that oft-cited finding about the relationship between knowledge and approval. That's a beautiful example of poor social science, yet it has passed quickly and without criticism into the public domain.

Phillip Finney *(Southeast Missouri State University)*: I've heard the judges speak about how juries might hold the social scientist in awe and take statements unequivocally, but I see another possibility: the jurors might feel the social scientist is trying to tell them what truth is and decide to reject his opinion. Is there a trend one way or the other? Do jurors accept the social scientist or reject him?

Stephan Michelson *(Econometric Research Inc)*: That is a researchable and important topic. The only pertinent research I know of was Rita James Simon's study of jury response to experts testifying about insanity. She says the jurors recognized the witnesses as experts but weren't in awe of them. The jurors accepted the testimony but did not consider it that important.

Michael Saks: The jury essentially ignored what the experts had to say.

Michelson: Yes. That's what she said.

REFERENCES

Axelrod, Robert M. 1977. The Use of Lie Detectors by Criminal Defense Attorneys. 3 *National Journal of Criminal Defense* 107.

Berry v. Chaplin, 74 *Cal. App. 2d* 652, 169 *P. 2d* 442 (1946).

Coleman, J. S. et al. 1966. *Equality of Educational Opportunity*. Washington, D.C.: Government Printing Office.

Commonwealth v. Fatalo, 346 *Mass.* 266 (1963).

Commonwealth v. Gilbert, 366 *Mass.* 18 (1974).

Commonwealth v. A Juvenile, 365 *Mass.* 421 (1974).

Commonwealth v. Lykus, 327 *N.E. 2d* 671 (1975).

Commonwealth v. Mascolo, 386 *N.E. 2d* 1311 (1979).

Commonwealth v. Vitello, 1978 *Mass. Adv. Sheets* 2603.

Frye v. United States, 293 *Fed.* 1013 (D.C. Cir. 1923).

Manson v. Brathwaite, 423 *U.S.* 96 (1975).

Skolnick, Jerome H. 1961. Scientific Theory and Scientific Evidence: An Analysis of Lie Detection. 70 *Yale Law Review* 694.

8

Overcoming Barriers to the Use of Applied Social Research in the Courts

DONALD L. HOROWITZ

CHARLES H. BARON

MICHAEL P. KIRBY

GEOFFREY W. PETERS

DONALD L. HOROWITZ*

There are major barriers to the use of social research in litigation, and, as in the case of many other phenomena, a number of different conditions at different levels of generality contribute to the barriers. Some of these obstacles can be eliminated, some of them can be eased, but many are inherent in the situation.

Certain courses that we might take in rectifying these problems would, I think, have some undesirable costs and consequences and I shall say a bit more about that later, but first I think it is incumbent on me to locate these barriers. It seems to me they lie in five rather arbitrarily chosen places:

in the nature of social research;
in the nature of the lawsuit as a controversy;
in the rules of evidence and in other rules of law that impinge on the use of social science research;
in the character of the adversary process and the use of expert witnesses;
in the background of judges.

I shall deal with these in order.

As to the nature of social research, it seems to me that, although this conference is focused on applied research, many of the same things can be said about basic research, which is also often relevant to judicial decision. Basic research, however, tends to be pitched at a completely different level of analysis from the level that is appropriate for the judicial decision. Applied research may well be pitched at a somewhat lower level of analysis, although not always. If so, this may mean that it has misconceived the research problem. It also often means that applied research is part of a hidden agenda, that it has some partisan quality to it and therefore may be suspect.

Somebody mentioned earlier the possibility of commissioning research specifically for purposes of litigation. That strikes me, as I think it did one of the speakers, as a most unsatisfying possibility. The time constraints and the methodology that would be dictated by those time constraints are unlikely to produce the kind of research that is sufficiently reliable to justify its utilization in litigation.

In general, what is litigated and what is studied are two completely different things, responding to two completely different sets of forces. Therefore, if there is an "answer" to a particular factual question that rests in the domain of social science, it is likely to be a partial answer, an answer based on inferences from proxies. Surrogate indicators and proxies, as we all know, have their own special hazards.

---

* Duke University School of Law.

It is also true, I think, that there are going to be more negative findings than positive findings, and that is not going to help the courts very much.

There is an interesting contrast in this respect between the courts and other governmental bodies. In other bodies the policy that emerges can be the result, at least in some measure, of social science findings. The courts, on the other hand, are at a disadvantage in this respect because they have to depend on the litigants. They do not self-start. They cannot wait for the findings to mature. They cannot act only when they are confident of the factual foundation for their action. They must decide. Unlike the legislative decision and often unlike the bureaucratic decision, the judicial decision is mandatory.

Perhaps, in view of this, courts would be better off on their own, operating without the dubious benefits of social science research. Here I want to turn to the second item—the nature of the lawsuit.

It seems to me that there is an inescapable tension between attending to the facts of the individual case and attending to the facts of a run of cases. Social science deals with recurrent patterns of behavior, whereas litigation is very often, although not exclusively, focused on the facts of individual cases. Two things, it seems to me, follow from this.

The behavior of a class of people cannot necessarily be inferred from the behavior of litigants. Nor can the behavior of litigants be inferred from general findings about whole classes of people. The reliance on one to infer the other is a very perilous venture.

The second thing that flows from this is that recurrent patterns can change, rendering social science findings obsolete. Can we predicate law, which is in principle, though not always in practice, immutable, on findings based on ephemeral patterns? At the extremes, I want to suggest that some important issues concerning the integrity of the judicial process lurk in this quest for the utility of social research in litigation.

One other aspect of the nature of the lawsuit vis-à-vis the nature of social research bears on this. I want to approach it through an example. The example is the case of *Lemon v. Kurtzman* (1971), which was decided by the Supreme Court in 1971. The case concerned the Establishment Clause of the First Amendment. The Supreme Court held it unconstitutional for a state to provide public funds for salaries for teachers of secular subjects in parochial schools.

There was an interesting tidbit in that case. The Court seemed to think that one reason why this ought to be a breach of the Establishment Clause was that the struggle of sectarian groups over material benefits in each annual session of the legislature was likely to grow and that this might prove divisive. One of the purposes of the Establishment Clause and of the separation of church and state was to prevent intersectarian strife. Therefore, legislatures should not provide funds to parochial schools because ultimately it would have this effect at every annual legislative appropriation session.

I think this factual assumption of the Court is probably unjustified. A good case can be made that the struggle over symbolic values will prove far more divisive than the struggle over mere material benefits, which, after all, can be compromised.

150

There is no definitive social science research on an issue this broad and there is not going to be any for a long time to come. In this respect, the Court found itself in that case and will find itself, it seems to me, recurrently in the position of using its experience and its intuition in order to be faithful to its responsibilities.

The third barrier consists of certain rules of evidence and other rules of law that pose hazards and obstacles to the sensible use of social science research.

One such hindrance is the hearsay rule. The federal rules of evidence tend to make social science studies, like other studies, inadmissible as evidence in chief. This tends to put the premium on the live testimony of expert witnesses. It makes the studies suspect. It tends to give judges the idea that they cannot be trusted to read anything but summaries. The rule also downplays the written word in favor of the spoken word; it downplays studies in favor of testimony about studies.

The federal rules also tend to favor official reports over other ways of presenting social science findings. The assumption, which I think is easily pierced, is that official reports have superior veracity. Government departments and commissions, as we all know, do not grind any axes when they write reports; they are just seeking the truth. It seems to me that official reports are often simplifications; they are often inferior versions of the things that they have summarized and that are themselves excluded from evidence. In short the rules of evidence tend to put a premium on secondhand and filtered information rather than on firsthand and original information.

The burden of proof is another device that has occasionally been misused where social science is involved. I want to illustrate this just briefly by an example.

In the case of *Hobson v. Hansen* (1971), which is a celebrated case in the District of Columbia, school officials were put to the burden of proving that unequal student test scores on standardized tests were not caused by inequalities in expenditures on teachers' salaries.[1] In that same lawsuit they were also put to the burden of proving that the unequal distribution of teacher experience was not related to differential student performance on standardized tests.

In both cases, you will observe, these were negatives that the school officials were called upon to prove. Worse yet, the affirmative propositions were extremely dubious to begin with. The burden of proof is a device that is obviously very sensibly employed in litigation where one party has made a factual presentation that seems to establish some connection between two conditions, A and B, and where it seems sensible to shift the burden to the other party to show that that factual connection is not there. But burden-of-proof rules are not always sensibly applied to dubious social science hypotheses. I think this is a real danger for the courts. They have not been sufficiently aware of it.

Another rule that impedes the intelligent use of social science research in the courts is the rule of appellate practice that shields from appellate review factual findings of the trial court, unless they are "clearly erroneous." That is a

151

showing that is always difficult to make on appeal. But where social science is involved, there are further difficulties. In social science, of course, nothing is clear; therefore, nothing can be either clearly correct or clearly erroneous. Consequently, the findings of fact of trial judges in social science matters are unlikely to be reviewed by the appellate courts. Yet I think a strong case can be made for having the appellate court pass on those findings of fact. I think it is a great mistake to apply a prudential rule like the clearly erroneous rule to findings of social science, but the extent to which it applies remains in doubt.

A fourth barrier is the adversary process and the use of expert witnesses. The experts, it has frequently been noted, tend to be partisans, and it is possible that more social science discoveries have occurred on the witness stand than in the library or the computer center or the laboratory.

Unfortunately, the adversary process has often intersected with social scientists' concern with current social issues and has given them carte blanche to "discover"—and I think that word is aptly put in quotes—that the research literature in fact confirms what they have been advocating all along.

The background of judges is the fifth barrier to use of social science research in the courts. By training, by recruitment, and particularly by the breakdown of their dockets, judges tend to be generalists. They cannot afford to learn too much about educational production functions, for example, because they will have only one such case every three decades. They cannot afford to invest too much time in becoming specialists in any field which is not a recurrent one for their docket. Judges of trial courts of general jurisdiction, therefore, have to be what they were when they ascended the bench, namely, generalists.

It seems to me, by the way, that there is a paradox here. Their character as generalists, as intelligent, impartial, informed generalists is what fits them as community representatives. It is what unfits them, however, as interpreters of specialized information, and social research is, to say the least, specialized.

What can be done about these barriers? As I said, some things can be done, some cannot, and some should not be done. Judges should be exposed to the original material. They should be exposed to the studies that purport to support the assertions made by the experts. In this respect, the rules of evidence should be altered, and the favorable treatment of government reports should be abolished because they are, as I said, inferior versions of the studies.

If judges are more exposed to the firsthand information, they will be somewhat less dependent on the testimony of social science advocates and on the social science translations contained in official reports.

Courts, it should be noted, do pretty well with some other bodies of specialized evidence based on recurrent experience. I am thinking of medical testimony, which the courts have more experience with than they do with social science. They can do much better with social science if they are exposed to it more frequently.

As to the nature of the lawsuit, that has been changing a bit. There has been less of a search for truth between the parties in recent years and more of a tendency to search for the right policy, using the lawsuit as a vehicle.

I suggested in *The Courts and Social Policy* (1977) that the courts do not necessarily do this very well. Ultimately, if they try to do it better, that is, if they devote the requisite energy to the search for the right policy, justice between the parties may well suffer. I think there is a tension between these two quests. It is a tension very clearly seen in the evidence that is relevant to the two different kinds of issues before the courts. Too much attention to one of these quests will tend to result in neglect of the other one.

The nature of social science, the first factor that I adverted to, is unlikely to change in response to the needs of litigation, unless litigation becomes a major source of research funding. Fortunately, this is unlikely, and it need not concern us.

This leaves the question of the adversary process and the use of experts. It is in that realm that most proposals for innovation have come—for social science masters; for social science staffs; for the use of dispassionate third-party experts, either ad hoc or on a continuing basis.

I am wary of these proposals. The beauty of the judicial process is that the judge himself actually decides. Where else does that happen in government these days? I am afraid that, by creating bodies of social science experts, we will tend to take the decision out of the hands of the judges, not formally, not officially, but tacitly and incrementally. I think the judges will have a strong tendency to defer to those social scientists whom they appoint to positions, if judges do the appointing, or to their organizational colleagues, if backup institutions are created.

In short, I think the problem with the adversary method of handling social science issues is the fact that it is both partisan and inconclusive, and the judge is left without a reliable answer; he is left with a choice between two polar positions. But the defects of proposals to find objective expertise may well be the opposite of this. Their perhaps too conclusive character, because of the deference factor that I mentioned, and their propensity for undercutting the participation of the parties in the decision-making process are two of their major problems. The availability of objective expertise, if that is what it is to be called, raises the possibility that the judge may refer to the objective expertise without the participation of the parties. That would be a fundamental alteration in our adversary system. If we are going to make it, we should first consider carefully the pros and cons of the adversary process, not merely in cases where social science is relevant but across the board.

If we do want to create a repository of specialized social science wisdom, I think perhaps the best approach is to integrate it into the adversary process, make sure that the parties have access to social science resources (a resource center, for example), and permit the parties to develop the material rather than encourage the judge to do so. If, on top of that, the rules of evidence are suitably altered to reduce judicial reliance on the expert witness and increase reliance on the studies themselves, the judge may be in a much better position to check the accuracy and the good sense of what the experts and the parties that hired them have said. This may well be the best that can be expected in a rather messy situation.

I am also wary of creating bodies of outside experts for the courts to call upon rather than merely for the parties to use, because those experts create the possibility of institutional rather than individually accountable decisions. Moreover, their very availability may increase the attention given to recurrent patterns and broad policies at the expense of what I take to be the generally commendable attention currently given to individual claims and grievances. The rules of evidence and the institutions for getting evidence before the judge have, in the end, substantive consequences.

CHARLES H. BARON[*]

I do not think that social scientists should, at least at the present time, be fighting the court system as it stands. Instead they should be trying to plug their data into the existing system at appropriate places. The system is so big and the forces operating within it are so powerful that reformers are likely to get much farther by exploiting appropriate points of entry into the system than by launching a frontal assault.

Several speakers have mentioned the difficulty that faces the lawyer or judge who wants to find out quickly what social research has already been done on a particular issue. Contrast this with the ease of locating legal research. The body of Anglo-American legal research materials is probably the best indexed system of written source materials in the world. Book publishers of long standing do a very good job of keeping that system well indexed. My suggestion is that this state of affairs presents us with opportunities for bringing about a manageable, uncontroversial reform which would provide great leverage for other reforms within the system. What is needed is some publisher who is willing to search out the existing published research findings, to put them in a form in which they can be used by lawyers and judges, and to index them in a way which makes them easy for lawyers and judges to find. The West Publishing Key Number Digest System does precisely this sort of thing with legal materials—principally reported court decisions. Each decision is analyzed as to its usefulness to future decision makers; for each possible use,

[*]Professor, Boston College Law School.

a headnote is prepared which expresses what the case stands for on that point. Each such headnote is indexed with others from other cases under appropriate topic headings, such as torts, contributory negligence, 4(6).

If social science research findings could be similarly analyzed and categorized under headings reflecting the possible use of that research as a basis for justifying arguments in a case, and if an index of those headings was put together, I think lawyers would use the research much more readily because they could get to it quickly. Judges and lawyers have to work very quickly and, as a result, they work with the material they can obtain most readily and with which they are most familiar.

To get this kind of enterprise started, I think one would need only to approach West Publishing or Commerce Clearing House. The publishers could take over from there; they would know what to do. One of the first things they would do, I think, would be to talk to the people at law schools who teach the basic course in legal research and writing. This course is typically taught by library staffs and young people who are just out of law school. They may have clerked for a couple of years, but this is their first teaching experience.

If West gave these teachers booklets which explained how the new social research indexing system worked and these people taught first-year law students to use social science research findings, the next generation of law school graduates would realize that winning lawsuits for their clients might be a function of their ability to use these materials. Experienced lawyers opposing the young graduates would find that to keep up with the new graduates they would have to start to use the materials as well.

In addition, having lawyers write briefs and offer evidence using these materials seems to me to be the best way to educate judges. Of course, there are other ways as well—judicial conferences on subjects of this sort and so forth—but for the most part I think the job of a practicing lawyer is that of an educator. He is in court to educate the judge with respect to what the law and facts are regarding his particular case, all of it, of course, from the point of view of winning the case for his client. Opposing counsel is there to educate the judge in ways that favor his client and to make sure that the judge is not miseducated by the first lawyer.

We've talked about cross-examination as a check on misuse of applied social research. I think there are other checks which haven't been noted. One of them is the power of an appellate court to reverse a decision. A still more important check occurs when judges review what was done in an earlier case and decide on the basis of hindsight whether what was done in that case should not have been done. I think Lord Mansfield once referred to this phenomenon as the common law working itself pure from case to case. Lawyers are used to the idea that lawyers and judges are going to make mistakes, so they tend to look at things from a long view. From this perspective, research misused in one case may be slightly less misused in the next case, and so on to the point where we arrive at what appears to be the best kind of use, something which approaches truth.

Another check on misuse of applied social research is provided by law review articles. My understanding is that law reviews are supposed to be fora in which scholars review the decisions of judges to point out what they think are mistakes or to praise a decision because of the good job that was done. Social scientists, as well as lawyers, ought to be reviewing cases in the pages of law reviews, which are themselves indexed in the index to legal periodicals and, as a result, are eminently available to lawyers and to judges.

Thus my suggestion is that we build into the adversary process a system which has considerable leverage for increasing geometrically in a relatively short period of time the amount of social science research used by lawyers and judges. It doesn't seem to me to be any more impossible than the task was for West Publishing Company when, years ago, it decided to index the existing body of American and English law.

Once social scientists become an intimate part of this adversary system, they will be able to suggest changes in the system from a more informed point of view and with more credibility than I think they can presently. Once they have become part of the process of contributing to legal change as part of the system, I think they will gain a kind of credibility which then will enable them to propose reforms of the system itself more effectively.

MICHAEL P. KIRBY*

The purpose of these comments is to provide a framework for understanding the effect and value of one form of applied social research, project evaluation, upon the criminal justice system. Evaluation is defined as those research activities meant to inform the management of an agency or the decision-making process used by government officials. Evaluation involves the application of techniques from both the academic and governmental sectors. Given the unique requirements of the decision-making process, many new procedures have been created to cope with practical difficulties, while others have changed substantially to improve the quality and timeliness of evaluation data. This hybrid called evaluation cannot be understood as having solely academic or governmental "roots"; rather it is an amalgamation of the two.

The complex task of bridging the two fields has created a discipline, still in its infancy, which has numerous flaws related to both utilization and proper research methods. Although there are numerous limitations to the quality of evaluation, this is not to deny that social research has probably had its greatest effect on policy through this area of project evaluation. Evaluation has been

---

*Associate professor of political science, Southwestern University, Memphis, Tennessee.

used to justify the continued existence of many good public agencies, to recommend the discontinuance of ineffective public agencies, and to improve the procedures and service delivery systems of many others.

Although these comments point to an important role for project evaluation, it is also a fair assessment that it has not reached its full potential. If widely and appropriately implemented evaluation could dramatically improve the quality of both management and decision making. Rather than blaming researchers, administrators, funding sources or decision makers for this state of affairs, it should be recognized that evaluation in criminal justice is a relatively young discipline which has been experimenting with a variety of procedures. As these experiences have accumulated, it is now possible to provide a framework to overcome some of the problems related to utilization and methods.

Several procedures can be used to make evaluation more effective.[2]

First, funding sources, administrators, and decision makers must understand evaluation concepts. They should be prepared to enforce accountability upon researchers so that evaluations are both useful and valid. Requests for proposals (RFPs) have to be written in such a way that they define what is expected of the researcher. It is not enough to draft RFPs which ask for an "evaluation." Various types of evaluation can be attempted and different levels of quality may result, thus not meeting the needs of the administrator or decision maker.

Second, research procedures have to be clarified in simple terms. Research is not a ritualistic exercise nor is it statistical by nature. Rather it is a logical system which can be understood by any consumer, as long as it is explained in simple terms. Complex statistics are only an adjunct to evaluation. Complex statistical techniques have corresponding simple substitutes, such as percentages, graphical techniques, and means.

Third, the research methods employed must fit the particular problem being examined. Certain problems require more rigorous methods than other problems. If the method suiting the problem cannot be executed, then it should be admitted that an evaluation is neither possible nor desirable. The philosophy that some data are better than no data should be eschewed as unreliable. Making decisions on the basis of erroneous or misleading information is a practice that can quickly discredit the evaluation discipline.

Finally, in the case of impact evaluations (which examine the effect of agencies on recidivism, court backlog, crime rates, and so forth) the use of experimental or quasi-experimental design is necessary for a valid evaluation. Without such designs, it is not possible to describe effectively and accurately the effect of an agency. However, experimental design does raise some apparent legal and ethical issues. This is an area which should be examined at much greater length by the legal community. Contrary to the conventional wisdom of the legal community, it appears that the courts would rule in favor of the careful use of experimental design.

In summary, evaluation has had a substantial effect on public policy. However, there is still a long way to go in producing consistently effective evaluations. Employing the above procedures will result in effective and useful evaluations.

GEOFFREY W. PETERS*

Many speakers have expressed concern about bad social science being used by courts that don't know any better. Let me suggest that that concern, although real, needs to be placed in perspective. The current legal literature reflects a great deal of concern on the part of the judiciary and the bar, if not the public, about the quality of lawyering which takes place in the courts. In other words, concern exists more right now about bad lawyering than about bad social science and it seems to me that the problem, while real, needs to be placed in that perspective.

Dr. Kantrowitz's remarks yesterday suggest to me that problems of adducing evidence exist in any scientific field and so social science should not expect to be any different in encountering these problems.

Much concern has been expressed about the tension between the role of the social scientist as an expert witness (a so-called co-opted victim of the adversary process, who is unable to present evidence with appropriate qualifications) and the role of the social scientist as the seeker of truth. I'd like to address this issue by differentiating some of the roles played by social scientists and their relationship to the courts.

There is the role of the expert witness in court. This is perhaps the most limited and restrained role that the social scientist might play. It is limited by the fact that the witness presents testimony elicited by advocates whose function it is to prevail in behalf of their client. Advocates do not necessarily seek truth. In fact, in criminal cases their role may well be to obfuscate truth. When the state presents its evidence, if defense counsel can obfuscate the truth to the point where the state cannot prove, by evidence beyond a reasonable doubt, the guilt of the defendant, then the defendant prevails and the government is not permitted to deprive the defendant of life or liberty.

The problems of co-optation of an expert witness in the intelligent analysis of testimony are very real. Co-optation is not likely to be easily solved. Social scientists who insist on the right to present a narrative with all of the qualifications and hedging that are necessary to a proper search for "truth" will simply find, perhaps fortunately so, that they are not used as expert witnesses.

---

*Deputy director for programs, National Center for State Courts, Williamsburg, Virginia.

In addition, remember that while a hundred social scientists might testify to the truth of a particular fact and only one would raise a doubt, in court you are likely to find only two expert witnesses, the one who would raise the doubt and one of the hundred on the other side. Thus, in court we don't necessarily seek to find the truth in evidence that is adduced through expert witnesses; what we do instead is try to give the defendants due process so that with their counsel, with their evidence, and with their expert witnesses they have an opportunity to present their views to a jury of their peers.

Social science plays a limited role in these circumstances because truth is a means to an end and not necessarily an end in itself. Lest that point be made too strongly, let me suggest that we look at the adversary process at its best.

The social scientist testifies and presents his evidence. Under direct examination the lawyer brings forth the evidence most favorable to his side of the case and may well explore some of the limitations on that evidence as a strategic device to defuse the cross-examination. Armed with social science experts of his own, opposing counsel then comes forth and asks pointed questions revealing the true weaknesses of the evidence presented on direct examination. In fact, using latitude granted to cross-examiners by law, the lawyer may ask questions which range from "When did you stop beating your wife?" to "It is true, is it not, that you failed to use the XYZ test to determine whether or not the data were in fact meeting the assumptions of your model?"

The direct examiner comes to the rescue upon redirect examination and does what lawyers call rehabilitation of the witness. The first question is, "You're not even married, are you?" and the response is, "No." The second question is, "Did you test your model using appropriate scientific techniques and find that the model was the most appropriate available?"

"Yes."

"Would the XYZ test have been appropriate?"

"No."

Thus, at its best, the adversary process does bring out all the sides that social scientists need to bring out in the search for truth in social science. Not in the search for truth, but rather in the just resolution of disputes (which may not necessarily involve truth), the social scientist can play a limited role in a properly operating adversary system.

Aside from appearing as an expert witness, the social scientist may act as a consultant to the court other than on an individual case basis. But here again there is the danger of co-optation. As one who has special talents and skills, the social scientist can help evaluate court programs, case-processing techniques, public perceptions of courts, and so forth. In this realm the social scientist has considerable latitude; he is not subjected to the adversary process directly, although I'm told that communicating with lawyers and judges often resembles it in any case. But, nevertheless, the ability of the scientist to add qualifications and caveats to the presentation of data is enhanced—enhanced but not complete.

Remember that social scientists are invited into the court to assist and are looked on with suspicion born of lack of understanding. They are not asked to tell the court what the problem is and why impoverished citizens shouldn't always lose. They are there only to evaluate whether master calendaring systems are improvements over individual calendaring systems, or other rather narrowly phrased questions. In short, they are limited as consultants to helping with specific problems rather than reporting on the state of justice in the courts.

The third role that a social scientist might play, as an academic scholar, is perhaps the least inhibitive. Bolstered by academic freedom, tenure, a sabbatical leave, and a grant from the National Science Foundation, the scholar can look long and hard at a court and see it for what it really is. Unhampered and unconstrained by loyalties and economics, the scholar can submit to the unrelenting truth of the crucible of peer review.

That sounds a little utopian, because the academic scholar yields to certain barriers within academic institutions which may well prevent the social scientist from taking that role. First, there are many barriers to academic interdisciplinary work.

Second, we know that to assure proper reception of research by one's academic colleagues, the research must frequently be deductive (that is, based on a theoretically derived test of a hypothesis) rather than inductive and descriptive, which may be more relevant to the problems of the court.

Third, to assure tenure, the results must be published in a refereed disciplinary journal rather than published in a place where courts are more likely to read it.

Fourth, tenure, sabbatical leaves, and NSF grants are hard to come by these days.

Finally, access to the courts themselves, as with any public bureaucracy, may well be problematic. Yet the role of the social scientist as consultant to the court, while it entails barriers, may solve some of the problems of the social scientist in the role of academic scholar.

Social scientists have the ability to effect important changes in the way the courts operate. Contrary to an earlier comment, I would suggest that social scientists who are perceived as being helpful, though demanding, will be cautiously welcomed to assist in court reform efforts. I do not mean to imply that social science evidence on a case-by-case basis will be welcomed; it will be subject to the problems that have been discussed throughout this conference. But the use of data relating to the way court systems operate may be welcomed by the courts much more easily and be subject to fewer constraints.

It seems to me that social scientists ought to be able to accept that role. A recent article suggested that integration of law and social science has proceeded extremely slowly, despite the glowing predictions of twenty years ago. We also have heard much about problems with the U.S. Supreme Court's use of social science evidence. We have catalogued the problems of the social scientist as an expert witness. Incidentally, despite the almost exclusive focus of this conference on federal courts, particularly on civil rights and class action cases, fewer than 3 percent of all the cases filed in the courts of this country are filed in federal courts and an even smaller proportion are civil rights actions. In short, I would suggest that a greater impact may be made by social scientists working with the state courts on problems of systematic improvement.

Putting social science into publications which are read by court personnel, and not necessarily just law reviews, and being prepared to present papers and communicate directly to court personnel would be valuable ways of interacting with the courts.

Don't be completely put off by court misuse of social science data in individual cases. Law reviews are replete with criticisms of instances where courts have misused legal precedent. The misuse of social science data is not any more novel in a court than the misuse of legal precedent.

Remember that, unlike social science, law is a tool which has to be invoked with finality. Every case must have an ending. Even the renowned IBM antitrust case will one day end. That means that the judge must make a decision under conditions of uncertainty using the best information available. Like the scholar, the judge can plead for future research at the end of his opinion. But unlike the scholar, for whom the search continues, the judge must end his opinion, at which point the case also ends.

Remember that, when doing research in areas important to the courts and society, the limitations of ethics and methodology, not to speak of resources, may inhibit or even preclude competent research. Random assignment of convicted defendants to sentences is ethically impossible, and yet methodological limitations on nonexperimental research designs may make causal inference impossible.

Don't be misled by your role in determining social policy. Austin Sarat was concerned with research which might lead to the adoption of personnel systems which would displace poor George, the eighty-year-old clerk over in the corner, who was the only one that knew the filing system. Sue Johnson's answer, appropriately, was, "We'll find a special title and a position for poor George in the adoption of the new system." In other words, social scientists and social science research are not so powerful that research results will overturn both common sense and the decision-making prerogatives of the manager or judge.

You will help judges by informing their decisions. You're welcome to submit evidence and information; you're not asked to replace the judge in deciding how it will be used or when.

DISCUSSION

Clark Abt *(Abt Associates Inc.)*: It is often asserted that we cannot use true experimental designs to determine the efficacy of a treatment for a population which, for reasons of ethics, must be treated equally. Therefore, we cannot do true experimental designs on, say, differential treatments of convicted felons to determine which legal remedy or which sentencing technique is the most efficacious.

This is not correct. We have found a way of achieving true experimental designs with random assignment of treatment and control groups consistent with ethics and equity. You formulate a treatment which is in scarce supply. Then you assign the treatment randomly, based on the ethical justification that it is a desirable treatment. And the fairest way of distributing anything desirable, of which there isn't enough to go around, is to distribute it randomly. You have thereby simultaneously met the requirements of true experimental design and equality.

Sue Johnson *(New York State Court System)*: Have any judges been persuaded to do that?

Shari Diamond *(University of Illinois)*: There was a plea bargaining study just done in Dade County, Florida (Heinz and Kerstetter 1979), where three judges agreed to have cases randomly assigned to pretrial conferences where the parties participated so that the plea bargaining was under the control of the court, the policeman, and the witness; the victim and the defendant were invited. There is also an old California study where people were, on a random basis, released from prison six months early.

Our justification for doing a study is that we don't know whether a touted treatment is going to have positive effects, and so randomly assigning people to alternate treatment conditions to compare the potential results can be justified on those grounds.

Geoffrey Peters: I leave to my Institutional Review Board and to the judges with whom we work the question of whether they will permit us to do this. I have no doubt but that true experiments are possible. In fact, the National Center is conducting at least two right now; neither of them, however, presents the ethical problems of the random assignment of defendants to different treatments. Whether that would pass ethical review within my institution or within the funding agency, and, ultimately, with the judges with whom we deal, is more doubtful.

I would ask the same question that Sue Johnson asked; that is, whether or not judges accept the experiment. It seems to me the biggest barrier will not be convincing social scientists that this is something that they can ethically undertake, but rather convincing judges that they can legally accept these experiments.

Carol Werner *(University of Utah)*: The equity issue is only part of the problem. What I see judges doing is limiting your pool, because if they see someone who they consider dangerous, or likely to be so, they just eliminate that person from the pool of potential recipients of a treatment.

Stuart Nagel *(University of Illinois)*: That was done in Stockton and Sacramento, where juveniles were put into three groups. One group consisted of those too dangerous to be released on probation; they were auto-matically incarcerated. A second group, too innocuous to incarcerate, was automatically put on probation. And the middle group was subjected to random incarceration and probation. A one-year follow-up conducted after the end of both the incarceration and the probation periods found that those who had been incarcerated were more likely to recidivate than those who had been given probation (Levin 1971). That was before *In Re Gault* (1967), though.

A really good, true experiment conducted by Mathematica had to do with giving unemployment compensation to people released from prison. In most states, if you're an ex-convict, you're not eligible for un-employment compensation, even though you legitimately can't find a job, are unemployed, and the unemployment compensation might hold you over for a while so you don't have to rob a gas station in order to stay alive.

What they're doing at Mathematica is randomly giving ex-convicts unemployment compensation. What is really interesting about that study is the way they're measuring recidivism. They're not measuring recidi-vism by just looking to see who gets arrested, because, using those measures, they feel that the only people who recidivate are the bunglers. They've hired streetwise ex-convicts to do the interviewing of these peo-ple to find out what crimes they've committed for which they haven't been arrested. At the Evaluation Research Society meeting last year the Mathematica people were saying informally that they've got all the rec-ords on rollers so that they can roll them into Pennsylvania if they're sub-poenaed by the State of New Jersey. They've got a subpoena exemption from the Attorney General of the United States—it's a Department-of-Labor-funded study—but they don't know whether that exemption will apply in the State of New Jersey—whether the doctrine of preemption will cover it. But it's an interesting example of a true experiment that involves all kinds of ethical problems and requires cooperation between lawyers and social scientists. It will be interesting to see the results.

Abt: Just a brief point of explanation for the non-social-scientists here. Any-thing less than a true—that is, randomized—experiment is always subject to grave doubts about the validity of causal inferences, and I think we can say that virtually all well trained social scientists would support that state-ment. That's why we're making such a fuss over this randomization issue, and many of us have been frustrated repeatedly in trying to implement randomized experiments by the counter-argument that it violates individ-ual equities.

Teb Marvell *(National Center for State Courts)*: There are many ways in which social science material can get into appellate courts. Of course, there are amicus briefs, but judges in some states will go out and talk with social scientists and informally get information. The court can also send

163

the case to a master or trial judge to take in evidence. The appellate judges can read anything they want to in the area since there are no evidence restraints on what judges can look at when making law.

In both Canada and Germany social scientists have written briefs and made oral arguments, and in Germany the courts have even gone so far as to commission social research for the courts. In addition, some judges have actually gone out and done social research for cases. So the appellate courts are wide open as to how materials can get into them.

Peters: That's something that has come up several times, and I have heard at least one person suggest that there was a statute which allows appellate courts to get information from the outside. I would remind you that there is a canon of judicial ethics which judges are bound by in almost every state. It specifically states that judges may not receive *ex parte* information on cases in which they are involved. I don't know how the statutes that have been cited square with that canon. I do know that there are judges who take that canon quite seriously and will refuse to discuss a case with anyone save their law clerk. That does not prevent a judge from going to the library and reading; it was never intended to do that. It was intended, however, to prevent the judge from independently securing information without letting both parties know. The obvious way around that is to provide notice to both parties.

A Member: I should say about thirteen states have changed that part of the code of judicial conduct to allow courts to get outside experts, and of course, as you say, they can tell the parties about what they have done and let the parties answer.

Donald Horowitz: That *ex parte* restriction, of course, was intended to cover something quite different—getting information about the controversy between the litigants. But what you are talking about, I take it, relates to a different kind of information, that which is relevant to the general rule to be invoked, rather than what has happened between those parties.

Even though I think that the canon does not cover the kinds of forays into the library or social research, or into expert gossip or expert advice, that you are referring to, in general, those are bad ways for courts to get their information. This is true not merely because such information often has an element of randomness—or worse, it may be skewed, depending on whom the judge speaks to—but because the parties are deprived of the opportunity to make their presentations on every aspect of the case that is of concern to them.

When Judge Charles Clark went to the Yale University organist to seek advice on a music copyright case (Schick 1970), I do not think it was terribly efficacious, but it was also rather foolish because he could have gotten far more balanced advice within the framework of the adversary process. And when Justice Murphy sent out his questionnaires in *Wolf v. Colorado*, he could have had far better questionnaires designed by people like the researchers who are sitting in this room.

So, on the whole, you are absolutely right: there are many ways that social science information, and other forms of information, for that matter, can find their way into appellate decisions. Most of them are not functional to the goals for which they are intended.

There is one other way in which social science material finds its way into appellate decisions, and it is probably far more common than those mentioned: when lawyers become aware of data on appeal that the trial lawyers were not aware of. They then sneak the data into the appellate brief. This, too, is unsatisfactory because the briefing schedules for responses are typically too short to enable those writing reply briefs to consult appropriate experts and come up with satisfactory rebuttals.

So, all in all, the regular modes by which social science information finds its way into decisions have their problems. The irregular ways have at least equal, if not greater, problems attached to them.

Same Member: I have one that I forgot to mention in my list which is probably the best way. A few appellate courts have had long discussions with attorneys and experts on all aspects of social science material.

When you get into the major lawmaking decisions, where all of the social science is going to the legislative facts, time is no concern. You can delay briefs, you can delay decision, you've got all kinds of time to do anything you want. They took years to get around to deciding *Brown*.

But it is an absolute misuse of social science for the judges to just take what the attorneys have shown them because it is liable to be very incomplete. They have to dig themselves.

Horowitz: I just want to say that you are much more cavalier about time than appellate judges tend to be when motions are presented to them for extensions of time, and I speak from bitter experience. They're not routinely granted; they are granted in some circuits, in the federal courts, for example, more than in others, and they are granted by some judges more than others. I rather doubt that in the run of cases motions for extensions of time will be granted merely because the appellant's lawyer had cited some social science data in his brief that wasn't in the record below, unless it's absolutely and critically central to the case.

Jeanne Katz *(Legal Times of Washington)*: I just thought I'd say something on behalf of attorneys. I have tried to use social science research and I have talked to a few attorneys, and lawyers would be willing to use a lot of this information if they could understand it. But social scientists must come down a step, especially if they want to publish in legal journals, to be able to talk about it in a way that wouldn't require one to have extensive economics training. Also, in most cases you just can't afford to go out and obtain the needed data from people who conduct these studies.

Peters: I don't agree at all. As a matter of fact, I would suggest the opposite. Lawyers are masters at learning a particular field in the period of time necessary to try a case. You see, for example, that lawyers who try personal injury cases are experts at anatomy because they have learned it in order to handle such cases on a routine basis. It seems to me that some lawyers may specialize in dealing with social science data on an evidentiary level. When and how that will happen, if it hasn't already, I don't know. It is quite possible that it has already happened, at least in some civil rights cases, where the lawyers involved are specialists and know what they're doing.

So I'm not at all convinced that social scientists must be able to simplify their work to such an extent that it is totally challengeable. I do think that social scientists should communicate well to lawyers and to judges. A lot of what social scientists and lawyers do, and any profession, perhaps, is to try to hide what they do behind a lot of unnecessary garbage and verbiage. But I question the idea that you could simplify, for instance, a factor analysis so that a judge with no background in social research will understand what you've done, and I question whether it would be useful to do so.

NOTES

1. I have discussed *Hobson* at length in my book, *The Courts and Social Policy* (1977).
2. Guidelines for implementing these suggestions are contained in Kirby (1979).

REFERENCES

Heinz, A. and Kerstetter, W. 1979. Pretrial Settlement Conference: Evaluation of a Reform in Plea Bargaining. 13 *Law and Society Review* 349.

Hobson v. Hansen, 327 F. Supp. 844 (USDC D.C. 1971).

Horowitz, Donald L. 1977. *The Courts and Social Policy*. Washington, D.C.: Brookings Institution.

In re Gault 387 *U.S.* 1 (1967).

Kirby, Michael. 1979. *The Role of the Administrator in Evaluation Alternatives—A Series.* Washington, D.C.: Pretrial Services Resource Center.

Lemon v. Kurtzman, 403 *U.S.* 602 (1971).

Levin, Martin. 1971. Policy Evaluation and Recidivism. 6 *Law and Society Review* 17-46.

Schick, Martin. 1970. *Learned Hand's Court.* Baltimore: Johns Hopkins Univ. Press.

Wolf v. Colorado, 338 *U.S.* 25, 44-6 (1949) (dissenting opinion).

9

Legal Concepts and Applied Social Research Concepts: Translation Problems

LEONARD SAXE
ROBERT POST
H. LAURENCE ROSS

LEONARD SAXE*

I am an unabashed social scientist and, despite participation in this conference, I speak and think a language called social scientese. I know a number of
dialects, best of which are social psychologese and evaluationese (based on
the subdiscipline of evaluation research). Basically, I speak and think as a
social scientist, although herein lies a central difficulty for those of us concerned with the use of applied social science by the legal system: we have an
important problem in communicating with one another.

To illustrate this difficulty, which is in part a language problem and in part
a thinking problem, let me comment on the fact that a session on translation is
occurring as the last program agenda. It's somewhat unfortunate, for if we
haven't been speaking the same language at this conference, what have we
been doing? Of course, it may be very useful to wrap up this conference with
a session on translation. Perhaps, during the conference we've come to
realize how social scientists and lawyers, judges, and legal scholars don't
really communicate, and we can now talk, from a more informed position,
about possible remedies.

While I think translation is at the heart of the problem of applied social
research in the courts, my thesis is actually more complex. I'd like to suggest
that there's a great deal more to translation problems than merely translating
one language into another. Although knowing one another's vocabulary is
certainly important, there are other critical aspects of communication. Thus,
there's more to understanding one another than lawyers knowing the meaning of "multiple regression," "cross-sectional" design, or even "reasonable
doubt." In addition to vocabulary, conceptual knowledge is critical to translation. Both vocabulary and concepts are different in social science and law.
These differences in the way we think may present the most important barriers to the effective use of social science in the courts.

Let me digress, briefly, from the central issue of law and social science by
developing several analogies. For example, consider what happens when
one travels to a foreign country. Let's pick France and let's assume we're visiting Paris. Depending on our past training and experience, within a very few
days we begin to pick up the French language. Words like *la ville, la cité, le
métro,* and *manger* that describe common places and things that we do
become a part of our vocabulary. The interesting aspect of this process is that
while these words can be directly translated into English, they don't have the
same meaning. Even when the words are identical—we have a Metro in
Washington, D.C., just like in Paris—the implications are very different. For
example, translating *manger* (to eat) from French to English doesn't really
communicate the different way in which eating is regarded in France and
America. Eating in France has a different social and cultural context and

---

*Assistant professor of psychology and senior research associate at the Center for Applied
Social Science, Boston University.

refers to a more central aspect of one's life. While there are certainly parallels, it's important to note that the culture affects how we react to other languages.

Perhaps this point will be even clearer when I shift from French to Yiddish. There is a series of Yiddish words which, over the past fifty years or so, has crept into common usage in English. For example, you may have heard the word *mishugana* or *schnorer* or *mensh*. If one asks a person to translate a Yiddish word, a typical comment is, "Well, it's really not translatable." There is a whole culture which underlies the simple definition. *Mishugana* doesn't just mean "crazy," it involves a set of contexts in which a particular kind of behavior occurs. It's not easy to actually understand the meaning unless you have a great deal of knowledge about how that word is used and you know something about the culture in which these words developed.

To extend the problem of translating different languages and cultures to the problem of social science and the law, I'd like to draw on Kuhn's concept of a paradigm (Kuhn 1970). It's a term that's been the subject of perhaps more controversy than it deserves, principally because it's been interpreted to mean many things. Other panelists are probably going to talk about paradigms more elegantly, but I use the word to mean a way of thinking about the world. I'm drawing on one of the at least seventeen ways Kuhn uses "paradigm." I'd like to suggest that the paradigm of social science, that which justifies sociologists, psychologists, economists, and political scientists in calling themselves members of the same community, is that they share a similar way of viewing problems. Although undoubtedly hard to describe, this paradigm contrasts with that used by members of the legal community.

To the degree that these paradigms are really different, and to the degree that they are held by people in the social science and law communities, talking with one another will not be very productive. Maybe we can provide translations of the words, but if we don't understand the culture, communication will not be very effective.

One of the striking features of social science that attracts me is that there are not as many rules as there are in other fields. I can frame my research in ways that some editors and reviewers of particular journals won't like, but I can usually find a home for any piece of research or thinking. No matter how deviant from the usual way of doing research, no matter how half-baked or irrelevant the underlying ideas may be, there's usually an outlet for such work in the social science community.

When I was a graduate student, I spent a good deal of my time reading philosophers of science. One of the most prominent of these contemporary philosophers, Abraham Kaplan (1964), talks about a principle which describes the perspective I've adopted. He refers to it as the "autonomy of inquiry." Basic to the logic of science (that is, the shared paradigm of social scientists) is an understanding that scientists are free to approach problems in any way that they think will answer their questions. While some principles serve as guidelines for conducting scientific inquiry, scientists are free to use whatever method or strategy best serves their purpose. Of course, this shouldn't be overstated; certainly within subcommunities of social scientists, particular ways of doing research are clearly specified.

Nevertheless, social science per se doesn't have rules, it only has heuristics which serve as general principles. To draw from Kuhn's idea of scientific revolution, the people who receive the highest rewards in the scientific community are not those who follow the rules but the individuals who figure out ways to break the rules and make sense of the world in a new way. These people—the Einsteins—break the patterns of "normal science" and create an intellectual and scientific revolution.

The idea of autonomous inquiry and principle-guided rather than rule-guided work suggests a basic difference between the way social scientists and legal people view problems. I'm sure that this underlies many of the specific difficulties that participants in this conference have described. The social scientist who, as an expert witness, wants to present all sides of an issue and does not want to make a definitive statement is being true (perhaps) to social science. However, this type of social science response creates a difficult situation for the court. A similar problem occurs when courts, acting according to their paradigm, try to determine what is acceptable methodology. This is hard to do and, in a sense, does fit with the culture of social science.

Another basic difference in the social science and legal paradigms is that social scientists attempt to understand and predict behavior in aggregate. They try to discover patterns that seem to explain the largest, but by no means entire, variance in situations. They're not necessarily concerned with specific cases. In other words, social scientists deal with nomothetic information.

In contrast, many of the cases that reach the courts are idiographic rather than nomothetic, and this is particularly true with respect to criminal offenses. Some of the most spectacular and difficult legal issues have arisen from recent events that seem clearly unpredictable, at least in terms of the ability of social science to predict or understand them. The Son of Sam murders in New York and the Florida case involving a teenager who murdered his neighbor after seeing a Kojak television episode are two examples. However desirable it would be to bring social science to bear on those kinds of cases, that's not what social science is about. Social science does not really have the tools to explain such aberrant behavior (that is, to determine whether it is due to insanity or external influences). While social scientists shouldn't neglect the study of such behavior, at the present time the paradigm of social science may make it impossible to provide the courts with much useful information.

In addition to the nomothetic aspect of social science, consider the conclusion of almost any empirical or theoretical social science report: "More research is needed on this topic." It's easy in this forum to make fun of such statements. However, conclusiveness just doesn't fit the paradigm of social science. It may fit the legal paradigm and, if it does, it may be the root of many of the difficulties in using social science in the courtroom.

To go back to the notion of visiting a foreign country or learning about another ethnic group, the only solution to these differences is cultural immersion. It's not going to be possible to correct the current difficulties of using social science in the courts by preparing a detailed dictionary of social science terms for use by attorneys and judges or even by offering a course in social science methods. Until those of you in the legal community have research experience and actually see an idea taken from its inception through an empirical test, you're not going to understand the context in which we, as social scientists, try to explain events. Until you understand our skeptical approach to explanation, you won't appreciate how we can really be used.

To be fair and deal with both sides of the problem, I admit that social scientists also need to learn more about the legal system. We need to learn not only your procedures but your culture. We need to search for precedents, learn to use language more precisely, and engage in the legal decision-making process. It's undoubtedly a complex solution, but no more so than the problem at hand.

ROBERT POST*

When we inquire into the relationship between social science research data and the law, we must first clarify what we mean by law. In this brief presentation I am not going to be talking about law as it is embodied in statutes, nor am I going to be talking about law as it is embodied in litigation (that is, in an attorney's presentation of facts before a court). I am also not going to be talking about law in the sense that it's practiced by academics, nor in the sense that it's practiced in the field of jurisprudence. I am instead going to be talking about law as it is embodied in legal decisions, in the opinions of judges who are settling disputes.

We do not have a very clear understanding of exactly what it means for a judge to settle a dispute, to issue law. Before the advent of the legal realists during the first third of the twentieth century, decisional law was thought to be determined by a series of scientific principles enshrined in precedents and revealed by reason. The legal realists shattered that notion.[1] But they did not replace it with a rigorous or even satisfying conception of what exactly a judge does when he writes an opinion. The question remains open, subject to many conflicting explanatory hypotheses.

The historical response to the legal realists has since been labeled the legal process school.[2] It included academics such as Herbert Wechsler, Henry Hart, and Alexander Bickel, who focused not so much on the outcomes of judicial decisions as on the process through which these outcomes were achieved. One might almost say—by way of parody—that for this school the law was functioning well if appropriate institutions were making decisions in appropriate institutional ways. According to the central premise of the legal process school, the function of judicial opinions is to legitimate the resolution

---

*Attorney and former law clerk to Chief Judge David Bazelon and Justice William J. Brennan, U.S. Supreme Court.

of certain social disputes, and that legitimacy can be achieved if the judiciary functions within clearly defined institutional constraints. From this perspective, the function of the courts, which operate in the realm of values and moral consensus, is chiefly cognitive.

The intellectual foundations of the legal process school were laid during the 1950s. Since that time, however, the nature of litigation in this country has undergone a vast transformation. Lawyers have increasingly used courts as tools to effectuate public policy ends. The path-breaking example is the litigation strategy used by the NAACP in the area of school desegregation. More generally, however, judicial review of agency regulation converts policy issues into questions for legal resolution. Thus, in our time courts have become conscious instruments of social policy.

Now this fact of social history has introduced certain tensions into our notion of what a court's opinion is supposed to do. Should a judge's opinion primarily perform a legitimating function in the sense of enunciating moral values (as Alexander Bickel put it in his book, *The Least Dangerous Branch*), or is it primarily an instrument to effectuate certain social policy aims?

The point I want to make is that these alternatives correspond to two different ways of discovering, appreciating, and assimilating facts. Helpful in understanding this difference is the work of Jürgen Habermas, one of the great figures of the Frankfurt school in Germany. In his early work, *Knowledge and Human Interests,* Habermas separates two distinct functions or modalities of knowledge. The first he labels "empirical-analytic." The distinctive quality of this form of knowledge is that it orders reality for the purpose of exerting "possible technical control over [the] objectified processes of nature" (Habermas 1971, p. 191). The second he labels "hermeneutic." In this modality knowledge is organized so as to maintain "the intersubjectivity of possible action-orienting mutual understanding" (Habermas 1971, p. 191). Hermeneutic knowledge, that is, centers on creating intersocial meaning; on reinforcing and understanding our own values; on trying to understand each other, speak to each other, listen and hear and make judgments together.

Habermas argues convincingly that these two modalities of knowledge correspond to two distinct ways of assimilating facts. Consider, for example, the contrasting roles played by facts in the empirical-analytic sociology of Émile Durkheim (1951) and in the hermeneutic sociology of Peter Winch (1970). The distinction has begun to penetrate jurisprudential thinking, as evidenced by the two kinds of judges introduced in Bruce Ackerman's *Private Property and the Constitution.* Ackerman distinguishes between the judge who is a "scientific policymaker," viewing values in an empirical-analytic way as susceptible of objective determination, and the judge who is an "ordinary observer," attempting to clarify our common intuitions.

The two modalities of knowledge identified by Habermas also correspond to two different relationships between decisional law and social science, because the social sciences acquire and organize their data largely for the purpose of acquiring technical control over the social environment. If decisional law is seen to have a similar purpose, it will assimilate and use in a fraternal manner the results of the social sciences. Indeed, as the primary resource our society has in meeting such needs, the social sciences will assume a privileged position, often dictating the results of particular cases. If, on the other hand, the function of decisional law is essentially moral—legitimating certain kinds of dispute settlements—then social science research data will not be elevated to such a privileged position.

In fact, if the function of law is to legitimate, we may expect to find in judicial opinions a certain skepticism toward social science research results. I am thinking here of an example that is often brought up by Senior Judge David Bazelon of the U.S. Court of Appeals for the District of Columbia Circuit. Judge Bazelon has dealt extensively with the question of how the law can know if a particular defendant is insane and thus not guilty of a crime. Judge Bazelon points out that the issue of insanity in a criminal trial is essentially the issue of responsibility. Because of our Judeo-Christian cultural heritage, we believe that we should not punish someone for acts unless he has been responsible for those acts. The notion of responsibility is at base a moral and political notion; it requires our society to define for itself when it will impose sanctions—when it will consider an individual responsible enough to be branded a criminal and punished accordingly (Bazelon 1976).

The psychiatrist's diagnosis of insanity is "scientific" in nature. It is an empirical-analytic judgment based on the need to predict and control the future behavior of the patient. Since the law is seeking a moral or hermeneutic judgment, it cannot rely exclusively on this diagnosis. Thus, the courts always reserve the question of insanity for a jury of lay citizens, because the question is considered to be political, not medical. Judge Bazelon correctly points out, however, that the social prestige of the psychiatrist is often so compelling that both judge and jury tend to forget this important distinction. Moreover, the intellectual foundation of the psychiatrist's medical expertise is opaque to the lay judge and jury, and there is no way of knowing whether the psychiatrist has unwittingly incorporated political considerations into his diagnosis. Among thoughtful jurists this has resulted in a certain skepticism concerning the role of the psychiatrist in the legal context (Bazelon 1978).

A second example of the relationship between decisional law and the social sciences is the decision of the Supreme Court in *Washington v. Davis* (1976). The question examined in that case was when it may be said that a government body is violating the Fourteenth Amendment by discriminating against blacks. Title VII of the Civil Rights Act of 1964 also prohibits discrimination against blacks, and before *Davis* there had been no clear distinction between constitutional and statutory analysis of this question. In the statutory area social science data had assumed an important, almost privileged role in the statistical proof of discrimination. Courts were accepting as determinative ever more sophisticated mathematical evidence.

Suddenly, however, in *Washington v. Davis* the Supreme Court sharply distinguished constitutional from statutory analysis by stating that only purposeful discrimination violates the Constitution. The concept of purposeful discrimination is vague and extremely difficult to apply to an institution. What does it mean to say that a legislature, a school, or a zoning board is purposefully discriminating? Does the concept reflect the subjective states of mind of the legislature's members? If not, how is it to be distinguished from the discriminatory effect social science statistics are so capable of disclosing? The Court offered no guidance on these questions.

Perhaps the Supreme Court merely wanted to reduce the possibility of finding constitutional violations. But to look at it another way, the Court may have been disturbed that the moral judgment of discrimination was becoming almost entirely dependent on social science statistics. Recognizing that the judgment of discrimination is moral, not merely technical, perhaps the Court wanted to make that judgment more receptive to the kinds of facts and perspectives that we normally use when making a moral judgment of discrimination. The Court thus deliberately imported the vagueness of ordinary moral discourse into the arena of constitutional adjudication.[3]

In contrast to these examples, there are areas of decisional law where the purpose is not so much to legitimate, as to impose systemic order to accomplish certain policy ends. One example is private dispute settlement in the field of torts. Traditionally, judicial opinions in the torts area were filled with discussions of moral questions. The doctrines of the field centered on concepts of rights and duties. But as society has increasingly come to organize itself through vast, impersonal matrices of relationships, this way of thinking has declined. For example, product liability, traffic regulation, and pollution control do not appear to us to be matters of rights and duties so much as systems of relationships in need of rational ordering for the achievement of social ends. This insight has been captured by such theorists as Guido Calabresi (1970) and Richard Posner (1973). The courts have responded by increasingly incorporating into their opinions social scientific analyses of the functioning of these social systems.

The example of Title VII points to another area in which the legitimation function of the courts is not primary. When a court is effectuating the policy of a congressional statute, it may often reasonably conclude that Congress has already enunciated basic moral decisions. The role of the court therefore is simply to implement the moral decisions and policies and address technical questions of compliance. Thus, in contrast to their approach to constitutional suits, the courts in Title VII suits have remained extraordinarily open to the use of social scientific data to resolve disputes.

At base, therefore, my point is very simple: to understand the relationship between social science data and law we must understand and carefully distinguish among the various functions that the law serves. In particular, it is crucial to understand the tension between the social policy function of law and the legitimation function of law. Since this tension is implicit in the multifarious purposes law serves, we should not expect an easy relationship between social science and the courts.

LEGAL CONCEPTS AND RESEARCH CONCEPTS

H. LAURENCE ROSS*

I will establish my expertise in this conference by saying that I'm a social scientist who has never done any research about the courts, nor have I ever appeared as an expert witness in a court. I have appeared as an expert before a legislature and, reflecting on the last comments, my experience was that the legislators listened politely and then did what they thought would impress their constituents. They did not care about what the expected effects of the legislation actually might be.

Let me note that the underlying theme of some common social science approaches to law is that the legal enterprise, particularly in a court, is seeking the truth, and social science ought to be useful to the courts in this enterprise, because it has something to add to the pursuit of truth.

I think that this is a partially valid statement, but it's an oversimplification of what the courts are doing. I think much of what has gone on in this conference can be summarized as an attempt to broaden and sharpen this simple-minded idea.

One goal of the legal process is the definitive disposition of a given complaint—definitive whether based on truth or on ignorance. I think it was Professor Rosen who made this point very well.

Another goal, as Professor Lind pointed out, is the pursuit of justice. As conceived by Lind, justice is measured by a subjective feeling of fairness. That avoids the necessity to provide a definition of justice. The important point is that the pursuit of justice goes beyond the search for truth.

If this were not the case, if the goals of law did not go beyond that of coming to the truth, we would be very surprised to find courts proceeding with institutions like the jury, a collection of twelve people whose main qualification seems to be that they know absolutely nothing about the case at hand.

In my opinion, some of the apparent misuse and nonuse of social science is therefore traceable to alternative legal agendas. I won't try to be terribly original in digressing upon this. I refer you to Norvell's article in the book by William Thomas, *Scientists and the Legal System* (Norvell 1974).

Policy may depend upon a legal fiction which would be destroyed by social science. We want to avoid the glaring light of truth in this situation, because we are proceeding on the basis of something that we all acknowledge is untrue. Norvell illustrates this in the court's pretense that a couple over seventy years of age can still have children, in order to make a point on the rule against perpetuities. The falsity of the premise is irrelevant to the decision. The social scientist is surprised by this only if he is dreadfully naive.

---

*Professor of sociology and adjunct professor of law, State University of New York at Buffalo.

In the Charlie Chaplin case (*Berry v. Chaplin* 1946) the results of a blood test were introduced into evidence. By scientific criteria, they definitively disproved Chaplin's paternity. Yet both the trial court and the appellate court seemed content to ignore the results of that test.

What explains this mystifying performance? Chaplin was a rich and famous person who associated intimately with a certain woman who was asking for some money to support her child. Was not the major question whether Mr. Chaplin ought to contribute to supporting this woman's child? For that question the scientific evidence was indeed irrelevant.

Legal personnel often express ethical reservations concerning certain scientific techniques. An example that was brought up in this conference was the polygraph. The one that I am most familiar with is chemical testing of breath for alcohol. These are seen to be relatively intrusive and distasteful techniques. Perhaps it is aversion to particular scientific techniques that is leading to what seems to a social scientist an unreasonable rejection of them by lawyers. Of course, the big question here is the survey. Both government agencies and the general public seem to be showing increasing resistance to social science's intrusion into personal beliefs through the survey. If that's the case, why not the courts as well?

It has been pointed out that social science is accepted in the legal system where the search for truth is primary. Mr. Peters and Mr. Wasby talked about administrative efficiency. The courts are eager to solve such problems as shortening the line of people waiting for trials and making the trials more efficient. To the extent that social science can provide relevant information, it's not going to be rejected.

Another matter that has been cited in this conference is giving definition to certain vague legal concepts, such as restraint of trade, and evaluating given situations in terms of these concepts as clarified. There is no problem here with rejection of social science.

Another area in which the courts seem to be receptive to social science is the prediction of consequences for alternative remedies. This is related, I think, to the relative openness of government to evaluation research in general.

Donald Campbell has depicted a future society where government will be experimental in the scientific sense (Campbell 1973). Administrators will commit themselves not to policy solutions but rather to social problems and will offer a variety of plausible solutions to which evaluation research will be applied. The results will lead either to more permanent adoption of a proposed technique or else to trying an alternative solution.

A criticism of this prediction, and I think an appropriate one, is that government needs the illusion of success in order to obtain reform in the first place. Commitment to social problems is not enough; government has to promise that it has a solution, or it won't receive the necessary resources. On similar grounds we can criticize the scientific perspective as a goal for adjudication. Courts also need illusions (as well as substance) in order to perform their varied functions in society.

177

DISCUSSION

Bernard Grofman *(University of California)*: One of the nicest comments made was that some of the concerns of applied social research are perhaps misdirected toward the courts. To what extent do we see overutilization of social science research in the courts because of an underutilization of social science research in the legislatures and in government generally?

Leonard Saxe: I'm not sure that there's a cause and effect relationship; that is, because social science isn't used by the legislature, adequate social policy isn't developed. I think that in some cases tough political questions are involved. School desegregation is one question that the legislature, not for want of data or expertise, has studiously avoided, and social policy questions have ended up in the courts.

Robert Post: The Sherman Act is the best example of an almost meaningless statute. Because of legislative inattention, the courts have in fact vacillated between effectuating a political determination—the protection of small businessmen—and enforcing a social scientific policy—the policing of economic efficiency in the marketplace.

H. Laurence Ross: I'd say one of the nicest points that has been made not only here but in the literature has been that courts act in part because legislatures dump problems at their feet. Legislatures very frequently are incapable or unwilling to act in the face of social problems and pass these problems on to somebody else.

Clark Abt *(Abt Associates Inc.)*: I'd like to ask Robert Post if he accepts Professor Ross's concept of the openness of the courts to evaluation research on the consequences of legal decisions and particularly the choice of remedies. I wonder whether you would really insist on your view that the court has to be skeptical of the application of social research if it sees its role as moral legitimizing, showing the possibly immoral or perverse consequences of some believed-to-be-moral concept?

Post: I don't think courts have to be skeptical. The only point I was making is that social science research may not have a privileged place in legal discourse. Such research presents facts which are, like any other facts, to be taken into account. We all feel a tendency to yield final judgment to the social sciences, and because of the reaction to that tendency one finds skepticism.

Your question about remedies is an interesting one because courts, having become instruments of social policy, have involved themselves necessarily in a whole new relationship to remedies. One thinks of Judge Johnson in Alabama restructuring Alabama schools (Fiss 1972), prisons (*Pugh v. Locke* 1976), and mental hospitals (*Wyatt v. Stickney* 1972). In undertaking such social reform courts have had to use the expertise of social scientists. There is some tension in this role, however, because, after all, courts are not here to run school systems or mental hospitals. There is thus an increasing tendency for courts to eschew, to the greatest extent possible, their assumed managerial responsibilities.[4] The rub is that constitutional violations often inhere precisely in the managerial decisions of institutional defendants.

Susan Burke *(Syracuse University)*: I just have a brief comment for Mr. Post. I appreciated here the distinction you made between the two functions of law, but I would just suggest that your choice of terminology risks confusing things. If I remember correctly, you distinguished between the legitimizing function and the social policy function, the social policy being the pragmatic running of things. But just in discussions in general the kinds of cases that you called the legitimizing cases are the ones that are usually referred to as social policy cases—school integration, death penalty cases, and so forth.

Post: This is a complicated problem because it entails the particular court level and the precise phase of a case one is talking about. Although Judge Garrity's management of the Boston school system entails issues of policy, the Supreme Court's rejection of state-sanctioned segregation in *Brown v. Board of Education* is not a question of policy in the same sense. Although the implementation of constitutional principles has often involved extensive reliance on social science expertise, the enunciation and justification of constitutional principles have had a somewhat more ambiguous relationship to that expertise, as the famous footnote in *Brown* demonstrates.[5]

Burke: So then it is quite likely that both functions might operate within a given case, with social science playing different roles at different stages in the case.

Post: Exactly. Law functions differently at the district court level than it does at the Supreme Court level. In cases involving school desegregation a major concern of a district court is with the implementation of remedies. This is rarely the main concern of the Supreme Court.

There is, of course, a constant interplay *between* these levels. A legal remedy is supposed to undo the effects of a legal harm. Thus, the Supreme Court's ruling in *Washington v. Davis* is likely to affect the shape of remedies issued by lower courts.

Joseph Sanders *(University of Michigan)*: You suggested that in the product liability cases we would move toward policy. In the school cases (a school case has been remanded on the basis of *Washington v. Davis*) there's a movement back in the other direction of moral legitimation. Do you have any thoughts about what causes these kinds of drifts to occur in the courts and why certain issues are turned into policy issues and then turned back again? It seems like an intriguing question for a sociologist to study.

Post: I agree; it is an intriguing question. My view is that in the field of torts, which concerns the area of private wrongs and which used to be discussed in the language of rights and duties, people began to find that the language didn't seem to relate to the realities of how obligations were ordered in our very complicated market economy. Alternative social policy approaches began to be articulated. An example of this trend is Calabresi's book, *The Costs of Accidents*, which was instrumental in illustrating that the way we distribute liability for auto accidents will structure the way people drive and the way insurance companies work. According to Calabresi, it was really a matter of thinking out the system of liability we wanted to govern cars and streets.

I don't think that the pullback in the area of school desegregation is in any way related. Its genesis lies much more directly in recent racial politics and in the sense of unease that this delicate area was being straight-jacketed by the statistical facts demonstrated by social scientists.

Saxe: The court does not directly set social policy when it does enunciate principles; it only happens in an indirect way. It is still deciding a single particular case, and in the most typical situation, one case at a time. So it's not clear how, for example, the recent *Bakke* decision relates to other cases and it's not clear precisely what the social policy implications are.

The courts undoubtedly have a social policy role but it's not a direct role and that confuses any attempt to analyze it.

Post: The situation is more complicated because by deciding a precedent a court also decides a rule, and the rule is to be applied in all future cases. So in that sense the court is not just deciding the case before it, it is deciding the principle by which all future cases will be decided, and that could easily be called a policy. You are right, however, in your observation that courts don't just follow precedent, they interpret past precedents.

Also, whether the principle enunciated in a case will be of sufficient scope to constitute a policy will depend in part on the level of the court. Areas of law which need clarification are treated by the Supreme Court through its choice of cases. It rarely chooses a case to decide it only on its own facts, and when it does so, as with *Bakke*, the Court is subject to criticism for misusing its function.

Michael Saks*(National Center for State Courts)*: I might point out that it sounds like the disagreement there has to do with the appellate versus the trial courts, wherein a court might try to sidestep the fact that it is making a policy decision by saying, "Well, we have to decide *this* case." Sometimes that is what an appellate judge is trying to do. Certainly, that's not what happens in the Supreme Court.

Geoffrey Peters *(National Center for State Courts)*: The kind of dichotomy you draw to explain the reluctance of the court to use social science data in certain cases is very useful. Until you explained that, I didn't understand my own unease with certain models that had been presented in the case studies, for example, the optimization model that Stuart Nagel had been using and the discussion of the two standard deviation rule. I had tremendous difficulty visualizing a court being willing to announce a statistical rule that it would use as precedential value for future rulings.

My immediate reaction was to say that they'd find a way to distinguish it. I think Mr. Post has found a way to distinguish it. The court is unwilling to use those kinds of social science rules as decision rules on a case-by-case basis but is willing to use them when it comes to the establishment of policy in appropriate kinds of cases. And I think that's an extremely useful distinction.

NOTES

1. See, for example, Gilmore (1961).
2. See, for example, Ackerman (1974).
3. For a discussion of the texture of ordinary moral discourse, see Pitkin (1972).
4. See, for example, *Newman v. Alabama* (1978).
5. *Brown* rested in part on the conclusion that state-imposed segregation in schools "generates a feeling of inferiority" in black students (347 U.S. at 494). The exact status of this statement—whether empirical or legal/moral—was not clear. In footnote 11, however, Chief Justice Warren supported this conclusion by the findings of social science research, thus raising the controversial possibility that the doctrine of "separate but equal" was rejected solely on empirical grounds. See Betsy Levin and Philip Moise, "School Desegregation Litigation in the Seventies and the Use of Social Science Evidence: An Annotated Guide" (1975).

REFERENCES

Ackerman, B. 1974. Book review of *Law and the Modern Mind*, Jerome Frank. 103 *Daedalus* 119-30.

_____ . 1977. *Private Property and the Constitution*. New Haven: Yale Univ. Press.

Bazelon, D. 1976. The Morality of the Criminal Law. 49 *S. Calif. Law Review* 385-405.

_____ . 1978. The Role of the Psychiatrist in the Criminal Justice System. In *Controversy in Psychiatry*, J. Brady and H. Brodie, eds. Philadelphia: Saunders.

Berry v. Chaplin 169 *P. 2d* 442 (Cal. 1946).

Bickel, A. 1962. *The Least Dangerous Branch*. Indianapolis: Bobbs-Merrill.

Calabresi, G. 1970. *The Costs of Accidents*. New Haven: Yale Univ. Press.

Campbell, D. T. 1973. The Social Scientist as Methodological Servant of the Experimenting Society. 2 *Policy Studies Journal* 72-5.

Durkheim, E. 1951. *Suicide*. New York: Free Press.

Fiss, O. 1972. *Injunctions*. Mineola, N.Y.: Foundation Press.

Gilmore, G. 1961. Legal Realism: Its Cause and Cure. 70 *Yale Law Journal* 1037-48.

Habermas, J. 1971. *Knowledge and Human Interests.* Boston: Beacon Press.

Kaplan, A. 1964. *The Conduct of Inquiry.* Scranton, Penn.: Chandler.

Kluger, R. 1976. *Simple Justice.* New York: Knopf.

Kuhn, T. 1970. *The Structure of Scientific Revolutions.* rev. ed. Chicago: Univ. of Chicago Press.

Levin, B. and Moise, P. 1975. School Desegregation Litigation in the Seventies and the Use of Social Evidence: An Annotated Guide. 39 *Law and Contemporary Problems* 50, 53-6.

Newman v. Alabama, 559 F. 2d 283 (5th Cir. 1977), cert. denied, 438 *U.S.* 915 (1978).

Norvell, R. 1974. Reception of Science by the Legal System. In *Scientists in the Legal System,* William A. Thomas, ed. Ann Arbor, Mich.: Ann Arbor Science Publishers.

Pitkin, H. 1972. *Wittgenstein and Justice.* Berkeley: Univ. of California Press.

Posner, R. 1973. *The Economic Analysis of Law.* Boston: Little Brown.

Pugh v. Locke, 406 F. *Supp.* 318 (M.D. Ala. 1976), aff'd in part and remanded in part *sub nom, Newman v. Alabama,* 559 F. 2d 283 (5th Cir. 1977), cert. denied, 438 *U.S.* 915 (1978).

Washington v. Davis, 426 *U.S.* 229 (1976).

Winch, P. 1970. *The Idea of a Social Science and Its Relation to Philosophy.* Atlantic Highlands, N.J.: Humanities Press.

Wyatt v. Stickney, 344 F. *Supp.* 373 (M.D. Ala. 1972), aff'd in part and remanded in part, as rev'd in part *sub nom, Wyatt v. Aderholt,* 503 F. 2d 1305 (5th Cir. 1974).

CLOSING REMARKS

MICHAEL J. SAKS*

I will not be so presumptuous as to suggest that I can summarize the many different and often competing views that we've heard.

I think there is a presumptive relevance of social science to the courts. Probably everyone would agree that somehow, in some way, these two enterprises are connected, simply because both are concerned with behavior and with consequences to future behavior and with things that will happen to people as a result of taking one course of action or another. They use different paradigms, they have different motives, they go about things in different ways, they have different methodologies, but that thing out there that both of them are concerned about is, at its base, the same thing.

We have heard about many different ways in which social science information can be introduced into the courts—sometimes into litigation and sometimes elsewhere. In terms of litigation, such information can be presented in expert testimony; it can be included in appellate briefs. Judges can take judicial notice of it. They can appoint special juries; masters for specific issues can be appointed.

Sometimes the courts are put under the social science microscope. Changes are made in the way the courts operate and those changes are evaluated, which is where social science research comes into play. That is why organizations like the Federal Judicial Center and the National Center for State Courts exist. Again, there is relevance between the two.

Nevertheless, as Leonard Saxe was suggesting, there is a culture gap between law and social science. It has been demonstrated at this conference, and I think it's demonstrated whenever social scientists and lawyers and judges get together. They're interested in the same things, at least in their essence, yet they differ in their pursuit of those things and their purposes for pursuit.

The suggestion I have for all of us is a modest one which I am perhaps stealing from Leonard Saxe. If we do not or cannot immerse ourselves in each other's fields, at least it would be useful for a judge or a lawyer to become involved in a social science research project from beginning to end. It would also be useful for the social scientist to spend some time with a lawyer or a judge, following a case through from beginning to end and trying to see the world through that other person's eyes. Perhaps in this way we could reduce some of the communication problems and close that cultural gap.

---

*National Center for State Courts.

Index